A Casebook on Roman Water Law

A Casebook on Roman Water Law

Cynthia Jordan Bannon

UNIVERSITY OF MICHIGAN PRESS
ANN ARBOR

Published in the United States of America by the
University of Michigan Press
Manufactured in the United States of America
Printed on acid-free paper
First published November 2020

A CIP catalog record for this book is available from the British Library.

Library of Congress Cataloging-in-Publication data has been applied for.

Library of Congress Control Number: 2020944268

ISBN 978-0-472-13207-2 (hardcover : alk. paper)
ISBN 978-0-472-03786-5 (paper : alk. paper)

dulcibus filiis

Contents

Introduction

The Romans are famous for aqueducts, canals, and dams but their law is also a lasting, if less visible monument to their attempts to control water. In fact, they began making water law long before building their first aqueduct. Both environmental and social needs drove Roman interventions in their hydraulic environment. In the Mediterranean climate annual rainfall amounts to about 800 mm but seasonal variation caused (and causes) summer droughts and winter floods. Where Romans depended on natural sources, access was not equal because springs and streams were unevenly distributed in the landscape. Where an aqueduct supplied water, its allocation and maintenance posed challenges. The Romans recognized water as a natural resource, a public good, and an economic commodity. Their law grappled with the intersections and incompatibilities of these categories.

The study of water resources offers valuable insights into Roman society and culture. For example, access to water affected not only health and sanitation but also economic productivity. Agriculture, manufacturing, and transportation all depended on effective management of water resources. In addition the control of water found ideological expression in private life—think of lavish fountains in aristocratic houses—and also in politics, especially for an emperor's public profile. These broader concerns inspired this project, and the book invites inquiry into them through directed readings of the sources. Although casebooks are not a thesis-driven genre, the cases collected here implicitly argue for the

Romans' creative efforts to manage their environment with law. Early in their history the Romans crafted laws and institutions to regulate water in both public and private contexts. In later eras they revised and adapted their law to fit changing economic, cultural, and physical environments of an empire that spanned the Mediterranean. The cases document the role of law in this history, and the study questions engage with key issues in legal and environmental history, ancient and modern. This casebook aims to cross historical and disciplinary boundaries by making the primary evidence for Roman water rights accessible. Reaching a wider audience is critical to the project because Roman law makes important contributions to contemporary debates about water rights and the management of the environment.

This casebook presents an analytical collection of Roman sources for water rights. The four chapters treat the legal institutions that regulated water in chronological order as they arose. The first two chapters examine institutions of Roman private law, the action for warding off rainwater (chapter 1) and servitudes or rights of use for water (chapter 2). The last two chapters broaden the perspective to include public laws and institutions, the interdicts on public rivers and the sea (chapter 3) and, finally, aqueduct administration (chapter 4). The cases are concerned with the regulation of water itself and rights to use it, but they do not cover all types of law relating to water, for example, maritime loans. A few cases address the impact of water on nearby land, such as river banks, because they are conceptually and physically connected with the legal treatment of water. To prepare for study of the cases, each chapter opens with an overview of its topic while this introduction presents the evidence for water rights and contextualizes them within historical and conceptual frameworks.

THE SOURCES FOR ROMAN WATER LAW

In Roman law on water, source can mean three different things. First, it can refer to the origin of the water, whether the source was natural (spring, stream, river) or man-made (aqueduct, canal). Second, a source is the authority that made the law. Third, sources are the evidence that informs us about Roman law.

Roman water law is known from several types of evidence: literature, inscriptions, legal writings. In turn, the nature of the evidence depends on the source of the law, that is, how it was made. For example, literary histories describe the lawmaking by Rome's magistrates and political bodies, while inscriptions record statutes and legal agreements. Legal literature is the richest source of legal rules and policy on water. Despite the variety of sources, it is difficult to write a comprehensive history of Roman water law because the evidence is scattered geographically and chronologically. Assessing historical change is also difficult because few sources survive from the early eras of Rome's history, while fuller, later sources often take an anachronistic view of the past. Consequently, water law can appear to be a timeless, synchronic system—as suggested by the cases in this book. In fact, it developed diachronically, and different political officials and legal bodies played a role in making and enforcing Roman water law in different eras. The following overview situates the cases within this institutional history and offers a chronological view of water law.

Early Law and the *Twelve Tables*

Roman water law developed along the trajectory of Rome itself—the law first applied to a small, agricultural community and was later adapted to an empire of cities and Mediterranean-wide trade. Romulus, Rome's founder, is credited with organizing Rome as a community of farmers and soldiers at a natural ford on the Tiber River, which connected the city with inland regions and the coast. The Romans traced their law back to this early era, although no sources survive from the period and later accounts probably project contemporary practice into the past. The first law on water appears shortly after the foundation of Rome's Republican government in 510 BCE.

Early in the Republican period, the Romans created their first written law code, the *Twelve Tables*, to resolve civic strife in 450 BCE. No direct evidence of this law survives because the original tablets were destroyed probably when the Gauls captured Rome in 387 BCE. But it was handed down through education and legal practices; portions of the *Twelve Tables* are also reported in Roman literature, legal and otherwise. Although later generations found the *Twelve Tables* obscure and difficult to interpret, they remained the basis for all Roman private law or *ius civile* throughout Rome's history. The *Twelve Tables* included two institutions relating to water: an action or legal claim to protect land from flooding (*actio aquae pluviae arcendae*; Case 1.1) and rights of use for neighbors who wanted to share a water supply (servitudes; Case 2.1). These are the topics of the first two chapters of this book.

Statutes, Ius Civile, and Ius Honorarium in the Republic

During the Republic (510–27 BCE), the Romans made law on water through three parts of their government: the Senate, elected magistrates, and citizen assemblies. Legislative power resided with the assembly of the plebs (*comitium plebis*), which enacted statutes or plebiscites, laws named for the magistrate who proposed the bill to the assembly. Only two Republican statutes on water are known. A *lex Sulpicia,* also known as the *lex Rivalicia* for its subject (*rivi* or water channels), was proposed by a Servius Sulpicius in either the mid-second or the mid-first century (Case 4.7). A second statute, a *lex Scribonia* of the first century BCE, prohibited *usucapio* of servitudes; that is, rights of use could not be acquired informally by long possession (Case 2.11).

While there was little Republican legislation on water, important laws were made by Rome's elected magistrates, especially the urban praetor. Starting in 367 BCE, the Romans elected praetors alongside consuls to shoulder executive and military responsibilities. One of the praetors, the so-called urban praetor, was in charge of the courts and had jurisdiction over private law in the city of Rome. At the start of his term, the urban praetor issued an edict listing all the legal actions that could be brought in his court. Rather than articulating abstract rights or substantive principles, Roman law typically encodes them in instructions for legal procedures or so-called actions. At first, these actions were based on the *ius civile* and the law of the *Twelve Tables*, but over time the praetor generated new actions known as *ius honorarium* or magistrate's law through his edict.

In his edict, the praetor framed legal claims or actions in a fixed verbal form or formula that represented the legal rights of the parties in an if-then expression. He posted the edict and held court in the forum where citizens could approach him and present problems for legal resolution. Formulary actions were a two-step process. First, the praetor presided over a preliminary hearing to assess the circumstances and determine whether or not there was a suitable legal remedy. If so, he gave a formula to the parties and supervised their selection of a judge (*iudex*) to preside over the trial, the second stage of the process. The judge was a layman who need have no legal expertise; he gave a judgment based on the formula and, in some cases, also set monetary compensation. The praetor could make new law by adapting the formula to give an analogous action (*actio utilis* or *in factum*) when he determined that the circumstances merited an action even though they did not exactly match his edict. The formulary system and the praetor's edict thus generated innovation in Roman law, allowing it to respond to the changing needs of Romans. In the area of water law, the praetor's edict included formulas for water servitudes and for the action for warding off rainwater. It also contained administrative actions known as interdicts that applied to rivers, springs, and canals, both public and private (e.g., Cases 3.11 and 3.12).

Aqueduct Administration in the Republic

In about fifty years after the creation of the urban praetorship, the Romans built their first aqueduct, the Aqua Appia named for the censor of 312 BCE Appius Claudius Caecus who supervised its construction. By the early third century CE, eleven aqueducts brought water to Rome, and most cities around the empire had at least one aqueduct.

In the Republic, Rome's aqueducts delivered most of their water to public basins and fountains, while delivery to private properties came with a fee to baths and fullers or as an honor to a few distinguished aristocrats. The Senate and Rome's magistrates shared legal duties related to the aqueducts. The Senate, a council of ex-magistrates, had no formal powers but broad authority over both domestic and international affairs. It controlled the treasury and thus also public works, such as aqueducts. The censors, elected every five years, not only conducted the census but also arranged contracts for public works, including repair and construction of aqueducts. Other city magistrates also played a role during their annual terms of office: aediles who were also in charge of city roads and markets, and praetors, who presided over the courts in Rome. Most of our knowledge about Rome's aqueducts comes from a treatise by Sextus Julius Frontinus, *On the Water-Management of the City of Rome* (*De Aquaeductu Urbis Romae*), which covers the history, engineering, and distribution, as well as the statutes and administrative law on the aqueducts.

Law and Empire

By the third century BCE, the Romans not only enjoyed four aqueducts in their city but they had also conquered most of the Italian peninsula, creating an empire while still enjoying a Republican form of government. During the next two centuries, the Romans extended their political dominion around the Mediterranean and eventually, around the turn of the millennium, the Roman state became an empire in name as well as fact. During the reign of the first emperor Augustus (27 BCE–14 CE), the Roman Empire stretched from the straits of Gibraltar to the Euphrates and from Britain to North Africa. The Roman Empire continued to exist in one form or another until late antiquity, and the legacy of its law extends into the modern era.

Throughout Rome's history, political conquest stimulated the economy, generating demand for goods and water. Agriculture was the largest sector of Rome's economy both because productivity was low and because the state amplified demand especially for grain, which the imperial government collected as a tax to supply the city of Rome and its armies. To meet these needs, landowners intensified and diversified production which further stressed the water supply. In the Mediterranean climate, even when annual rainfall is adequate, seasonal precipitation means dry summers when few crops thrive without irrigation. Although Romans practiced dry farming, they also often irrigated their crops, even grain in some parts of the empire. Manufacturing also used water, for example, milling grain or making ceramic jars for transport and storage. More significant demand for water arose near cities and towns where irrigated crops such as garden vegetables and flowers earned profit in local markets. Urbanization itself increased demand on water resources not only for economic activity but also for domestic use and display. Roman cities and towns, like Rome itself, managed local water resources, often building a civic aqueduct that supplied both urban residents and rural farms in the city's hinterland.

As they built and governed their empire, the Romans used law to organize communities and natural resources. After military conquest, they established provinces or administrative units and founded colonies and towns (*municipia*) as civic centers. They also reorganized their rural territories, distributing land to colonists and assigning rights to rivers, streams, and springs. The Romans introduced law into these communities through town charters or municipal laws which prescribed the civic institutions for the towns as well as legal rules for civic aqueducts and water rights like those in Rome (e.g., Cases 2.4, 3.33, 4.4). The Romans also brought the census to the provinces to record legal status and property holdings as a basis for the land tax that was often paid in crops. In the provinces, all land and water was public property of the Roman people through conquest. Consequently, in the provinces residents could possess their land but not own it, except in special cases (for example, a Roman citizen living in the province), in contrast to Italy where Roman citizens could own land. The regulation of water was thus connected with the legal status of people and Rome's social structure.

Roman society was hierarchical, with an emperor at the top and a small group of wealthy and politically connected elites, and below them many more free people of lesser means, both citizens and foreigners, and at least as many slaves. Within this hierarchy, most Romans used law in face-to-face communities where everyone knew everyone else, or at least someone who knew someone. While elites often controlled resources including land and water, poorer free citizens farmed their own land, sharing the same water supply and participating in the same markets as their wealthy fellow citizens. These social and economic relationships shaped Roman water law in cities and rural areas around the empire, and legal status mattered: slaves were considered property and only citizens had access to private law (*ius civile*) to protect their physical safety, family welfare, and economic interests. As they conquered new territory, the Romans granted citizenship as a reward to local elites who then helped to govern the empire, more rarely enfranchising entire communities. These new citizens had Latin rights, a limited form of citizenship that brought no political rights but allowed them to own land, enforce contracts, and form legal marriages. Strictly speaking, only citizens could exercise these rights, but in practice, the Romans often accorded to local laws the same force as Roman law, so that individuals across the empire had similar access to law even before the emperor Caracalla granted universal citizenship in 212 CE.

Emperors and imperial government changed the legal system both directly and indirectly. The praetor's edict continued to structure private law, but it acquired a fixed form in the early second century CE. For Rome's aqueducts, there was a new imperial office, the water commissioner (*curator aquarum*) who was responsible for delivery and distribution of the water as well as maintenance of the infrastructure; he also had jurisdiction over the aqueducts, serving as judge in legal disputes about them (Case 4.8). The aqueducts supplied water not only to the residents of Rome but also to imperial properties (such as palaces and baths) and to private individuals. Their administration required technical knowledge as well as political finesse because the water supply of Rome was of prime importance to emperors as a symbol of their power and beneficence.

Emperors also participated directly in the legal system. They made law through their decrees, known as imperial constitutions. A few constitutions concerned water law, mostly for aqueducts at Rome and Constantinople, although a few also addressed rivers and private water sources (e.g., Cases 3.42, 4.26). Through imperial law, emperors attempted to impose accountability on the administration of civic water systems while burnishing their own reputations. Emperors also took the role of judge in trials. They served as a court of appeal that opened access to the law to people from around the empire through the petition system. An individual who was unhappy with the decision of a local court could send a petition to the emperor asking him to rehear the case. The emperor gave his judgment in a written response or rescript, which came to have the force of law. To advise the emperor on law and assist in responding to petitions, there was an imperial office staffed with legal experts or jurists.

The Jurists and Legal Literature

In addition to magistrates and emperors, the jurists or legal experts were an important source of Roman private law. They were sources in two senses: they both made law and produced literature that transmitted the law to later generations. A jurist (*iuris consultus* or *iuris peritus*) was a legal expert who advised litigants as modern lawyers do but did not appear in court as advocate. Jurists advised magistrates and emperors on the law; some played influential roles in imperial government as head of the emperor's legal office (*ab epistulis*) or on his advisory board (*concilium*). They also studied and taught law. Their work introduced the systematic analysis of law that we call jurisprudence. The jurists wrote treatises in which they interpreted statutes and analyzed both real and hypothetical legal cases. Their writings are the most important source for Roman water law although only a fraction of it has been handed down.

Most of the jurists' writings are known from a compilation made in the late Empire during the reign of Justinian (527–565 CE). The jurists in Justinian's legal office selected excerpts from several centuries of legal literature to create the *Digest of Justinian.* Although some passages were edited to align with current law, for the most part the law of the *Digest* represents Classical Roman law that was in force from the first century BCE through the early third century CE. Justinian also created a textbook, *Institutes,* and collected imperial constitutions in his *Codex* and *Novellae,* which replaced earlier collections, such as the one made by the emperor Theodosius in 438 CE, *The Codex of Theodosius.*

Many of the cases in this book come from the jurists' writings. But water law is also documented in inscriptions, texts written on durable materials such as stone and bronze. These inscriptions record both public and private law on water, and they vary in form and origin. Only a few cases come from them, but they merit a separate treatment to explain their legal and historical contexts, which appears at the end of this introduction.

WATER RIGHTS AND PROPERTY LAW

In Roman law, water was treated as property, *res*, a physical thing that could be owned, used, or leased. When the Romans categorized property, they began by distinguishing the human and the divine (see, e.g., Gaius, *Institutes* 2.2–11). Sacred or religious law governed things that belonged to the gods, while human or civil law governed everything else. Sacred waters dedicated to deities or religious functions were outside the scope of civil law and thus are also not included in this casebook. Other water resources were sorted into three legal categories. Private property (*res privata*) included water that rose or flowed on privately owned land, and it was owned by the person who owned the land. Public property (*res publica*) included water in public rivers or civic aqueducts and all resources on public land. But the law sometimes treated public water as if it were no one's property (*res nullius*), that is, anything that could be converted to private property when a person took control of it, such as wild animals and fish which became the property of the person who caught them through the legal mechanism of *occupatio* (e.g., Case 3.6). It is difficult to apply this model directly to water because its fluid nature resists capture, and because simply keeping water in a reservoir precludes its use.

Both practically and conceptually water was hard to contain within the institutions of property law, especially ownership. In theory an owner had broad legal powers over his property, but in practice Roman ownership was limited in a number of ways that posed particular challenges when water was involved. For example, landowners had to take into account their neighbor's interests in managing runoff or sharing a water source. The Romans adapted ownership-based institutions to these environmental and social circumstances of private water resources but public property posed additional challenges for water law. In theory everyone owned the water in public rivers and aqueducts; in practice, it was difficult for everyone to use a public source as if it were his own. Simply conceptualizing the law for public water proved difficult, and the Romans discussed various concepts of public use and the common good to solve this problem. Their solutions inform the following discussion of the legal institutions for water in relation to Roman property law generally.

Water as Private Property

The earliest water law appears in the *Twelve Tables* (c. 450 BCE), the actions for warding off rainwater and servitudes. Both institutions seem designed to serve the priorities of Rome's agricultural society. One addresses the problem of too much water, the other of too little. The action for warding off rainwater (*actio aquae pluviae arcendae*) provided a remedy against future harm caused by rainwater flowing from a neighbor's land. It applied only to rainwater, only on rural land, and only when the defendant had done some work that increased the risk of damage. There was, however, an exception for work that cultivated the land, such as plowing and digging ditches to irrigate or drain fields. Improvements such as these were common, and the structure of the action rewarded landowners who were proactive about the condition of their fields and incentivized neighbors to manage runoff cooperatively so as to avoid the costs of legal action.

The action for warding off rainwater also illustrates the remedy-based nature of Roman law. As noted above, it addressed only threatened or future damage on rural land. If rainwater had already caused damage, there was a different remedy, established by the *lex Aquilia* around 300 BCE. Or if runoff caused damage in town, yet another remedy.

Like the *actio aquae pluviae arcendae,* servitudes were an old institution known already in the *Twelve Tables,* but they mostly addressed scarcity not flooding. Ideally, a farm would have its own resources, consistent with the Roman ideal of self-sufficiency. The environment created a different reality: water resources were not distributed evenly, and the climate generated seasonal drought. The Romans responded to these environmental constraints with servitudes to articulate access to water.

A servitude was a praedial right of use, meaning that the right-holder did not own the water, only the right to use it. There were three servitudes for access to water: *aquaeductus* to conduct water, *haustus* to draw water, and *pecoris adpulsus* to water animals. There was also a servitude to discharge water (*stillicidium* or *flumina*). These water rights were included among the praedial servitudes, so-called because they were attached to estates (*praedia*). The right-holder owned the dominant estate to which the servitude was attached, while his neighbor owned the servient estate or the parcel of land whence the water came.

A praedial servitude equipped its holder with rights similar to an owner's. In its early form, *aquaeductus* combined ownership of a water source and a right to conduct the water. By the late Republic, the two components were combined in a single right similar to a right of use in modern law, but their character was somewhat paradoxical. Servitudes were incorporeal, like other rights of use, notably usufruct or a life interest in property. But unlike usufruct, servitudes were property rights more like ownership than contracts. The Romans grouped them with other real property that served agricultural productivity, such as land, slaves, and draft animals (*res mancipi*). Praedial servitudes were governed by the same legal mechanisms as other res mancipi. To create servitudes, the Romans used conveyances or legal procedures for transferring ownership of res mancipi (*mancipatio, in iure cessio*). Or, to claim ownership of a servitude, the right-holder used a modified form of *vindicatio*, the procedure for confirming ownership.

Servitudes were tightly connected with the agricultural communities in which they operated. Like other *res mancipi*, they facilitated farm work, for example channeling water for irrigation or granting access to water livestock. Praedial servitudes were attached to the land they served and transferred with it to a new owner when the property was sold or inherited. They were also restricted to adjacent land: that is, only neighbors could benefit from a servitude, ensuring that these rights were supported by close and steady social relationships. The parties to a servitude could also make agreements about how and when the water was to be used, using the law to define and support their common use of water. No written record was required to record the creation of a servitude, though some landowners will have recorded their servitudes on wax tablets or stone or bronze tablets. When disputes arose, neighbors relied on social norms and shared history to resolve questions about water rights. In turn, the social and economic needs of these local communities shaped the law on both private and public water sources.

Public Property

In Roman law, public property (*res publica*) could be owned by the state or open to all. Public places were usually open to all citizens for free use, for example, a public road, bath, or theater. The oceans, however, were also open to all, but not even the Romans believed that they owned the sea, although they sometimes claimed ownership of the sea shore. To add to the confusion, *res publica* was also the usual term for the Roman state itself. These ambiguities created some lack of clarity in Roman law on public property. To address the issues, the jurists worked with terms such as public benefit (*publica utilitas*) or common use (*usus communis*) and eventually developed a concept of common property (*res communes*).

Some water resources were strictly public property, such as the water in civic aqueducts. They were built with public funding or for the public with private funds, and they served public needs and were usually connected with a city. Ongoing civic administration reinforced the public nature of the water. Although imperial policy emphasized a free and full supply, actual allocation of water was more complex. At Rome, the aqueducts delivered water to public basins and fountains, imperial properties, and private individuals. Water flowed continuously in public fountains and was free and open to all. Some individuals had rights to tap the aqueducts and have water delivered to their private property. The emperor had water delivered to his own property both for his own enjoyment at palaces and for public use in monumental fountains and baths.

To manage the aqueducts' water, the Romans enacted statutes or decrees of the Senate, which are known from Frontinus' treatise and summarized in Tables 1 and 2. Similar laws are known from other cities and towns around the empire. Most of these laws focused on limiting individual access and protecting the physical structures themselves. Many of these laws attempt to control the water supply by imposing fines for illegal use. Sometimes, the law even offered half the fine to the individual who prosecuted a violation as an incentive for policing.

There was significant administrative law regulating delivery to private individuals. At Rome there was a multistep process that seems aimed at accountability, as outlined by Frontinus (Aq. 105–6). A right to private delivery from the aqueducts was both similar and different from a servitude. They were both rights of use but only personal rights applied to aqueducts' water. A personal right was like a contract or lease, although there was not always a fee or rent paid for city water. A right to city water was not attached to the land and lasted only as long the person owned the property to which the water was delivered. The laws on the aqueducts testify to competition over a scarce and economically valuable resource. Frontinus reports rampant fraud and profiteering from illegal taps on the aqueducts. The problem was not restricted to Rome, as reflected in imperial constitutions from Constantinople and Antioch (see Cases 4.17 and 4.18). Nor were aqueducts the only kind of public water to generate competition.

Public rivers were important sources of water across the empire. The

Table 1. Provisions of the Senate Decree of 116 BCE

prohibits illegal withdrawal of water	(*Aq.* 97.1)
prohibits watering the Circus Maximus without permission of aediles or censors	(*Aq.* 97.2)
prescribes as penalty confiscation of fields illegally irrigated with public water	(*Aq.* 97.3)
prescribes a fine for a contractor who fraudulently diverts water	(*Aq.* 97.4)
prescribes a fine for polluting the aqueducts' water	(*Aq.* 97.5–7)
orders aediles to appoint two landowners per city district to oversee the water supply	(*Aq.* 97.8)

Based on Frontinus, On the Water-Management of the City of Rome (*Aq.*)

jurists defined a river as public if it flowed year round (*perenne*), in contrast to seasonal torrents. In addition, all rivers in conquered territory were public because all land was owned by the local civic community or Rome itself. Public rivers were free and open for all citizens to use, like other public property. But a river is different from a theater or public bath, for example, and consequently raised different legal problems. Moreover, rivers were important for transportation, agriculture, and industry, as well as tax revenue, and these social needs generated conflict over rights to use public rivers.

To manage these varied policy aims, the Romans began to regulate public rivers through the praetor's edict early in the second century BCE. The law on public rivers developed as part of the ius honorarium, specifically through interdicts. An interdict was an administrative order issued by a magistrate (usually the praetor) to a private individual seeking legal protection. If an individual—the plaintiff—was prevented from

Table 2. Imperial Laws on the Aqueducts

11 BCE Senate Decrees	
establishes office of *curator aquarum* and honors, powers, and funding	(*Aq.* 100)
orders curator to maintain and inventory constant number of public fountains	(*Aq.* 104)
prescribes administration and infrastructure for grants to private individuals	(*Aq.* 106)
prohibits alienation or transfer of grants to *privati*	(*Aq.* 108)
orders compensation to landowners for materials used in repairing aqueducts	(*Aq.* 125)
orders clearway to be reserved around aqueducts and penalty for violations	(*Aq.* 127)
9 BCE lex Quinctia	
prescribes penalties for damage, jurisdiction for claims, and rules for clearway	(*Aq.* 129)
before 97 CE Imperial Instructions (*mandata*)	
restricts use of lapsed water (*aqua caduca*) to grants	(*Aq.* 111)

As presented in Frontinus, On the Water-Management of the City of Rome (*Aq.*)

using the river by another person's work in or around the river, he could present his situation to the praetor, who would decide whether or not to grant an interdict preventing the activity. Interdicts protected possession and use of property rather than ownership, and were thus available to both owners and nonowners. For this reason they were a flexible remedy that could protect the use of both public water, which individuals did not own, and private water, when ownership was in doubt, a not infrequent circumstance in the Roman world where there was no consistent system of title. By the second century BCE the praetor's edict contained several interdicts relating to water use (listed in Table 3).

Access to public rivers for sailing was an early focus of the interdicts, emphasized by comparisons with public roads (Case 3.17). The analogy was, however, more than a legal argument because boats were often towed upstream by animals or humans who walked along towpaths lining the river front. Subsequently, the jurists broadened the river interdicts, taking a holistic approach that addressed other interests in and around the river, starting with flood control. Soon interdicts also protected diversion of water and maintenance of hydraulic infrastructure (e.g., canals, drains). While the praetorian interdicts addressed practical concerns about the right to use public rivers, the jurists' discussions of

Table 3. Interdicts on Water

Interdicts on Public Rivers	
Flow	*Ne quid in flumine publico fiat, quo aliter aqua fluat, atque uti priore aestate fluxit* (*D.* 43.13)
Navigating	*Ut in flumine publico navigare liceat* (*D.* 43.14)
Shoring up banks	*De ripa munienda* (*D.* 43.15)
Interdicts on Private and Public Water	
Shoring up banks	*De ripa munienda* (*D.* 43.15)
Rivers	*De fluminibus. ne quid in flumine publico ripave eius fiat, quo peius navigetur* (*D.* 43.12)
Daily and Summer Water	*De aqua cottidiana et aestiva (D.* 43.20)
Canals	*De rivis* (*D.* 43.21)
Springs	*De fonte* (*D.* 43.22)
Drains	*De cloacis* (*D.* 43.23)

them reveal the conceptual difficulties of fitting water into Roman property law.

Common Property

Public rivers posed legal problems because they were freely accessible, an idea that bridged law and traditional Roman ideas about the natural world. Popular wisdom held that the sea and running water were free and open to all, like the air and the light of the sun and the moon. The earliest Roman evidence for the idea appears in Plautus' comedies in the second century BCE (*Asinaria* 198; Rudens 969–75), although idea of the sea as open access can be traced to Plato's *Laws* (7.824b). Cicero grappled with the question in his treatise *On Duties* (1.52), where he asserted that "running water [was] first among the common goods that all humans share." Although the other items in Cicero's list (fire, good advice) do not figure in the jurists' discussion, he framed the issues that persist in legal treatments of common property.

The jurists' discussion of free and open resources began with the sea and its shores. The Republican jurist Quintus Mucius endorsed the sea as free and open to all (*D.* 7.4.23 Pompon. 26 *ad Q. Muc.*). The legal status of the sea was, however, hard to reconcile with Roman property categories. It is sometimes associated with *res nullius,* which also included wild animals or fish in the sea.[1] While *res nullius* were free and open for all, the sea was different: anyone could take fish but no one could own the sea. The sea shore was sometimes considered public property, because everyone could use it. Public rivers were also free and open for all to use, like other public property, such as roads or theaters. But the shore and rivers are different from other public property because they are natural resources. The jurists recognized this difference when they theorized open access as part of natural law, *ius naturale,* that is, principles grounded in the physical reality of the world and sometimes associated with the Stoic conception of divine cosmic rationality. While *ius naturale* offered a philosophical framework for these legal concepts,

1 The term *res nullius* first appears in the middle of the second century CE in Gaius' textbook (*Inst.* 2.9), although earlier jurists discuss the concept.

it did not resolve the difficulty with applying property law to natural resources.

The problem centered on the character of public property. It was owned collectively, but individuals had a right to use it. The idea is conceptually simple yet hard to implement. For example, when seasonal drought lowered the level of rivers leaving not enough water for both shipping and irrigation, how was it possible for everyone to use it as if he owned it? The jurists addressed the problem with the concepts of common use (*communis usus*) or public utility (*publica utilitas*) to give a legal basis for rights in water resources. The jurists' discussions of these concepts led to the creation of a new property category, *res communes* or common goods. As defined by the Severan jurist Marcian *res communes* included the air, the sea, and the sea shore and, probably, running water. There was some disagreement about running water, but Marcian uses the same term (*aqua profluens*), as Cicero did, signaling a continuity between the law and cultural ideas about resources. Marcian's definition of *res communes* was endorsed in Justinian's law (*Institutes* 2.1.1) and has proved influential in later legal approaches to water resources. In turn, scholarship on modern law helps to frame the Roman evidence.

MODERN APPROACHES

Modern approaches to law and the environment illuminate the study of Roman water law, despite some historical and conceptual differences. Contemporary law confronts a broader range of hydraulic technology than the Romans deployed, as well as different economic contexts. In countries with civil law traditions, modern law codes drew from Roman law as did jurists of the early common law. In both common and civil traditions, contemporary scholarship on environmental law often begins from Roman property categories—private, public, common. Ancient and modern concepts of public and private are a fairly close fit, although the Roman state did not have the regulatory system that most modern nations enjoy. In addition, both modern and ancient law encounter some of the same difficulties with defining and applying the concept of common property.

Commons and Common Pool Resource

The jurists' approach to water rights belongs within more recent scholarship on the commons and common pool resources. In early modern England, a commons was shared grazing land that everyone in a village could use freely. The "commons" became a symbol of environmental destiny in Garrett Hardin's essay, "The Tragedy of the Commons," which argued that a commons would inevitably self-destruct through unregulated overuse. The idea of the commons was refined in subsequent scholarship, particularly by Elinor Ostrom, who demonstrated that tight-knit communities could successfully manage a commons. Ostrom's work created an influential paradigm for the study and governance of the environment and especially, common pool resources. A common pool resource is a shared resource which is difficult to regulate and which is characterized by subtractability, that is, each person's use of it decreases what is available to others. A common pool resource may be "open access," that is, everyone can use it freely. But more often, common pool resources are managed by custom or law or by a combination of both law and social norms. Small, tight-knit communities tend to be more successful at avoiding the tragedy of the commons and regulating their shared resources.

"Commons" and "common pool resource" are not strictly legal terms but broader concepts that operate in legal, historical, and political discussions of the environment. They are useful because water does not fit neatly into legal categories of property, as the Romans recognized. The physical fluidity of water poses problems whether it is classified as a common good owned by everyone (*res communes*) or public property owned by the state (*res publica*) or as property that is owned by no one at all (*res nullius*). The concept of a commons transcends categories, informing Roman approaches to both public and private property. In turn, Roman ideas about common property are informed by the legal concepts of possession and ownership. Since the Roman concept of ownership (*dominium*) is less fully theorized than its modern analogue, modern conceptual frameworks can help to fill in the gaps in our understanding of the Roman evidence.

The Environmental Bundle

The Roman concept of ownership (*dominium*) was long thought to represent the property owner's monolithic power over property. More recent scholarship recognizes its composite nature—that is, that ownership is composed of a bundle of component rights; Honoré's 1961 essay is an essential starting point. The idea of component rights is especially useful for understanding the law of common pool resources, because it allows legal authority to be shared among users as the resources themselves are shared. Environmental scholars have identified a particular set of component rights which is sometimes called the environmental bundle of rights.

The environmental bundle is composed of the rights of access, withdrawal, management, exclusion, and alienation. Access means getting to or into a source of water; for example, approaching a spring to draw water or sailing on a river. Withdrawal involves taking some of the resource, for example, diverting water from a river or aqueduct. Management refers to maintenance or repairs of infrastructure necessary for exercising rights of access or withdrawal. A right of exclusion empowers a person to exclude others from using the resource, while the person with a right of alienation can transfer ownership to another person.

The environmental bundle and the notion of a common pool resource together provide a useful framework for studying Roman water rights. The Romans did not have a term equivalent to a "commons" in the historical sense, although they often exploited grazing land communally. They used the adjective *communis*, "common," with a meaning similar to "commons" to describe natural resources that were free and open to all. The closest Roman analogue to common pool resource is the legal category *res communes*, which included the air, the sea, the sea shores, and running water.

Even though they did not use the same language, the Romans grappled with the same problems of managing water rights and worked with ideas that correspond to modern concepts. For example, Cicero prefigures the concept of subtractability, when he explains that we use resources such as running water, as common goods but that we also must limit sharing because, although supply of these resources is limited, demand is not (*On Duties* 1.51). Moreover, when the Romans regulated water, whether it was public, private, or common, they began from ownership and rights consonant with the environmental bundle. Adopting these modern concepts allows us to interrogate ideas implicit in the Roman sources and thus to develop a fuller understanding of Roman water law. Moreover, this analytical framework facilitates comparison of ancient and modern legal approaches to issues that were as highly contested in ancient Rome as they are today.

WATER LAW IN INSCRIPTIONS

The cases include evidence from six Roman inscriptions, three from Spain, two from Italy, and one from North Africa. All four inscriptions belong to the period of Classical Roman law, approximately 27 BCE—250 CE. They are important documentary evidence for the practice of law which complements the analytical writings of the Roman jurists. One inscription records the municipal law or town charter with laws on both private water resources and a civic aqueduct, two texts record decrees about civic aqueducts, and three inscriptions record resolutions to disputes about water rights.

The *Tabula Contrebiensis* records an agreement about the construction of an aqueduct or canal in 89 BCE on the south bank of the Ebro River in northeastern Spain (*CIL* 1^3.2951a; Case 4.3). The inscription is named for Contrebia, a community whose leaders served as judges or arbiters in a dispute between three other communities. The Salluienses wanted to purchase a strip of land on which to build the aqueduct from the Sosinestani, but the Allavonenses protested their right to sell it. The agreement authorizes the purchase, describes the land, and gives instructions for the process of arbitration. The Roman authorities played a role in resolving the dispute when the Roman governor, Gaius Valerius Flaccus, assigned jurisdiction over the dispute. In addition, the agreement is framed in Roman legal language, which represents some of the earliest evidence for the adaptation of Roman law for communities in the provinces.

The *lex rivi Hiberiensis* (*lrH*) or Ebro irrigation decree records bylaws for an irrigation community on the Ebro river in Roman Spain during the reign of Hadrian (117–138 CE). The irrigators diverted water from the river into a main canal, the Ebro canal or *rivus Hiberiensis* (Case 3.29). The water was then distributed by gravity flow to subsidiary canals serving individual parcels of land along the main canal. The *lrH* records the settlement of a dispute between upstream and downstream irrigators and outlines the legal rules that guided their practices, such as contributions for repairs, allocation of water, procedures for making decisions and enforcing the rules. The legal mechanisms and administrative structure are recognizably Roman but the substance of the legal rules probably reflects local practice.

The Lamasba decree records resolution to a dispute within an irrigation community in the territory of Lamasba in Roman North Africa during the reign of Elagabalus (218–222 CE) (*CIL* 8.18587 = 4440; Case 3.25). The community shared water from a spring or a seasonal stream, the Aqua Claudiana, which was impounded in two different reservoirs. The inscription includes a brief preamble explaining that local leaders authorized a special commission to investigate water use and that this decree records the allocation of water. The bulk of the inscription contained a register of allocations, although only a small part of it is preserved. The Lamasba decree is similar to two fragmentary inscriptions from Italy that record schedules for water delivery; they are presented in chapter 2 as figures 2.1 and 2.2. Although these inscriptions do not use legal language for the allocation of water, they provide important evidence for the practices that Roman law regulated.

The *lex Coloniae Iuliae Genetivae* (Urso law, *CIL* 1^2.5, Cases 2.4, 3.33, 4.4, 4.10) is a town charter enacted by Rome to prescribe and authorize the law for the colony for Caesar's veterans near Urso (Osuna) in southwestern Spain around 44 BCE. The inscription records a revised version of the charter from the midfirst century CE when the Flavian emperors reorganized the Roman communities in Spain. A colony or *municipium* had political and legal institutions modeled on Rome's. Two annual executive magistrates, *duumviri* (or *duoviri*) supervised the town like consuls and presided over the local assembly of councilmen (*decuriones*). *Decuriones* joined the assembly after election to the office of quaestor or aedile, both with functions similar to their Roman analogues. These civic officials were in charge of water rights in both rural territory and the civic aqueduct.

Inscriptions also document aqueduct laws for two cities in Italy, Amiternum and Venafrum. Augustus gave an aqueduct to Venafrum when he established a colony there after 17 BCE. It is possible that there was an earlier civic aqueduct, since Cicero mentions the collapse of an underground aqueduct at Venafrum (*Letters to His Brother Quintus* 3.1.3). The aqueduct brought water from springs at Volturno to the city in a channel that ran both above and below ground. A long inscription records a decree enacting laws on this aqueduct from sometime in the years 16–10 BCE (*CIL* 10.4842; Cases 4.31–35). It was discovered on a stone built into a building at Venafrum (Venafro) in 1846, and subsequently moved to a local museum. Although only about half of the decree survives, it provides details about the regulation of the city's water supply. There have also been found several boundary stones that originally marked the clearway of the Venafrum aqueduct.

Amiternum was an important town in the upper Aterno valley in central Italy. Its aqueduct was either constructed or repaired in the first century CE when the inscription was erected. The inscription was discovered near the town during the first archaeological excavations of the site in 1888–1889 (*CIL* 12.1853; Case 4.25). It describes the route of the aqueduct from its collection basin through a series of reservoirs located on private estates. Remains of an aqueduct on the west side of town may belong to the structure regulated by this law.

NOTE TO INSTRUCTORS

While writing this casebook, I tested it in the classroom with my students at Indiana University. They responded enthusiastically to the topic, and their questions and comments helped me to revise both study questions and translation. I assign students to write out answers to the study questions as they prepare the cases for each class as homework. In class, we work through cases in a Socratic discussion, but I find that my students are better able to participate after they have discussed the cases briefly in small groups. Over the years I have found that writing better than discussion reveals what students understand, or don't understand, about the law. Consequently I assign both formal papers and informal in-class writing assignments.

To help students gain a fuller picture of Roman law, I assign Borkowski's *Textbook on Roman Law*, revised and expanded by Paul du Plessis, 5th ed. (Oxford: Oxford University Press, 2015). I also assign to students a law school primer on legal reasoning: D. S. Romantz and K. E. Vinson, *Legal Analysis: The Fundamental Skill*, 2nd ed. (Durham, NC: Carolina Academic Press, 2009). Although Romantz and Vinson use contemporary law and situations, they effectively model deductive and inductive reasoning and introduce categories of policy goals that help students to analyze Roman law.

Students are particularly interested in aqueducts and I usually assign supplementary materials. Frontinus' treatise presents much that is essential for understanding the policy concerns that motivated the laws. Students can read the entire work in print translated by H. B. Evans, *Water Distribution in Ancient Rome* (1994) and online translated by R. H. Rodgers, http://www.uvm.edu/~rrodgers/Frontinus.html. Rodgers' print edition (2004) is invaluable for both Latin text and notes on technical, historical, and administrative issues.

Learning about the material remains of aqueducts helps students to appreciate the challenges of regulating them. For the city of Rome, P. Aicher's book, *Guide to the Aqueducts of Rome*, is a good place to start, or his short introduction on Nova, https://www.pbs.org/wgbh/nova/article/roman-aqueducts/.

Digital resources are also useful. Photos, information, and bibliography on many hydraulic installations are compiled at the Roman Aqueducts website, http://www.romanaqueducts.info. A digital map of Rome's aqueducts by K. W. Rinne can be found at Aquae Urbis Romae: The Waters of the City of Rome, http://www3.iath.virginia.edu/waters/. The Atlas Project of Roman Aqueducts at https://www.romaq.org/ has mapped the routes of hundreds of aqueducts around the empire, including the ones discussed in this case book.

The essential guide to Roman hydraulic engineering is A. Trevor Hodge, *Roman Aqueducts and Water Supply*. With caution I use a short video created by Gary Robbins, professor of geology in the Department of Natural Resources and the Environment at the University of Connecticut, "Modeling the Art and Engineering of Roman Aqueducts with Lego Bricks" (https://www.youtube.com/watch?v=xAcQ1r3UEAQ). I screen this video in class so that I can address its errors and correct any misunderstanding; despite its flaws, it gives students a simplified overview that we can refine through our study of more specialized readings and discussion.

Students and instructors alike can actively engage with the Roman evidence because the cases include background on legal doctrine and cultural history. The bibliography guides further study. Study questions help students practice legal reasoning, examine the internal logic of the law, and evaluate its response to the challenges of managing water in the Roman world. Studying Roman law with a casebook builds the analytical skills that are central to the liberal arts and legal study in particular.

NOTE ON TRANSLATIONS

Translations of cases from the legal sources and inscriptions are my own. In translating the *Digest of Justinian* and *The Codex of Justinian*, I have learned much from the editions by A. Watson (2009) and B. W. Frier (2016) respectively, but my translations are somewhat freer in places to improve clarity without misrepresenting the Latin meaning.

Robert H. Rodgers graciously allowed me to use his translation of Frontinus' treatise on Rome's aqueducts:
http://www.uvm.edu/~rrodgers/Frontinus.html

CHAPTER 1

The Action for Warding Off Rainwater

The *Actio Aquae Pluviae Arcendae* or Action for Warding Off Rainwater was aimed at protecting land from erosion and flooding. It provided a remedy against future harm caused by water flowing from a neighbor's land. A landowner could bring the Action for Warding Off Rainwater against a neighbor if he feared the impact of some activity or work on his neighbor's land. If his action was successful, his neighbor could be compelled to remove the work or at the very least to allow its removal. A defendant who ordered his slave to do the work could be compelled to hand over the slave to the plaintiff.

In order to hold a landowner liable under the Action for Warding Off Rainwater, several conditions had to be met. First, as noted above, the Action for Warding Off Rainwater addressed only threatened damage. There was a different remedy if damage had already occurred under the lex Aquilia, an early third-century BCE statute covering all kinds of wrongful loss. Second, the potentially harmful work could be either an activity or a man-made structure, and there could be an action for a structure even if no one knew for certain that it was man-made. Third, the work usually had to be located on land adjacent to the plaintiff's land. Last and most importantly, the work had to change the way the water flowed downhill, altering its natural course. This last condition occasioned juristic discussions of the dynamic relationship between humans and the natural environment.

The Action for Warding Off Rainwater can be traced to the *Twelve*

Tables, Rome's first law code, ca. 450 BCE (*XII Tab.* 7.8). Although only part of the original law is preserved, much is known about the Action for Warding Off Rainwater from the treatment by the jurists, as excerpted in the *Digest of Justinian*, where the action is most often referred to with the phrase *aquae pluviae arcendae*.

While the Action for Warding Off Rainwater protected land and property, it was not a property action (*in rem*) but a personal action (*in personam*). In a personal action, when the defendant was found liable, he had to make good the situation not with monetary compensation but by his own effort—for example, removing the structure or ceasing the activity that threatened damage. In a personal action, the legal right and liability attached to individuals and did not continue when they no longer owned the property. If a potential plaintiff sold his land, he lost his right to bring a claim under the Action for Warding Off Rainwater; conversely, a potential defendant who sold his land could no longer be held liable.

I. Scope of the Action for Warding Off Rainwater (*actio aquae pluviae arcendae*)

Case 1.1. Statutory Basis of the Action

D. 40.7.21 pr Pomponius, libro septimo ex Plautio

> sic et verba legis duodecim tabularum veteres interpretati sunt "si aqua pluvia nocet," id est "si nocere poterit."

Pomponius, in the seventh book from Plautius

> Earlier jurists understood the words of the *Twelve Tables*, "if rainwater causes harm," to mean "if it could cause harm."

1. In this case, Pomponius quotes part of the wording of the action for warding off rainwater from the *Twelve Tables* (ca. 450 BCE). The *Twelve Tables* provided a basis in statute for the action for warding off rainwater. It was an action in the *ius civile*, in the *legis actio* form. Which clause from the law does Pomponius quote? What exactly does it mean?

2. How did jurists of the Republican period (*veteres*) interpret the clause from the *Twelve Tables*? Explain the difference between the original wording and the later interpretation.
3. How did the Republican jurists change the scope of the action? Who benefits from this change? Does this change make the action more useful? Why or why not?
4. Does the Action for Warding Off Rainwater provide a remedy for damage that has already occurred or for damage that might occur in the future? In Roman law, there was a separate action for damage to property. A plaintiff could sue for compensation for damage to his property with a claim based on the lex Aquilia, a third-century BCE statute. What are the pros and cons of having separate actions for damage already done and potential future damage?

Case 1.2. What Is Rainwater?

D. 39.3.1 pr Ulpianus, libro quinquagensimo tertio ad Edictum

Si cui aqua pluvia damnum dabit, actione aquae pluviae arcendae avertetur aqua. aquam pluviam dicimus, quae de caelo cadit atque imbre excrescit, sive per se haec aqua caelestis noceat, ut Tubero ait, sive cum alia mixta sit.

Ulpian in the fifty-third book on the Edict

If rainwater will cause harm, it can be prevented with the action to ward off rainwater. We say that rain is water that falls from the sky and comes from a rainstorm, whether rainfall could cause harm by itself or, as Tubero says, when other water is combined with it.

1. What is the purpose of the action for warding off rainwater?
2. What is rainwater? Or, what is NOT rainwater? Answer with a few examples.
3. How does Ulpian define rainwater? Come up with a few examples that test the definition.
4. Ulpian quotes Tubero to clarify the purpose and scope of the action, or does Tubero's qualification raise as many questions as it answers? Explain.

5. An earlier Republican jurist, Quintus Mucius also discussed the Action for Warding Off Rainwater, and explained how rainwater should be defined for this action:

If we consider "rainwater" only water which we see collected from rain, then Mucius would come along to say that all water which was increased by raining should be warded off, because the words "rain" and "raining" are etymologically related (si aquam pluviam eam modo intellegeremus quam imbri collectam videremus, veniret Mucius, qui, quia coniugata verba essent pluvia et pluendo, diceret omnem aquam oportere arceri quae pluendo crevisset). (Cicero, *Topica* 38)

How does Mucius' definition differ from Tubero's and Ulpian's? Which definition would make it easier to prove that rainwater was involved in a legal dispute? Which makes better law? Why?

6. In another case, Ulpian offers diagnostics to help a potential plaintiff identify rainwater: "And that a body of water is regarded as being swollen by rain if it changes color when it increases in quantity (*D.* 39.3.1.16 Ulp. 53 *ad Ed.*). What qualities does Ulpian use to recognize rainwater? How helpful is his diagnostic? Can you think of a situation in which it would <u>not</u> work?
7. Can the Action for Warding Off Rainwater be used if the water is hot? Jurists disagreed: Trebatius allowed it but Ulpian disagreed because rainwater was not hot (*D.* 39.3.3.1 Ulp. 53 *ad Ed.*). Are you persuaded by Ulpian's rationale? Why or why not? Compare Labeo's approach to hot water in irrigation (Case 3.23, Study Question 5).

Case 1.3. Rural or Urban?

D. 39.3.1.20 Ulpianus libro quinquagensimo tertio ad Edictum

Apud Labeonem autem invenio relatum, si ex agro meo aqua fluens noceat loco qui est intra continentia, hoc est aedificio, non posse me aquae pluviae arcendae conveniri: quod si ex continentibus profluens in meum agrum defluat eique noceat, aquae pluviae arcendae esse actionem.

Ulpian in the fifty-third book on the Edict

> I find it reported in Labeo that I cannot be sued under the action for warding off rainwater if water flowing from my field could harm a place that is within the city limits, that is, built-up. But if water flowing from the city limits onto my field and could harm it flowing down, there is an action for warding off rainwater.

1. The Action for Warding Off Rainwater did not apply everywhere: Where could it be used? Did it matter where the water came from? Or was it the type of land that was affected? Cicero knew the action applied on rural and not urban land (Topica 43).
2. Labeo does not mention towns or cities directly but refers to the built-up area (*continentia*) which can be interpreted as urban space when we read it with Cassius' opinion comparing the Action for Warding Off Rainwater with another action that applies to water flowing from an urban structure (*ex aedificio urbano, D.* 39.3.1.19 Ulp. 53 *ad Ed.*, and see Case 1.23). Rome was bounded by the pomerium (a religious perimeter) and by two rings of walls. But the city extended beyond these boundaries with a suburban zone of dense settlement and farms and villas. How easy would it be to apply Labeo's rule to determine where the Action for Warding Off Rainwater applied? What does his rule reveal about the Roman concept of a city?
3. Does it make sense to treat cultivated land differently from land built-up like a town? What factors could justify the different treatment, for example, the nature of the locations, typical activities in these locations. Try to think of at least one additional factor.
4. Nearly two centuries after Labeo, Ulpian quotes and affirms his rule about the Action for Warding Off Rainwater and the city (*D.* 39.3.1.17 Ulp. 53 *ad Ed.*). What circumstances might have made it necessary to reiterate the rule? Can we assume that the city landscape changed over that time? Or do other factors better explain the legal discussion? In this case, Ulpian characterizes the Action for Warding Off Rainwater as "specific," citing Labeo and Cascellius for these descriptions. In what sense is the Action for Warding Off Rainwater "specific"? Why does it make sense to have an action that applies only on rural land?

Case 1.4. Potential Harm from Work

D. 39.3.1.1 Ulpianus, libro quinquagensimo tertio ad Edictum

Haec autem actio locum habet in damno nondum facto, opere tamen iam facto, hoc est de eo opere, ex quo damnum timetur: totiensque locum habet, quotiens manu facto opere agro aqua nocitura est, id est cum quis manu fecerit, quo aliter flueret, quam natura soleret, si forte immittendo eam aut maiorem fecerit aut citatiorem aut vehementiorem aut si comprimendo redundare effecit. quod si natura aqua noceret, ea actione non continentur.

Ulpian in the fifty-third book on the Edict

This action is applicable when harm has not yet occurred but when some work has already been done, that is, when harm is feared from this work. It is valid as often as water is about to cause harm because of some man-made work, that is, when someone builds so that water flows otherwise than it naturally used to flow; for example, if by releasing the water he makes it accidentally greater or quicker or stronger or if by retaining it he makes it overflow. But if water could cause harm naturally, it is not prevented by this action.

1. The Action for Warding Off Rainwater applied before damage occurred. What other conditions must be met? Draw up a comprehensive list of conditions based on Cases 1–4.
2. Which of these conditions would be the most difficult for a plaintiff to prove? Why?
3. The Action for Warding Off Rainwater applied on private land, but a different legal remedy was available when runoff from public land posed a danger. In this situation, Ulpian recommends that the landowner arrange a *cautio* or guarantee against anticipated injury with the contractor doing the work on public property (*D.* 39.3.3.3 Ulp. 53 *ad Ed.*). This *cautio* was a formal promise in which the party undertaking construction promised to make good any damage to property that might occur as a result of his work. If damage occurred, the *cautio* was grounds for a claim. How does the *cautio* differ from the Action for Warding Off Rainwater? Which one would a landowner prefer, if he had a choice? Why?

II. Procedural Issues

A. Plaintiff and Defendant

Case 1.5. A Personal Action for Property

D. 39.3.6.5 Ulpianus, libro quinquagensimo tertio ad Edictum

Aquae pluviae arcendae actionem sciendum est non in rem, sed personalem esse.

D. 39.3.7 pr Paulus, libro octavo decimo ad Edictum

Is cum quo aquae pluviae arcendae agitur, quod opus fecit, licet cedere loco paratus sit, cogitur accipere iudicium, quoniam et suo nomine convenitur, ut opus tollat.

Ulpian in the fifty-third book on the Edict

We must understand that the action to ward off rainwater is not a property action but a personal action.

Paul, in the eighteenth book on the Edict

Although person may be prepared to withdraw from the site, when an action for warding off rainwater is brought against him, because he made a work, he is compelled to accept an order to remove the work, since [the action] was brought in his name.

1. What does the plaintiff get if he wins his suit under the Action for Warding Off Rainwater? What must the defendant do if he is found liable?
2. What does Paul mean by "withdraw," when he writes that the defendant "is prepared to withdraw from the site"? Is he suggesting that the defendant would give up ownership of the land or simply stop the work? Why is it not enough for the defendant to "withdraw from the site"?
3. Although the Action for Warding Off Rainwater protected property, it was not an action *in rem* but an action *in personam*, as Ulpian indicates in the first part of this case. How does Paul indicate the personal liability of the defendant? Why might an action *in rem* be expected?

Personal liability was attached to the defendant and not to the property, similar to liability on a contract. Ordinarily, plaintiffs might prefer *in rem* actions because they could bring greater financial compensation than *in personam* actions which were limited to the amount of the contract. What circumstances made a personal action more appropriate for rainwater than a property action?

Case 1.6. Who Can Be Plaintiff?

D. 39.3.1.13 Ulpianus, libro quinquagensimo tertio ad Edictum

Item sciendum est hanc actionem vel superiori adversus inferiorem competere, ne aquam, quae natura fluat, opere facto inhibeat per suum agrum decurrere, et inferiori adversus superiorem, ne aliter aquam mittat, quam fluere natura solet.

Ulpian in the fifty-third book on the Edict

In addition we must understand that this action is available to higher against lower, so that [the owner of the lower land] does not prevent water from running down across his field by building something, and to lower against the higher, so that [the owner of the higher land] does not release water in any way other than it usually flows naturally.

1. In this case, "higher" and "lower" refer to owners of land on different levels. Which owner can be plaintiff in a claim on the Action for Warding Off Rainwater? Which owner can be defendant?
2. Why would the owner of lower land bring the Action for Warding Off Rainwater?
3. Why would the owner of higher land bring the Action for Warding Off Rainwater?
4. Does this case mean that the Action for Warding Off Rainwater is available only for land on a slope? Explain.

Case 1.7. Who Can Be Defendant?

D. 39.3.4.2 Ulpianus, libro quinquagensimo tertio ad Edictum

Idem Iulianus scribit aquae pluviae arcendae actionem non nisi cum domino esse idcircoque, si colonus ignorante domino opus fecerit,

> dominum fundi nihil amplius quam patientiam praestare debere, colonum autem interdicto quod vi aut clam impensam quoque restituendi operis et damnum, si quod ex eo datum fuerit, praestare cogendum. si tamen dominus desideret caveri sibi damni infecti ab eo, ex cuius praedio nocet, aequissimum erit caveri oportere.

Ulpian in the fifty-third book on the Edict

> The same Julian writes that there is no action to ward off rainwater except with the owner, and for this reason if a tenant builds something without the owner's knowledge, the owner of the farm has to provide nothing more than permission, but the tenant must be compelled with an interdict against force or stealth to pay the cost of restoring the work and the loss, if any has come from it. Nevertheless if the owner wishes a guarantee to be given against threatened damage by the person whose land is the source of harm, it will be most just to require a guarantee.

1. Who can be a defendant in a claim on the Action for Warding Off Rainwater?
2. Under what circumstances can a tenant and not the landowner be defendant? What happens if the tenant builds a threatening structure with the landowner's knowledge?
3. The interdict against force or stealth was an administrative order that authorized a plaintiff to bring a claim for restoration of his property. Reconstruct the rationale behind Ulpian's opinion. What problems could arise? Does his solution adequately take into account the economic situation of the parties? Is it fair?
4. Who bears the risk of damage from runoff in this case, the landowner or the tenant? What are the pros and cons of this allocation of risk?
5. In the second sentence Ulpian suggests an alternate remedy, the *cautio* against anticipated injury. If a landowner (or potential plaintiff) was concerned about run-off risk from work on neighboring land, he could ask the neighbor to give a guarantee to cover the cost of potential damage. Is the *cautio* a better solution than a claim on the Action for Warding Off Rainwater? Why or why not? See Case 1.4 for the use of a cautio for run-off risk from work done on public property. Does it make sense to apply the same legal remedy for work on both public and private land the same way? Explain.

Case 1.8. An Agreeable Neighbor

D. 39.3.19 Pomponius, libro quarto decimo ad Quintum Mucium

Labeo ait, si patiente vicino opus faciam, ex quo ei aqua pluvia noceat, non teneri me actione aquae pluviae arcendae:

D. 39.3.20 Pomponius, libro trigensimo quarto ad Sabinum

Sed hoc ita, si non per errorem aut imperitiam deceptus fuerit: nulla enim voluntas errantis est.

Pomponius, in the fourteenth book on Quintus Mucius

Labeo says that if I do some work, with my neighbor's permission, and rainwater could cause harm because of the work, I am not liable to an action to ward off rainwater.

Pomponius, in the thirty-fourth book on Sabinus

But this is so only if he was not misled by error or ignorance, since there is no consent when someone makes a mistake.

1. Why does Labeo decide that the defendant should not be liable under the Action for Warding Off Rainwater? Do you agree? Explain.
2. How does Pomponius qualify Labeo's opinion? Does his qualification broaden or narrow the standard for the Action for Warding Off Rainwater? That is, does it make it harder or easier to hold a defendant liable under the Action for Warding Off Rainwater?
3. What assumptions do Labeo and Pomponius make about the relationship between neighbors? How realistic are their assumptions? What sticking points might make it difficult to get a neighbor's permission to undertake a particular work project?
4. A landowner might informally agree to let water run to his property from a neighbor's land, as Labeo suggests in this case. Alternatively he could arrange a servitude that gave his neighbor a right to discharge water onto his land (see Case 1.23). Labeo agreed with Ofilius that there could be no claim if there was a servitude, unless the damage was "above average" (*ultra modum, D.* 39.3.2.10 Paul. 49 *ad Ed.*). Can you explain why? (For servitudes, see chapter 2)

Case 1.9. The Persistent Neighbor

D. 39.3.14.4 Paulus, libro quadragensimo nono ad Edictum

De eo opere, quod post litem contestatam factum est, novo iudicio agendum est.

D. 39.3.15 Paulus, libro sexto decimo ad Sabinum

Sed interdum opus et quod post litem contestatam factum est tolletur, si id quod antecessit tolli sine eo non potest.

Paul, in the forty-ninth book on the Edict

Work that is done after legal action is begun must be litigated in a new trial.

Paul, in the sixteenth book on Sabinus

But sometimes even a construction made after the joinder of issue will be removed, if work that was done earlier cannot be removed without removing it.

1. What legal recourse do I have if my neighbor does more work even after I bring a claim under the Action for Warding Off Rainwater against him? Under what circumstances must I bring a second claim under the Action for Warding Off Rainwater for the new work?
2. How practical is Paul's solution to this problem? What difficulties might the parties encounter in determining whether a second action is necessary?
3. What costs does Paul's solution involve? Who bears these costs, plaintiff or defendant? Is this allocation of costs fair? Why or why not?
4. How effective is Paul's solution likely to be in deterring the persistent neighbor? Or in promoting cooperation between neighbors? Explain.

Case 1.10. Buyers and Sellers

D. 39.3.6.4 Ulpianus, libro quinquagensimo tertio ad Edictum

Si quis prius, quam aquae pluviae arcendae agat, dominium ad alium transtulerit fundi, desinit habere aquae pluviae arcendae actionem eaque ad eum transibit, cuius ager esse coepit: cum enim damnum futurum contineat, ad eum qui dominus erit incipiet actio pertinere, quamvis, cum alterius dominium esset, opus a vicino factum sit.

Ulpian in the fifty-third book on the Edict

If someone transfers ownership of a farm to another person before he brings an action to ward off rainwater, he ceases to have the action, and it will pass to the person to whom the field belongs. For the action will begin to concern the person who will be the owner since it involves future damage, even though the work was done by a neighbor when ownership belonged to another person.

1. Can a person who has sold his land bring a claim under the Action for Warding Off Rainwater? Why or why not?
2. Why might a seller want to pursue the Action for Warding Off Rainwater even after he had sold the land? Why is it a better solution for the new owner to bring an action?
3. There was a lively real estate market in Roman Italy. A productive estate with a well-appointed villa could fetch a high price, especially if it was located in easy reach of town. How would a risk of damaging runoff affect buyers and sellers in this market? Who has a greater financial interest in preventing water damage, the buyer or the seller? Why?

B. Consequences of Liability

Case 1.11. Removing the Work

D. 39.3.1.2 Ulpianus, libro quinquagensimo tertio ad Edictum

Neratius scribit: opus, quod quis fecit, ut aquam excluderet, quae exundante palude in agrum eius refluere solet, si ea palus aqua pluvia ampliatur eaque aqua repulsa eo opere agris vicini noceat, aquae pluviae actione cogetur tollere.

Ulpian in the fifty-third book on the Edict

Neratius writes: he will be compelled by an action on warding off rainwater to remove a work that he has made to keep out water that used to flow back onto his field when a swamp flooded, if this swamp swells with rainwater and this water could harm his neighbor's fields because it is kept back by the work.

1. Why does Neratius find the defendant liable in this case? What conditions must be met in order to find him liable?
2. Which of the definitions of rainwater in Case 1.2 seems most consistent with Neratius' opinion in this case?
3. What must the defendant do, if he is found liable? How good an outcome is this for the plaintiff? What difficulties might he have enforcing the verdict?

Case 1.12. Who Pays?

D. 39.3.6.7 Ulpianus, libro quinquagensimo tertio ad Edictum

Celsus scribit, si quid ipse feci, quo tibi aqua pluvia noceat, mea impensa tollere me cogendum, si quid alius qui ad me non pertinet, sufficere, ut patiar te tollere. sed si servus meus fecerit, servum quidem noxae dedere debeo: quod autem is cui heres sum fecit, perinde est, atque si ipse fecissem.

Ulpian in the fifty-third book on the Edict

Celsus writes that if I myself built something so that rainwater could harm you, I am to be compelled to remove [it] at my own expense. But if someone who has no connection to me [did it, he writes that] it is enough for me to allow you to remove it. But if my slave did it <or a person to whom I am heir> I should hand over the slave in noxal surrender. But if a person to whom I am heir did it, then it is as if I myself had done it.

1. When a defendant lost in a case on the Action for Warding Off Rainwater, he could be compelled to remove the harmful work, but he did not always have to do it himself or cover the costs. Celsus considers four different scenarios. Describe them as fully as you can. Who built the structure in each case? What is the defendant's relationship to the builder?
2. When was defendant responsible for removing the work himself? What are the alternatives? Does it make sense to treat these situations differently? Why or why not?

3. Why does Celsus impose different consequences when the landowner did not construct the harmful work himself? Would a plaintiff prefer to deal with a defendant who had built the work himself? Why or why not?
4. Noxal surrender is one of those institutions of Roman law that reveal the oddities of the law on slavery. Although a slave was classified as property in Roman law and could not be a party to a lawsuit, he or she could bear liability. When a slave was determined to be liable, his owner had a choice either to pay the compensation or to give the slave to the plaintiff in a procedure called noxal surrender. In a suit on the Action for Warding Off Rainwater, when a slave had built the harmful work, Celsus gives the defendant the option of noxal surrender. In what sense is the slave liable for the damage? Does the option of noxal surrender give more advantage to the defendant or to the plaintiff? Explain.
5. In Roman law on inheritance, the heir assumes the legal personality of the deceased, both its advantages (e.g., property ownership) and its disadvantages (e.g., debts). How does Celsus' opinion take this principle into account? What complications could arise in bringing the Action for Warding Off Rainwater against an heir?
6. What does this case reveal about the organization of labor in the Roman world?

III. Work and Causes of Action

A. Farm Work

Case 1.13. Exemptions

D. 39.3.1.3–5 Ulpianus, libro quinquagensimo tertio ad Edictum

De eo opere, quod agri colendi causa aratro factum sit, Quintus Mucius ait non competere hanc actionem. Trebatius autem non quod agri, sed quod frumenti dumtaxat quaerendi causa aratro factum solum excepit. (4) Sed et fossas agrorum siccandorum causa factas Mucius ait fundi colendi causa fieri, non tamen oportere corrivandae aquae causa fieri:

> sic enim debere quem meliorem agrum suum facere, ne vicini deteriorem faciat. (5) Sed et si quis arare et serere possit etiam sine sulcis aquariis, teneri eum, si quid ex his, licet agri colendi causa videatur fecisse: quod si aliter serere non possit, nisi sulcos aquarios fecerit, non teneri. Ofilius autem ait sulcos agri colendi causa directos ita, ut in unam pergant partem, ius esse facere.

Ulpian in the fifty-third book on the Edict

> Quintus Mucius says that this action is not available for work done with a plow to cultivate a field. Trebatius however excludes from the action work done with a plow not to cultivate a field but only to seek a crop. (4) But Mucius says that ditches (*fossas*) to drain fields are made to cultivate the farm, but the ditches should not be made to channel water into a single stream. For [he says, the farmer] ought to make his own field better without making his neighbor's field worse. (5) But that if someone is able to plow and sow also without trenches for water (*sine sulcis aquariis*), he is to be held liable if any [harm could come] from them, even though he seems to have made them to cultivate his field. But if he is not able to sow in any other way except if he made trenches for water, he is not liable. Ofilius, however, says that it is right to make water trenches oriented so that they run to one part [of the field] to cultivate it.

1. This case reports the views of three Republican jurists (Quintus Mucius, Trebatius, Ofilius) on work that could be exempt from the Action for Warding Off Rainwater. Why was some work exempt? Do they agree? Explain?
2. What do jurists mean by "cultivating a field"? How do their examples help to define this standard?
3. What qualification does Ofilius add to Mucius' definition? Why should water channels (*sulci*) be treated differently from the ditches (*fossae*)? Why might these types of "work" have caused disagreement?
4. Around the same time as Ofilius gave his opinion, another case tested the definition of exempted work when the Action for Warding Off Rainwater was found to be available against a defendant who planted willows which then caused water to back up onto his neighbor's land

(*D.* 39.3.1.6 Ulp. 53 *ad Ed.*). Was this the right decision? Why or why not? In his handbook on farming, Cato recommended growing willow in swampy places and using their branches for a vine trellis (*On Agriculture,* 6.4, 9.1). Does the law adequately take account of this practice? Explain.

5. In the first century CE three jurists, Labeo, Sabinus, and Cassius affirmed the definition proposed by Mucius (*D.* 39.3.1.7–8 Ulp. 53 *ad Ed.*). Which jurist's rule do you think is better law? Why?
6. The examples in this case are likely to have come from actual lawsuits. How helpful would the jurists' discussion be to a potential plaintiff in deciding whether or not he could bring a claim? How could a defendant prove that his work was aimed at cultivating a crop? How could a defendant use their discussion to avoid liability under the Action for Warding Off Rainwater?

Case 1.14. Irrigation

D. 39.3.3.2 Ulpianus, libro quinquagensimo tertio ad Edictum

Si vicinus, qui arvum solebat certo tempore anni rigare, pratum illic fecerit coeperitque adsidua irrigatione vicino nocere, ait Ofilius neque damni infecti neque aquae pluviae arcendae actione eum teneri, nisi locum complanavit eoque facto citatior aqua ad vicinum pervenire coepit.

Ulpian in the fifty-third book on the Edict

If my neighbor, who used to irrigate his field at a specific time of year, made a meadow there and began to harm the neighboring [field] with constant irrigation, Ofilius says that he cannot be held liable either for anticipated injury or under the action for warding off rainwater, unless he leveled the place and, after this was done, the water began to arrive more quickly at the neighboring [field].

1. Ofilius considers two types of irrigation. Which kind of irrigation can be grounds for liability under the Action for Warding Off Rainwater? Why?

2. The Romans knew how to grade land to create a constant gentle slope that moved water from higher to lower parts of a garden. Would this kind of irrigation lead to liability under the Action for Warding Off Rainwater? Why or why not? To what extent is Ofilius' opinion about leveling consistent with other cases on exempted work?
3. This case raises questions about the timing of the action. When exactly does Ofilius expect the plaintiff to file action? Can his opinion be justified legally? Why or why not?
4. Does Ofilius' opinion broaden or narrow the standards for the Action for Warding Off Rainwater? That is, does his opinion make it harder or easier to hold a defendant liable for work that threatened to cause damaging runoff?
5. Ofilius also considers the possibility of an action based on the *cautio* against anticipated injury. Recall that a landowner could use this *cautio* to protect himself against damage from his neighbor's planned construction (see Case 1.4). Why does Ofilius reject the *cautio* as a remedy for the neighbor's change in irrigation practices?
6. What interests or policy considerations might have motivated this approach to liability under the Action for Warding Off Rainwater?

Case 1.15. Washed Away?

D. 39.3.3 pr Ulpianus, libro quinquagensimo tertio ad Edictum

Apud Trebatium relatum est eum, in cuius fundo aqua oritur, fullonicas circa fontem instituisse et ex his aquam in fundum vicini immittere coepisse: ait ergo non teneri eum aquae pluviae arcendae actione. si tamen aquam conrivat vel si spurcam quis immittat, posse eum impediri plerisque placuit.

Ulpian in the fifty-third book on the Edict

In Trebatius it is reported that a man, on whose land water rose, set up a fullery around the spring and began to release water from it onto his neighbor's farm. He [i.e., Trebatius] said that he was not liable under the action for warding off rainwater. However if he channeled the water together or if he sent anything dirty, many [jurists] agreed that he could be stopped.

1. A fullery was a laundry where woven wool cloth was finished by washing it in vats of urine, then rinsing and drying it before it was dyed and made into garments. In this case, the owner of the spring used its water for the rinsing process and then let it run downhill to his neighbor's farm. According to Trebatius, can the neighbor use the Action for Warding Off Rainwater to stop the fulling? Why or why not?
2. Fulleries were located both in town and in rural areas, as were other industries, such as tanneries that used water in processing animal hides. Why did the jurists disagree about allowing the Action for Warding Off Rainwater for runoff from such industries? Which view do you think is correct, and why?
3. Releasing water could inconvenience a neighbor and in modern law it can be treated as a legal nuisance, that is, an activity that interferes with a person's enjoyment of his property. While the Romans did not use the term nuisance, a legal opinion by the second-century CE jurist Aristo is often cited in modern legal discussions of nuisance (*D.* 8.5.8.5 Ulp.[Aristo] 17 *ad Ed.*). The case likely derived from an actual dispute that occurred in the town of Minturnae, on the bay of Naples, where there was a cheese shop that released foul smoke that bothered residents on upper stories of nearby buildings. Aristo compares smoke floating up with water flowing down, and determines that their release could be prohibited. Does Aristo's analogy help to explain the dissenting opinion about the fullery? Is the fullery's release of water more like smoke from a cheese shop or runoff from a field? Explain.

Case 1.16. Diverting a Torrent

D. 39.3.2.9 Paulus, libro quadragensimo nono ad Edictum

Idem Labeo ait, si vicinus flumen torrentem averterit, ne aqua ad eum perveniat, et hoc modo sit effectum, ut vicino noceatur, agi cum eo aquae pluviae arcendae non posse: aquam enim arcere hoc esse curare, ne influat. quae sententia verior est, si modo non hoc animo fecit, ut tibi noceat, sed ne sibi noceat.

Paul, in the forty-ninth book on the Edict

Therefore Labeo says that if a neighbor diverted a torrent to stop the water reaching him, and in this way it happened that his neighbor could be harmed, it is not possible to bring an action for warding off rainwater against him. For warding off water means to take care that it does not flow onto [one's land]. This opinion is more consistent with the facts, if any way he did it not with the intention to harm you but to not harm himself.

1. A torrent is a seasonal stream or arroyo: much of the year it looks like a dry gulley but in the rainy season it fills with fast-moving water. Could diverting a torrent lead to liability under the Action for Warding Off Rainwater? Why or why not?
2. What additional condition does Labeo add for a liability under the Action for Warding Off Rainwater? How could a plaintiff prove his neighbor's intent in diverting the torrent? What arguments could a defendant make to prove his intentions?
3. At the end of the case, Paul affirms Labeo's opinion and suggests that not all jurists took the same view. What reason does Paul give for supporting Labeo? Why might other jurists disagree?
4. The Action for Warding Off Rainwater imposed some limit on the rights of a landowner to do as he wished on his land. What limit does Paul set? How easy would it be to apply his limit? Explain.
5. Ulpian addresses the same issue in another case, writing that "no one is forbidden to help himself as long as he does not harm someone else" (*D.* 39.3.1.11 Ulp. 53 *ad Ed.*). How does Ulpian's rule differ from Paul's rule? Which do you think makes better law, and why?

Case 1.17. Dam Right!

D. 39.3.2.5 Paulus, libro quadragensimo nono ad Edictum

Item Varus ait: aggerem, qui in fundo vicini erat, vis aquae deiecit, per quod effectum est, ut aqua pluvia mihi noceret. Varus ait, si naturalis agger fuit, non posse me vicinum cogere aquae pluviae arcendae actione, ut eum reponat vel reponi sinat, idemque putat et si manu factus fuit neque memoria eius exstat: quod si exstet, putat aquae pluviae arcendae actione eum teneri. Labeo autem, si manu factus sit agger, etiamsi memoria eius non exstat, agi posse ut reponatur: nam hac actione neminem cogi posse, ut vicino prosit, sed ne noceat aut interpellet facientem, quod iure facere possit. quamquam tamen deficiat aquae pluviae arcendae actio, attamen opinor utilem actionem vel interdictum mihi competere adversus vicinum, si velim aggerem restituere in agro eius, qui factus mihi quidem prodesse potest, ipsi vero nihil nociturus est: haec aequitas suggerit, etsi iure deficiamur.

Paul, in the forty-ninth book on the Edict

Likewise [Alfenus] Varus says: the force of water pushed down an earthen embankment which was in my neighbor's field, and as a result, rainwater could cause me harm. Varus says that if the embankment was natural, I cannot use the action for warding off rainwater to compel my neighbor to replace it or to allow it to be replaced. And he thinks that it is the same if it was man-made and there is no memory of [i.e., of its construction]. But if there is memory, he thinks that [the neighbor] can be held liable in an action for warding off rainwater. Labeo, however, thinks that there can be an action [to compel] him to replace it, if the embankment was man-made, even if there is no memory of it. For no one can be compelled by this action to benefit his neighbor but only not to cause harm or to interfere with his doing what he could do by right. Although the action for warding off rainwater fails, I still think that an analogous action or an interdict is appropriate against a neighbor if I wish to rebuild on his land a dike which, once rebuilt, could bring me a benefit but will do no harm to him. Fairness suggests this, even if we lack a right.

1. In this case, Paul reports opinions about earthen dikes or embankments given by two earlier jurists, Alfenus Varus and Labeo. Which type or types of dike create liability under the Action for Warding Off Rainwater? Why?
2. What rationales does Paul advance to support the opinions of Alfenus Varus and Labeo? What is the "clear legal right" that Paul mentions? What kind of legal right does the plaintiff lack? How consistent is Paul's approach with other cases?
3. What alternative legal remedies does Paul offer? The interdict in question is probably against force or stealth (see Case 1.7). An *actio utilis* or analogous action was a mechanism for broadening claims to

make them applicable in more situations than were strictly covered by the original action. What considerations does Paul cite to support his extension of the Action for Warding Off Rainwater? Do you agree with his reasoning? Why or why not?

Case 1.18. Too Much or Too Little?

D. 39.3.1.21 Ulpianus, libro quinquagensimo tertio ad Edictum

Sicut autem opus factum, ut aqua pluvia mihi noceat, in hanc actionem venit, ita per contrarium quaeritur, an posset aquae pluviae arcendae agi, si vicinus opus fecerit, ne aqua, quae alioquin decurrens agro meo proderat, huic prosit. Ofilius igitur et Labeo putant agi non posse, etiamsi intersit mea ad me aquam pervenire: hanc enim actionem locum habere, si aqua pluvia noceat, non si non prosit.

Ulpian in the fifty-third book on the Edict

As work done to keep rainwater from harming me comes within the scope of this action, so conversely it can be asked whether it is possible to bring an action for warding off rainwater if a neighbor did work so that water would not benefit my field which otherwise did benefit it by running down. In that case Ofilius and Labeo think that there can be no action, even if it is in my interest that the water come to me. For this action has a place if rainwater could cause harm not if it does not provide a benefit.

1. Can a defendant be liable under the Action for Warding Off Rainwater if his work stops water that benefits the plaintiff? Why or why not?
2. How can you distinguish "removing a benefit" from "causing harm"? Try to come up with a couple of hypothetical situations to test your rule.
3. Ulpian affirms an opinion shared by two earlier jurists, Ofilius and Labeo. How consistent is their view with other cases? Explain.
4. In another section of his commentary, Ulpian quotes an opinion by another earlier jurist, Marcellus, about a similar situation in which the plaintiff had sought an action on fraud (*de dolo*):

Next, Marcellus writes that there can be no action against someone who diverts his neighbor's spring while digging on his own land. And of course he ought not to have even the action for fraud, if he did it with the intention not of harming his neighbor but of improving his own field. (*D.* 39.3.1.12 Ulp. 53 *ad Ed.*)

The action on fraud was a kind of delict or civil wrong. In order to be liable for fraud, the defendant had to have an intention to harm the plaintiff. Does Ulpian require the same standard for the Action for Warding Off Rainwater? Would such a standard be consistent with other cases on liability under the Action for Warding Off Rainwater? Why or why not?

5. This case as well as the cases on exempted work involve evaluating the defendant's intent. How easy would it be to determine his motives? Does this subjective standard make the Action for Warding Off Rainwater more or less fair? Explain.

B. Natural Causes

Case 1.19. The Nature of the Site

D. 39.3.1.10, 14 Ulpianus, libro quinquagensimo tertio ad Edictum

Idem aiunt, si aqua naturaliter decurrat, aquae pluviae arcendae actionem cessare: quod si opere facto aqua aut in superiorem partem repellitur aut in inferiorem derivatur, aquae pluviae arcendae actionem competere. . . . (14) Huic illud etiam applicandum numquam competere hanc actionem, cum ipsius loci natura nocet: nam (ut verius quis dixerit) non aqua, sed loci natura nocet.

Ulpian in the fifty-third book on the Edict

The same authorities say that the action to ward off rainwater does not apply if water flows down naturally. But if, after work is done, water is either pushed back onto the higher ground or diverted onto lower ground, the action for warding off rainwater is appropriate. . . . (14) We should add that this action is never appropriate when the nature of the site itself causes harm; in that case (as someone might say more precisely) the water does not cause harm but the nature of the site.

1. At the start of this case, when Ulpian refers to other jurists ("the same authorities") he probably means Sabinus and Cassius, whom he names in a preceding extract (*D.* 39.3.1.8 Ulp. 53 *ad Ed.*, and see Case 1.13, Study Question 5). How did these jurists limit the application of the Action for Warding Off Rainwater? What effect on the environment must the work have in order to bring an action?
2. What does "the nature of the site" mean? How convincing is Ulpian's explanation that the "nature of the site" causes the damage and not the water? How would you explain it?
3. What does "flows down naturally" mean in this case? Does Ulpian adopt the same meaning of "naturally" in this case as in Case 1.4? Why or why not?
4. Based on this case, how did the Romans understand the relationship between humans and their environment? How much control did they believe humans had over the natural world?

Case 1.20. Defect of the Site

D. 39.3.14.1 Paulus, libro quadragensimo nono ad Edictum

Cum agitur aquae pluviae arcendae, de facto quod nocet quaeritur: ideoque si vitio loci pars aliqua soli subsedit, quamvis per eam causam aqua pluvia inferiori noceat, nulla competit actio. idem fortasse dicitur, si in agro manu factum aliquid subsederit.

Paul, in the forty-ninth book on the Edict

When there is an action for warding off rainwater, the question concerns what was done to cause harm. For this reason if some part of the land subsides because of a defect in the site, even though rainwater could harm the lower ground for this reason, no action is appropriate. The same perhaps is said if something built in a field subsided.

1. Paul considers two situations involving work and the nature of the site. Describe each situation carefully and identify key differences. In which situation or situations can the defendant be held liable in an Action for Warding Off Rainwater? What is the rationale in each situation?

2. Which party, plaintiff or defendant, benefits the most from Paul's opinion? How could Paul's opinion help a plaintiff prove his case? How could a defendant use Paul's opinion to defend himself from liability?
3. Compare the previous case: would Ulpian agree with Paul that "the nature of the site" caused the damage? Explain.

Case 1.21. Natural Changes

D. 39.3.2.6 Paulus, libro quadragensimo nono ad Edictum

Apud Namusam relatum est, si aqua fluens iter suum stercore obstruxerit et ex restagnatione superiori agro noceat, posse cum inferiore agi, ut sinat purgari: hanc enim actionem non tantum de operibus esse utilem manu factis, verum etiam in omnibus, quae non secundum voluntatem sint. Labeo contra Namusam probat: ait enim naturam agri ipsam a se mutari posse et ideo, cum per se natura agri fuerit mutata, aequo animo unumquemque ferre debere, sive melior sive deterior eius condicio facta sit. idcirco et si terrae motu aut tempestatis magnitudine soli causa mutata sit, neminem cogi posse, ut sinat in pristinam locum condicionem redigi. sed nos etiam in hunc casum aequitatem admisimus.

Paul, in the forty-ninth book on the Edict

It is recorded in Namusa that if flowing water blocks its path with muck, and harm could come to the high ground from backed-up water, it is possible to bring an action to compel the owner of the lower land to allow it to be cleared away. For this action applies not only to man-made work but also to all work which is not according to the landowner's wishes. Labeo approves an opinion contrary to Namusa: he says that the nature of the field itself can be changed of its own accord and for this reason, when the nature of the field has changed by itself, each and every person should bear it calmly, whether his situation is made better or worse. Therefore, if the condition of the land is changed by an earthquake or a tremendous storm, no one can be compelled to allow it to be restored to its previous condition. But we also allow fairness to be considered in this case.

1. In the case described by Namusa, what "work" caused the threat of damaging runoff? What reason does Namusa give for allowing an action in these circumstances? Do you agree with his rational? Why or why not?
2. Can it be said that the backed-up water in Namusa's case was caused by "nature"? If so, what concept of nature is at play? Or how is "nature" defined in this case?
3. Why do Namusa and Labeo disagree about applying the Action for Warding Off Rainwater in this case? Whose opinion, Namusa's or Labeo's, would a plaintiff prefer? a defendant? Explain.
4. Typically, when nature or an act of god causes damage, there is no liability, as Paul explains in the last part of the case. How and why does Paul modify this rule?
5. Which jurist's opinion (Namusa's or Labeo's or Paul's) is more consistent with other cases on the Action for Warding Off Rainwater? Explain.
6. What advice does Labeo offer to potential plaintiffs? What does his advice reveal about the Romans' view of the relationship between humans and the environment?

Case 1.22. The Lay of the Land

D. 39.3.1.22–23 Ulpianus, libro quinquagensimo tertio ad Edictum

Sed et si vicinus opus tollat et sublato eo aqua naturaliter ad inferiorem agrum perveniens noceat, Labeo existimat aquae pluviae arcendae agi non posse: semper enim hanc esse servitutem inferiorum praediorum, ut natura profluentem aquam excipiant. plane si propter id opus sublatum vehementior aqua profluat vel corrivetur, aquae pluviae arcendae actione agi posse etiam Labeo confitetur. (23) Denique ait condicionibus agrorum quasdam leges esse dictas, ut, quibus agris magna sint flumina, liceat mihi, scilicet in agro tuo, aggeres vel fossas habere: si tamen lex non sit agro dicta, agri naturam esse servandam et semper inferiorem superiori servire atque hoc incommodum naturaliter pati inferiorem agrum a superiore compensareque debere cum alio commodo: sicut enim omnis pinguitudo terrae ad eum decurrit, ita etiam aquae incommodum ad eum defluere. si tamen lex agri non inveniatur, vetustatem vicem legis tenere. sane enim et in servitutibus hoc idem sequimur, ut, ubi servitus non invenitur imposita, qui diu usus est servitute neque vi neque precario neque clam, habuisse longa consuetudine velut iure impositam servitutem videatur. non ergo cogemus vicinum aggeres munire, sed nos in eius agro muniemus: eritque ista quasi servitus, in quam rem utilem actionem habemus vel interdictum.

Ulpian in the fifty-third book on the Edict

But also if a neighbor removes a structure, and after the removal water flowing naturally to the lower land could cause harm, Labeo thinks that it is not possible to bring an action for warding off rainwater. For there is always a servitude on lower estates to receive water flowing onto them naturally. Clearly if the water flows with more force or in a single stream because this structure is removed, Labeo allows that there can be an action for warding off rainwater. 23. Then he says that certain rules were agreed on the conditions of the fields so that I can have embankments or ditches in fields that have large streams, even in your field. If, however, an agreement was not made for a field, [he says that] the nature of the field is to be respected and that the lower field always is servient to the upper and the lower field should allow this disadvantage naturally from the upper field and make up for it with another advantage. For just as all richness of the soil runs down to it, so the disadvantage of the water also flows down to it. If again no agreement on the field is found, long-standing practice holds in place of an agreement. Of course we follow the same rule for servitudes that, where no servitude is found to have been established, someone who used a servitude for a long time and not by force, stealth, or favor, seems to have a servitude established by long custom as if by right. Therefore we will not compel a neighbor to shore up his embankments, but we will build them in his field: it will be like a servitude for which we have an analogous action or an interdict.

1. In this extract, Ulpian quotes an exceptionally long, continuous piece of legal reasoning by the jurist Labeo. Consequently, we can follow the logic of Labeo's argument and probe his understanding of the relation-

ship between law and the environment. Labeo begins from the same situation as in Case 1.19, The Nature of the Site, in which the Action for Warding Off Rainwater cannot be used because the water flows downhill "naturally." How does Labeo modify the rule here? What rationale does he give for changing the rule?

2. Labeo considers agreements or contracts between neighboring landowners that govern the hydraulic infrastructure on their land. How effective are these legal agreements at managing the flow of water? Under what circumstances might such regulations not be adequate to the challenge of managing runoff?
3. In some situations, Labeo privileges nature over law. That is, the legal rights of the landowners must accommodate the lay of the land and even be determined to some extent by the physical landscape. What rationale does Labeo give to support this approach? What counterarguments can you think of?
4. Labeo authorizes the downhill neighbor to build embankments or ditches on the uphill neighbor's land. To justify this intrusion on the owner's rights, Labeo proposes an analogy with servitudes. A servitude was a kind of property right that gave one landowner limited rights to use his neighbor's land or water (see chapter 2). Labeo compares the uphill neighbor's right to a servitude established by long use. How compelling is the analogy? Does the right seem to be based more in nature or social custom?
5. What assumptions does Labeo make about "nature" and the relationship between humans and the physical environment in this case? Compare his ideas about nature with those of other jurists.
6. What alternative remedies does Ulpian suggest in the last sentence of the case? On what basis are these remedies appropriate? The interdict in question is probably against force or stealth (see Cases 1.7 and 1.17). An analogous action (*actio utilis* or *in factum*) was appropriate when circumstances merited a remedy even though they did not exactly fit the legal requirements, as in this case where the landowner does not have a legally established servitude. See the next case for the servitude to release or accept water.

Case 1.23. Stillicidium

D. 39.3.2.10 Paulus, libro quadragensimo nono ad Edictum

Illud etiam verum puto, quod Ofilius scribit, si fundus tuus vicino serviat et propterea aquam recipiat, cessare aquae pluviae arcendae actionem, <sic tamen, si non ultra modum noceat.> cui consequens est, quod Labeo putat, si quis vicino cesserit ius ei esse aquam immittere, aquae pluviae arcendae eum agere non posse.

Paul in the forty-ninth book on the Edict

But I also hold that view which Ofilius wrote that, if your farm is servient to a neighbor and for this reason receives water, there is no action for warding off rainwater, <at least unless it causes more than average harm.> It follows, as Labeo believed, that if someone grants a right to his neighbor to release water, he cannot sue him under the action for warding off rainwater.

1. Paul affirms the opinions of two earlier jurists, Ofilius and Labeo. Under what specific circumstances do they deny an action under the Action for Warding Off Rainwater?
2. When Labeo mentions a right to release or discharge water, he means a servitude or right to use someone else's property. Ofilius' expression, that the plaintiff's land is servient, means the same thing. In fact, there were probably two servitudes: one for receiving more than the usual amount of water, and another for not receiving any water at all. Which servitude is at issue in this case? For servitudes, see chapter 2, esp. Case 2.13.
3. The bracketed sentence is marked as an interpolation, that is, it was probably not part of the original case but added later by Justinian's compilers. How does it change the rule established by the earlier jurists? Do you think it appeared in the original opinion or not? Explain.
4. Gaius gives two names for this servitude, *flumina* and *stillicidium*, "flowing water" and "eavesdrip," which may represent respectively rural and urban applications (*Institutiones* 2.14). The servitudes for discharging water appear in only a few cases in the *Digest of Justinian*,

usually in connection with other urban servitudes. The urban servitude probably arose first to supplement the action for warding off rainwater. Can you explain why? Should the law on discharging water be different in rural and urban places? Why or why not?

5. Varro, a politician and scholar contemporary with Cicero, reports an etymology for *stillicidium: "stillicidium* comes from what falls in drops, *flumen* [from] what flows continuously" (Varro, *L.* 5.27). Does the etymology help you to understand the nature of the right to discharge water? Why or why not?
6. Review Aristo's opinion in the case about the cheese shop in Case 1.15, Study Question 3. Aristo compares releasing smoke with the right to discharge water. How robust is Aristo's analogy? Should the law treat air and water differently? Why or why not?

CHAPTER 2

Servitudes

Private water was governed by ownership and servitudes. The landowner owned all water sources on his land and had, at least in theory, exclusive rights to them. In practice, neighbors often shared water, and used servitudes to articulate their access to this valuable resource. A servitude was a right of use that gave a nonowner a right to use a resource on neighboring property. It created a relationship between two parcels of land, the dominant estate (land owned by the right-holder) and the servient estate (an adjacent parcel of land owned by someone else). For example, the landowner might have a right to conduct water from a spring on his neighbor's land to his own property.

The legal structure of servitudes for water use was paradoxical in some ways. They were among the praedial servitudes, so-called because they were attached to estates or *praedia*. Servitudes were classified as property, yet they were incorporeal rights of use. Consequently, ownership of a servitude could not be transferred by delivery, which required physical possession. Instead, a right of use had to be exercised in order for its holder to keep the right. In turn, servitudes could be lost by non-use, when the right-holder did not exercise his right for a legally prescribed period of time (loss by non-use). A servitude could also be lost if its holder became the owner of the servient estate (loss by merger).

There were two kinds of praedial servitudes, rustic and urban. Rustic praedial servitudes were probably in existence at the time of the *Twelve Tables*, Rome's earliest written law code, ca. 450 BCE. At first, there were four rustic praedial servitudes, three rights of way (*via*, *iter*, *actus*) and the right to conducted water (*aquaeductus*). Over the course of the Republican era, additional rustic praedial servitudes were developed to meet the needs of Roman landowners—for example, the right to draw water (*haustus*), the right to dig clay or sand, and so on. At the same time, the urban servitudes were created to regulate relations between neighbors in cities and towns, for example, for light or for inserting a beam into an adjacent house. There were also servitudes for discharge of water (*stillicidium* and *flumina*) that were introduced in chapter 1 because of their connection with the Action for Warding Off Rainwater (Case 1.23). These servitudes appear in too few extracts in the *Digest of Justinian* for full treatment. Instead, they feature in the study questions to this chapter illustrating the principles of water servitudes.

Whereas urban servitudes applied in cities and towns, the rustic praedial servitudes were closely connected with Rome's agricultural communities. They were included among res mancipi, a legal category of property necessary for cultivating the land. A rustic praedial servitude could be established only on a neighboring estate, ensuring that social ties closely supported the legal relationship. Only the landowner could bring legal action to protect or protest a servitude, but anyone connected with cultivation of the land (tenant, usufructuary) could exercise the right and thus maintain it.

Disputes about servitudes were resolved through a property or *in rem* action that took the form of a modified *vindicatio*, the usual procedure for claiming ownership. In post-Classical law, this action was renamed the *actio confessoria* when plaintiff was the owner of the dominant estate and the *actio negatoria* when the owner of the servient estate. Additional actions were available through the praetorian interdicts which covered both public and private water rights. An interdict was a magistrate's order that could resolve a legal dispute in a single hearing or provide temporary relief while the parties proceeded to litigation. Several interdicts concerned water rights, such as the Interdict on Daily and Summer Water and the Interdict on Canals; see also chapter 3.

I. Servitudes as a Kind of Property

Case 2.1. Rustic Praedial Servitudes

D. 8.3.1 pr–1 Ulpianus libro secundo Institutum

Servitutes rusticorum praediorum sunt hae: iter actus via aquaeductus. iter est ius eundi ambulandi homini, non etiam iumentum agendi. actus est ius agendi vel iumentum vel vehiculum: itaque qui iter habet, actum non habet, qui actum habet, et iter habet etiam sine iumento. via est ius eundi et agendi et ambulandi: nam et iter et actum in se via continet. aquae ductus est ius aquam ducendi per fundum alienum. (1) In rusticis computanda sunt aquae haustus, pecoris ad aquam adpulsus, ius pascendi, calcis coquendae, harenae fodiendae.

Ulpian in the second book of his Institutes

These are the rustic praedial servitudes: *iter*, *actus*, *via*, and *aquaeductus*. *Iter* is a person's right of walking or going on foot but not driving an animal. *Actus* is the right of driving either an animal or vehicle, and so someone who has *iter* does not have *actus*, but someone who has *actus* also has a right to go (*iter*) without an animal. *Via* is the right of going and driving and walking, for *via* includes in itself both *iter* and *actus*. *Aquae ductus* is the right of conducting water across another person's farm. (1) The rights of drawing water, driving animals to water, grazing, cooking lime, and digging sand are counted among the praedial servitudes.

1. The four "original" rustic praedial servitudes were known already at the time of the *Twelve Tables*, ca. 450 BCE, when Rome was a small, agricultural community centered around a ford on the Tiber River. What activities do these four "original" servitudes govern? How clearly are they distinguished?
2. Servitudes give us insight into how the Romans understood ownership and the rights that owners had over their land. What owner's rights are implied by the rustic servitudes?
3. How did a servitude limit the owner's rights over his land? Why would a landowner agree to such limitations? Try to give at least a preliminary answer, but keep thinking about the pros and cons of servitudes as you work through the subsequent cases.

Case 2.2. Praedial and Praedium

D. 8.4.1.1 Ulpianus libro secundo Institutum

Ideo autem hae servitutes praediorum appellantur, quoniam sine praediis constitui non possunt: nemo enim potest servitutem adquirere vel urbani vel rustici praedii, nisi qui habet praedium.

Ulpian in the second book of his Institutes

> These servitudes are said to belong to estates because they cannot be established without estates. In fact, no one can acquire a servitude on either a rustic or an urban property unless he has an estate (*praedium*).

1. Ulpian explains the category of "praedial servitudes" with an argument from the derivation of the word the Latin noun *praedium*, a general term for "property" or "estate," as in real estate. Why are servitudes called praedial rights?
2. A praedial servitude creates a relationship between two estates or farms: the dominant estate (owned by the right-holder) and the servient estate (owned by someone else). The servient estate is encumbered by a servitude which benefits the dominant estate. In what sense does the servient estate 'serve' the dominant estate? What benefit does each of the rustic praedial servitudes give to the dominant estate?
3. The servitude, *aquaeductus*, began as a combination of ownership of the spring and a right of passage. Later *aquaeductus* was formulated as a unified right of use. How does the concept of praedial servitudes reflect their origin in ownership?
4. A servitude was not the only way to bring water onto a farm that had none. One Roman landowner, Mummius Niger Valerius Vegetus, used sale and ownership to acquire water for his Villa Calvisiana in Etruria (Tuscany): he purchased the land around the spring, as well as a corridor where he built an aqueduct to carry water almost six miles through a combination of arches and pipes. Vegetus recorded these arrangements in a long inscription which specifies the width of corridor (ten feet for arches, six feet for pipes) and names all ten farms and the owners from whom he purchased the land (*CIL* 11.3003 = *ILS* 5771). Given these circumstances, why did Vegetus choose to buy the land and water instead of arranging a servitude? What advantages does owning the water and land offer? What purposes does the inscription serve? For another legal factor, consider the adjacent only rule (see Case 2.16).

Case 2.3. Rights of Use

D. 8.5.4 pr Ulpianus libro septimo decimo ad Edictum

Loci corpus non est dominii ipsius, cui servitus debetur, sed ius eundi habet.

Ulpian in the seventeenth book on the Edict

The physical place does not belong to the ownership of the very person to whom the servitude is owed, but he has a right to go [there].

1. This case concerns *iter* (*ius eundi*) not *aquaeductus* but it is the clearest evidence that the jurists understood servitudes as rights of use. In what sense is the right-holder an "owner" of the servitude? How does a servitude differ from ownership?
2. The Roman jurists classified praedial servitudes as property rights, because they were governed by the legal mechanisms relating to ownership (see Cases 2.9 and 2.34). How is a servitude different from other property?
3. In Roman law, property could be corporeal or incorporeal. Were servitudes corporeal or incorporeal? Why might their classification seem contradictory?
4. In explaining which category servitudes belong to, Ulpian uses the Latin word for body, *corpus*, that is etymologically related to the English term. How does this etymology help to explain the legal categories?
5. In another case, Pomponius considers water arising in a water channel governed by a servitude. The right-holder gets the benefit of it (*D.* 43.20.3.3. Pompon. 34 *ad Sab.*). Can you explain why? How does Pomponius' opinion help to explain what it means for a servitude to be a right of use? Another way to understand Pomponius' opinion is through the concept of a residuary right. Typically the owner recovers residuary rights to property after a right-holder ceases to exercise a right over it. Why does the right-holder apparently have a residuary right to water rising in the water channel?

Case 2.4. Servitudes in a Roman Colony

Corpus Inscriptionum Latinarum 1².5 ch. 79

> qui fluui riui fontes lacus aquae stagna paludes
> sunt in agro, qui colon(is) h[ui]usc(e) colon(iae) diuisus
> erit, ad eos riuos fontes lacus aquasque sta-
> gna paludes itus actus aquae haustus iis item
> esto, qui eum agrum habebunt possidebunt, uti
> iis fuit, qui eum agrum habuerunt possederunt.
> itemque iis, qui eum agrum habent possident ha-
> bebunt possidebunt, itineris aquarum lex ius-
> que esto. vacat

Charter of the Colony Julia Genetiva, ch. 79

> Whatever rivers, streams, springs, lakes, ponds, and swamps are on land that will have been assigned to colonists of this colony, there is to be [a right of] going on foot, driving animals, [and] drawing water at those streams, springs, lakes, ponds, and swamps for those who will have and possess this land as the same as it was for those who had and possessed the land. Likewise there will be legal authority and right and authority of conducting water (*iter aquarum*) for those who have and possess and who will have and will possess this land.

1. This case comes from the charter for the Roman colony, Urso, founded in Spain for Caesar's veterans. What kinds of water resources does the charter address? Who had legal rights to these resources?
2. Which rights to water are governed by the charter? Consider rights of access, withdrawal, management, exclusion, alienation. What exactly does a landowner at Urso "have and possess" when he has a right to water?
3. Did the charter change water rights at Urso? Why might the Roman authorities decide to affirm preexisting water rights?
4. The charter treats water rights at Urso as if they were servitudes in *ius civile*, and its language suggests the early two-part form of the servitude for aquaeductus (see Case 2.2). Yet water rights were probably subject to local law or custom even after the foundation of the colony.

Traditional water sharing arrangements persist because they are typically embedded in social relationships and community institutions.

Case 2.5. Haustus

D. 8.3.3.3 Ulpianus libro septimo decimo ad Edictum

Qui habet haustum, iter quoque habere videtur ad hauriendum et, ut ait Neratius libro tertio membranarum, sive ei ius hauriendi et adeundi cessum sit, utrumque habebit, sive tantum hauriendi, inesse et aditum sive tantum adeundi ad fontem, inesse et haustum. haec de haustu ex fonte privato. ad flumen autem publicum idem Neratius eodem libro scribit iter debere cedi, haustum non oportere et si quis tantum haustum cesserit, nihil eum agere.

Ulpian in the seventeenth book on the Edict

A man who has a right to draw water (*haustus*) seems also to have a right of going by foot (*iter*) to draw water, as Neratius says in the third book of his *Parchments.* Whether a right of drawing water and a right of entering are granted to him or only a right of drawing water, he will have both rights; [he writes that] in this right there is both entry at least going as far as to the spring and drawing water. This is about drawing water from a private spring. In the same book Neratius also writes that a right of going on foot to a public river should be granted but that granting a right of drawing water is not necessary and that he has no claim if someone granted only a right of drawing water.

1. Describe the different situations that Neratius considers. Which servitudes are involved in each situation?
2. How is *haustus* different from *aquaeductus*? In what circumstances would *haustus* be more useful than *aquaeductus*? or why would a person choose *aquaeductus* over *haustus*?
3. What kind of servitude was needed to draw water from a public river? Why was a servitude for *haustus* not necessary? This case is usually understood to mean that public rivers were "open access" resources in Roman law, that is, everyone had a right to take water from a public river. Explain how this conclusion can be inferred from Neratius' remarks. For more on access to public rivers, see chapter 3.

Case 2.6. Use It Like You Mean It

D. 8.6.25 Paulus, libro quinto Sententiae

> Servitute usus non videtur nisi is, qui suo iure uti se credidit: ideoque si quis pro via publica vel pro alterius servitute usus sit, nec interdictum nec actio utiliter competit.

Paul in the fifth book of Sentences

> A person does not seem to use a servitude unless he believes that he is exercising his own right. Consequently, if a man exercises a servitude as if he were using a public roadway or a servitude belonging to someone else, neither an interdict nor an analogous action is available.

> Hypothetical fact pattern: *Titius channeled water in a canal on land owned by his neighbor Seius. Titius thought that another neighbor, Quintus, had a servitude of aquaeductus to use this water. When Seius prevents Titius from channeling water, Titius would like to bring a legal action to claim a servitude. Can he do so?*

1. How would Paul decide about the hypothetical fact pattern? If Titius cannot bring action against Seius, would Paul allow Quintus to do so? Why or why not?
2. Since a servitude was a right of use, the right-holder had to exercise the right in order to keep it. But simply using a right was not enough to maintain the servitude. What else does Paul require?
3. How do the comparisons—using a public road or someone else's right of way—help to clarify what is required of the person "using" a servitude?
4. Paul considers possible legal remedies available to a person who thought he was using a public road or someone else's servitude, and he rejects both options (an interdict or an analogous action on the servitude). Paul is probably thinking of the interdict on public places (*D.* 43.8.2 pr Ulp. 68 *ad Ed.*) which individuals could use to protect their right to use public property. Why does it not apply here? Why is an analogous action on the servitude also impossible? Several actions were available to protect servitudes (see section III.C, this chapter).
5. The Interdict on Daily and Summer Water protected servitudes for

channeling water: a person could ask the praetor to issue an interdict if someone interfered with his use of the water. Aristo thought the interdict could be granted to a person who thought he had a right (*D.* 43.20.1.19 Ulp. [Aristo] 70 *ad Ed.*). Would Paul agree? Explain. For more information on this interdict, see section II.C on Irrigation in chapter 3 (Cases 3.19–26).

Case 2.7. Who Owns the Water?

D. 39.3.21 Pomponius, libro trigensimo secundo ad Quintum Mucium

Si in meo aqua erumpat, quae ex tuo fundo venas habeat, si eas venas incideris et ob id desierit ad me aqua pervenire, tu non videris vi fecisse, si nulla servitus mihi eo nomine debita fuerit, nec interdicto quod vi aut clam teneris.

Pomponius in the thirty-second book on Quintus Mucius

If water that has underground streams from your land emerges on my land, and you cut off these underground streams and for this reason the water stops coming to my land, you do not seem to have acted with force, if no servitude is owed to me for this water, and you will not be held liable with the interdict on force or stealth.

1. Where is the source of the water located, on "your" land or "my" land? Is it the "I" or the "you" in the case above? Remember that the landowner owns everything on, under, or attached to his land.
2. If you cut off the flow of water from your land to my land, can I bring a claim against you? Why or why not?
3. Pomponius writes that "I" would have a claim if I had a servitude. He is presumably thinking of the servitude *aquaeductus*, the right to channel water. How would a servitude change "my" rights in this case?
4. Pomponius considers whether "I" can use the interdict on force or stealth to compel you to restore the water system to its prior condition. That is, were you interfering with my right to water when you cut off the flow from your land? Who has a right to control the water on my land, you or I? Explain.

5. Why might a landowner want to keep the water from his spring for himself? An imperial constitution addressing a similar situation as this case identifies irrigation as a powerful motive (*CJ* 3.34.6, 269 CE). The constitution affirmed a landowner's right to water from a spring on his land and disallowed his neighbor's diversion of it. The emperor's language was dramatic: the owner's land is thirsting, and the diversion of water is harsh and cruel, both morally wrong and without legal right (*iniuria*). It is not clear whether the neighbor had a servitude or not. How can we account for the urgency of the emperor's decree?

Case 2.8. Classification of Property

Gaius, *Institutiones* 2.12–14a

Quaedam praeterea res corporales sunt, quaedam incorporales. (13) <Corporales> hae < sunt> quae tangi possunt, uelut fundus, homo, uestis, aurum, argentum et denique aliae res innumerabiles. (14) Incorporales sunt quae tangi non possunt, qualia sunt ea quae in iure consistunt, sicut hereditas, ususfructus, obligationes quoquo modo contractae. . . . eodem numero sunt iura praediorum urbanorum et rusticorum. praediorum urbanorum iura sunt velut ius altius tollendi aedes et officiendi luminibus vicini aedium aut non extollendi, ne luminibus vicini officiatur; item fluminum et stilicidiorum ius, id est, ut vicinus flumen vel stilicidium in aream vel in aedes suas recipiat; item cloacae immittendae et luminum immitendorum; praediorum rusticorum iura sunt velut via, iter, actus; item pecoris ad aquam adpulsus; item ius aquae ducendae. haec iura tam rusticorum quam urbanorum praediorum servitutes vocantur. (14a) est etiam alia rerum divisio: nam aut mancipi sunt aut nec mancipi. Mancipi sunt velut fundus in Italico solo, item aedes in Italico solo, item servi et ea animalia quae collo dorsove domari solent, velut boves, equi, muli, asini; item servitutes praediorum rusticorum. nam servitutes praediorum urbanorum nec mancipi sunt.

Gaius, from the second book of his Institutes

Moreover some things are corporeal, some are incorporeal. (13) Corporeal things are those that can be touched, such as a farm, a person, clothing, gold, silver, and really countless other things. (14) Incorporeal things are those that cannot be touched but that exist in law, such as inheritances, usufructs, obligations however arranged. . . . In the same category are rights belonging to urban and rural estates. There are rights belonging to urban estates, such as the right of building houses higher and of blocking light to a neighbor's house, or of not building higher so as not to block a neighbor's light; likewise a right of flowing water and of eavesdrip, that is, so that a neighbor receive flowing water or eavesdrip on his land or his houses; also [a right] of inserting a drain and of opening windows. There are rights belonging to rustic estates, such as the right of way and of driving a vehicle and of driving animals; also a right of driving animals to water and of channeling water. These are called servitudes of both rustic and urban estates. (14a) There is also another classification of things: they are either *res mancipi* or *res nec mancipi*. *Res mancipi* are for example a farm on Italian land and likewise a house on Italian land, also slaves, and animals that are usually domesticated for draft or burden, such as oxen, horses, mules, donkeys. In addition servitudes belonging to rustic estates are *res mancipi*; to be sure servitudes belonging to urban estates are *res nec mancipi*.

1. Make a list of the examples that Gaius uses to define the various kinds of property: *corporeal, incorporeal, res mancipi, res nec mancipi*. How helpful are Gaius' examples in clarifying the scope of these categories? Which category is most exclusive? In Classical Roman law, there were both praedial and personal rights of use (*D.* 8.1.1 Marcian. 3 *Reg.*). In post-Classical law, all servitudes were treated as personal rights, probably by assimilation with rights to use public water which were always personal (see chapter 4).
2. To which categories of property does Gaius assign rustic praedial servitudes? Is it inconsistent to classify servitudes as both praedial and incorporeal? Why or why not?
3. Which servitudes can be either rustic or urban? How can we explain their inclusion in both categories?
4. Usufruct is personal right of use or life interest in property owned by someone else that lasted until the right-holder's death. What are the pros and cons of the two kinds of right of use? Which seems better suited to a resources like water? Why?

5. Gaius seems to add servitudes to the category of *res mancipi* almost as an afterthought. Why might he have hesitated to classify them in this way? Why does it make sense to do so?
6. How are rights of use different from other kinds of property? Why is it difficult to slot them into the categories that work for other things? Begin to grapple with this issue and keep it in mind as you work through the cases on servitudes.

II. Rules for Rights of Use

A. How to Establish a Servitude

Case 2.9. Conveyances

Gaius, *Institutiones* 2.18–19, 22, 28–29

> Magna autem differentia est inter mancipi res et nec mancipi. (19) Nam res nec mancipi ipsa traditione pleno iure alterius fiunt, si modo corporales sunt et ob id recipiunt traditionem. . . . (22) Mancipi vero res sunt quae per mancipationem ad alium transferuntur; unde etiam mancipi res sunt dictae. . . . (28) <Res> incorporales traditionem non recipiere manifestum est. (29) Sed iura praediorum urbanorum in iure cedi <tantum> possunt, rusticorum vero etiam mancipari possunt.

Gaius, from the second book of his Institutes

> There is however a great difference between *res mancipi* and *res nec mancipi.* (19) For *res nec mancipi* become the property of another person with full title by delivery alone, if they are corporeal at least and are subject to delivery for this reason. . . . (22) But *res mancipi* are things that are transferred to another person by *mancipatio,* from which they take their name. . . . (28) It is evident that incorporeal things are not subject to delivery. (29) But while rights belonging to urban estates can only be created by *in iure cessio,* rights belonging to rustic estates can also be created by *mancipatio.*

1. Gaius explains that the Romans used different legal mechanisms or conveyances to transfer ownership of different types of property.

Mancipatio was the conveyance in Roman law and it involved fictional sale where a coin was placed on a scale while the parties pronounced formulaic statements in a kind of ritual. *Cessio in iure* was also an old and formal procedure performed by the parties before a magistrate. *Traditio* or delivery was the least complicated and most common method of transferring ownership, which happened when the new owner took physical possession of the property. Which conveyance did the Romans used for *res mancipi*? *Res nec mancipi*? Corporeal property? Incorporeal property? Servitudes?

2. When the owner of the servient estate established a servitude, he used a conveyance to transfer the right to the owner of the dominant estate. Which conveyances were used to establish rustic praedial servitudes?
3. What rationale does Gaius present to explain why rustic praedial servitudes can be conveyed by either *mancipatio* or *in iure cessio*?
4. Gaius thinks it is self-evident why it was not possible to establish a servitude by delivery. Can you explain the logic?

Case 2.10. Servitudes in the Provinces

Gaius, *Institutiones* 2.31

Sed haec scilicet in Italicis praediis ita sunt, quia et ipsa praedia mancipationem et in iure cessionem recipiunt. alioquin in prouincialibus praediis siue quis usumfructum siue ius eundi agendi aquamue ducendi vel altius tollendi aedes aut non tollendi, ne luminibus vicini officiatur, ceteraque similia iura constituere uelit, pactionibus et stipulationibus id efficere potest; quia ne ipsa quidem praedia mancipationem aut in iure cessionem recipiunt.

Gaius from the second book of his Institutes

But these (i.e., conveyances) are like this on Italian estates because the estates themselves are subject to *mancipatio* and *cessio in iure.* In a different way on provincial estates if someone should wish to establish usufruct or a right of *iter, actus, aquaeductus,* of raising a building higher or of not raising it so that it blocks a neighbor's lights, and other similar rights, he can do it by pacts and stipulations because the estates themselves are not subject to *mancipatio* or *in iure cessio.*

1. Gaius explains how to establish servitudes in Italy and in the provinces. Which legal mechanisms does he recommend for each location?
2. The different legal mechanisms accommodate the different status of land in Italy and the provinces. In Italy, Roman citizens could own land as property as defined by the ius civile. In the provinces, the state (Rome itself or local communities) owned most land in the provinces while individuals possessed land according to local law or custom. How do these circumstances explain the legal mechanisms used to create servitudes in each place?
3. In the provinces water rights were not praedial servitudes but personal rights established by two kinds of contract, pacts and stipulations (cf. *CJ* 3.34.3). Compare contracts and conveyances for water rights. Which is more advantageous, and why?
4. The parallel between praedial servitudes in Italy and personal servitudes in the provinces reflects Roman efforts to accommodate their law to circumstances in the provinces. From a legal perspective, the land regimes made it impossible to establish praedial servitudes in the provinces. From a practical perspective, why might the Romans have wanted farmers in the provinces to be able to have the legal protection of a servitude for water use?
5. Servitudes in the provinces may have differed from praedial servitudes in other ways, as suggested by the case that is typically cited as the model for provincial servitudes (*D.* 8.3.33.1 African. *9 Quaest.*). It describes a servitude for *aquaeductus* that enables the right-holder to channel water over a series of estates, in apparent breach of the adjacent only rule (see Case 2.16). Compare also water rights in the irrigation community in Roman Spain (Case 3.29).

Case 2.11. Not by **usucapio**

D. 8.1.14 pr Paulus libro quinto decimo ad Sabinum

Servitutes praediorum rusticorum etiamsi corporibus accedunt, incorporales tamen sunt et ideo usu non capiuntur: vel ideo, quia tales sunt servitutes, ut non habeant certam continuamque possessionem: nemo enim tam perpetuo, tam continenter ire potest, ut nullo momento possessio eius interpellari videatur. idem et in servitutibus praediorum urbanorum observatur.

Paul in the fifteenth book on Sabinus

> Servitudes belonging to rustic estates, even though they attached to corporeal property, are nevertheless incorporeal and so are never acquired by *usucapio*; or it may be because servitudes are the kind of thing that does not have sure and continuous possession. For no one can go by foot so endlessly and continuously that his possession never appears interrupted. The same rule applies to servitudes belonging to urban estates as well.

1. A person acquired ownership by *usucapio* when he maintained possession of property for a specific period of time: one year for moveable property, two years for immoveable property or real estate. Could a servitude be acquired by *usucapio*? Why or why not?
2. *Usucapio* was particularly useful because records of title to land were inconsistent and incomplete in the Roman world, and ownership brought legal advantages. To what extent does Paul base his opinion on legal principles rather than practical necessity or the needs of landowners?
3. Paul's opinion may be connected with the *lex Scribonia*, a law of the first century BCE which prohibited the *usucapio* of servitudes. Why do you think the issue was still debated in the third century CE when Paul was writing?
4. By the end of the second century CE, there was another legal mechanism to acquire water rights by holding possession for a specific period of time, *longi temporis praescriptio* or prescription, as explained in an imperial constitution of 397 (*CJ* 11.43.4, Arcadius and Honorius, 397 CE; cf. *CJ* 3.34.1, 211 CE). *Praescriptio* is similar to *usucapio* except that in the provinces, possession had to be continuous for ten years if both parties lived in the same province, twenty years if different provinces (*CJ* 3.34.13, Justinian 531 CE). What are the pros and cons of the different periods of possession for usucapio and for praescriptio?

Case 2.12. Beyond Memory

D. 43.20.3.4 Pomponius, libro trigensimo quarto ad Sabinum

> Ductus aquae, cuius origo memoriam excessit, iure constituti loco habetur.

Pomponius in the thirty-fourth book on Sabinus

When a [servitude] for conducting water has outlived the memory of its origin, it is considered to have been established as a right.

Hypothetical fact pattern: Seius had been diverting water from Maevius' stream for a long time. Neither man remembered going to the praetor to establish a servitude, and there were no records of either mancipatio or in iure cessio. Maevius tries to stop Seius from using his water, and Seius brings a legal claim for his right to water.

1. How would Pomponius decide the case in the hypothetical? Would he allow Seius to bring a claim for the servitude? Does Seius have a legal right to channel water from Maevius' stream? Why or why not?
2. What is the legal basis of the right to channel water in this case? Water sharing practices are often informal, undocumented, and based on custom or practice. How does Pomponius' rule respond to this reality? What other solutions are possible?
3. Why might the Romans have thought it a good idea to recognize custom or long practice as the basis of a legal right? An imperial constitution from 286 CE authorized a right to water on the basis of longstanding custom, because it provided water for irrigation (*CJ* 3.34.7). What other issues should be considered when custom is the basis for water rights?
4. Is this case consistent with the previous one? The ius civile contained some inconsistent rules, in part because it was a dynamic institution that changed over time, but also because the jurists did not achieve a fully systematic analysis of the law, despite their self-conscious rationalizations and debates about principle. Is it more important for a legal system to be internally consistent or responsive to changing social needs? Can it be both? Explain.

B. Where, When, and How

Case 2.13. From the Source

D. 8.3.9 Paulus, libro primo Sententiae

Servitus aquae ducendae vel hauriendae nisi ex capite vel ex fonte constitui non potest: hodie tamen ex quocumque loco constitui solet.

Paul from the first book of his Sentences

> A servitude for conducting or drawing water cannot be established except [starting] from a source or spring. At present, however, a servitude is usually established [starting] from any place whatsoever.

1. What types of water sources can be governed by a servitude for *aquaeductus* or *haustus*? Generalize from Paul's examples: what characteristics define a water source that is suitable for a servitude? Why might it be a good idea to restrict servitudes to natural sources? What costs does the rule impose?
2. In another case, Ulpian defined a water source, *caput aquae*, as the place where water arose, and gave as examples a spring or a diversion from a river, lake, or canal (*D.* 43.20.1.18 Ulp. 70 *ad Ed.*). How helpful is this definition? Come up with two hypothetical situations to test his definition.
3. To access groundwater the Romans usually developed springs, that is, they built structures around them to contain and collect the water. Does Paul's rule seem out of touch with these practices? Could a developed spring be the source for a servitude? Why or why not?
4. The jurists considered natural sources to be permanent or perpetual causes, as Paul explained in a case about an urban servitude that created a right to discharge rainwater (or *stillicidium*; see Case 1.23). This servitude could not be established on a hole at the bottom of a wall used for washing the floor, "if no water should come into this place from the sky (because what is produced by a man's labor does not have a perpetual cause). On the other hand, although rainwater does not fall constantly, it still has a natural cause and so is deemed to be constantly produced. All praedial servitudes must be grounded on causes that perpetually exist. Thus, a servitude cannot be created giving the right to channel water from a tank or standing pond. A natural and perpetual cause must also lie behind the right to discharge eavesdrip" (*D.* 8.2.28 Paul. 15 *ad Sab.*). How persuasive is Paul's rationale? Does it make sense to apply the same rule about perpetual cause to both *aquaeductus* and the right to discharge water? Why or why not?

Case 2.14. Natural Cause or Social Custom?

D. 8.4.2 Ulpianus, libro septimo decimo ad Edictum

De aqua per rotam tollenda ex flumine vel haurienda, vel si quis servitutem castello imposuerit, quidam dubitaverunt, ne hae servitutes non essent: sed rescripto imperatoris Antonini ad Tullianum adicitur, licet servitus iure non valuit, si tamen hac lege comparavit seu alio quocumque legitimo modo sibi hoc ius adquisivit, tuendum esse eum, qui hoc ius possedit.

Ulpian in the seventeenth book on the Edict

Some [jurists] doubted that there were no servitudes for raising or drawing water from a river with a waterwheel or if someone would establish a servitude on a cistern. But in a rescript of the emperor Antoninus to Tullianus, it is added that the right-holder should be protected, although the servitude is not legally valid, if however he acquired it by this law or in some other legal way.

1. In this case Ulpian reports the emperor Caracalla's rescript or response to a petition from an individual who sought protection for his right to draw water (*haustus*). The case presents two situations, though only one may belong to the original case. Describe the two situations and the legal problems they raise. Use the term "perpetual cause" in your answer. Did the emperor recognize a servitude for *haustus* in either situation? How did he justify his decision?
2. The emperor's rationale suggests that the case came from the provinces or at least that the parties were not Roman citizens because they acquired servitudes not by a *ius civile* conveyance but by a law (the rescript itself or a contract?) or "some other lawful way" (review Case 2.10). The emperor validates these customary water sharing arrangements by equating them with servitudes. What costs and benefits can be associated with giving local custom the same authority as Roman law? For example, does assimilating customary servitudes to Roman law weaken the concept of perpetual cause? Are these intellectual problems outweighed by the practical advantages of more consistent law and less conflict over water?

3. Sometimes legal questions came to the emperor because there was a disagreement about interpreting the law. What different interpretations were possible in this case? Which interpretation makes better law? What does "better" mean? more fair? more efficient?

Case 2.15. Utility

D. 8.1.8 pr Paulus, libro quinto decimo ad Plautium

Ut pomum decerpere liceat et ut spatiari et ut cenare in alieno possimus, servitus imponi non potest.

Paul in the fifteenth book on Plautius

A servitude cannot be imposed to allow us to pick fruit or stroll or picnic on another's land.

1. Servitudes could not be created for just anything, and Paul mentions a few excluded activities. What principle or quality unites all his examples? Why would someone engage in these activities?
2. Paul's excluded activities function as a negative definition; that is, they show what a servitude was *not*. We can use his examples to formulate a positive definition: what kinds of activities were appropriate for servitudes? Try to come up with a general principle as well as a list of activities that fit your definition.
3. Rustic praedial servitudes were classified as *res mancipi*, a legal category limited to property closely tied to farming. Is Paul's opinion consistent with this classification? Why or why not?

Case 2.16. Self-Sufficiency and Adjacent Land

D. 8.3.5.1 Ulpianus, libro septimo decimo ad Edictum

Neratius libris ex Plautio ait nec haustum nec appulsum pecoris nec cretae eximendae calcisque coquendae ius posse in alieno esse, nisi fundum vicinum habeat: et hoc Proculum et Atilicinum existimasse ait. sed ipse dicit, ut maxime calcis coquendae et cretae eximendae servitus constitui possit, non ultra posse, quam quatenus ad eum ipsum fundum opus sit.

D. 8.3.6 pr Paulus, libro quinto decimo ad Plautium

> Veluti si figlinas haberet, in quibus ea vasa fierent, quibus fructus eius fundi exportarentur (sicut in quibusdam fit, ut amphoris vinum evehatur aut ut dolia fiant), vel tegulae vel ad villam aedificandam. sed si, ut vasa venirent, figlinae exercerentur, usus fructus erit.

Ulpian in the seventeenth book on the Edict

> Neratius said in his books on Plautius that [a person] cannot have *haustus* or *adpulsus* or [a right] of digging clay or burning lime on someone else's land unless he owns the neighboring farm. He says that Proculus and Atilicinus held this opinion, too. But Neratius himself says that a servitude for burning lime or digging clay can be established only as far as is necessary for this farm itself.

Paul in the fifteenth book on Plautius

> For example, if it has a pottery in which containers were made to ship the farm's produce (as in certain cases it happens that wine is transported in amphorae or that storage jars are made), or roof tiles or [materials] for building the farmhouse. But if the pottery is run to sell jars, [the right] will be usufruct.

1. In the first part of this case, Ulpian quotes Neratius' opinion about the scope of servitudes. What two limits does Neratius impose on servitudes? Evaluate the impact of these limits. Why might they have been controversial?
2. Neratius suggests that not all jurists endorsed the limitation to adjacent land. In fact, Paul expressly says that it was possible to establish *haustus* on a nonadjacent farm if the owner of the intervening land grants a right of access (*D.* 39.3.17.4 Paul. 15 *ad Plaut.*). It is possible that *aquaeductus* was limited to adjacent land but not other rustic praedial servitudes. Does it make sense to apply limit only to aquaeductus? Why or why not? Review the Vegetus inscription in Case 2.2, Study Question 4 for a work-around to the adjacent only rule.
3. The Romans prized self-sufficiency and pursued it as an economic goal. In preindustrial economies like ancient Rome's, self-sufficiency is a typical strategy for dealing with limited technology and low produc-

tivity. How do servitudes help landowners to achieve self-sufficiency?

4. In the second part of this case, Paul introduces the manufacture of ceramic jars to illustrate the need of the dominant estate. How do the landowners use these jars? Which legal institution (servitude or usufruct) governs digging clay for each use of the jars? How does the comparison with usufruct help to clarify the scope and definition of a servitude?
5. In another case, Papinian explained the distinction between servitudes and usufruct in terms of farming practice: a servitude for watering animals was praedial if the estate primarily produced livestock, otherwise it could be personal (i.e., usufruct, *D.* 8.3.4 Papin. 2 *Resp.*). Which jurist defined the scope of servitudes most narrowly? Which definition responds more adequately to the landowner's economic interest in natural resources?

Case 2.17. Indivisible: No Shares

D. 8.1.17 Pomponius libro singuli Regularum

Viae itineris actus aquae ductus pars in obligationem deduci non potest, quia usus eorum indivisus est: et ideo si stipulator decesserit pluribus heredibus relictis, singuli solidam viam petunt: et si promissor decesserit pluribus heredibus relictis, a singulis heredibus solida petitio est.

Pomponius in his only book of Rules

A part of *via, iter, actus,* [or] *aquaeductus* cannot be made subject to an obligation because the exercise of these rights is indivisible. Likewise if a man who has stipulated for one of these rights died, leaving a number of heirs, any one of them can claim the whole right of way (*via*). Similarly, if a man who promised [to grant] one of these servitudes dies, leaving a number of heirs, it can be claimed from any one of them.

1. The question of dividing servitudes seems to have arisen in relation to inheritance. When the owner of the dominant estate died, several heirs inherited the estate. Can all the heirs exercise the servitude? Do they inherit the servitude as a whole or in shares?
2. Alternatively, what happens when the owner of the servient estate dies and several heirs inherit the estate? Do they all have to agree to allow exercise of the servitude? Or can one speak for the group?

3. What does Pomponius mean when he writes that the exercise of servitudes is "indivisible"? How does this description explain his opinions about inherited servitudes?
4. The jurist Paul agreed with Pomponius, but explained the outcome differently with reference to via: "there is a single servitude for *via*, because by its nature it has an interval" (*D.* 33.2.12 Paul. 13 *ad Plaut.*). Paul seems to admit that servitudes were somewhat paradoxical, single yet exercised on multiple occasions. Does his explanation clarify what Pomponius meant when he described servitudes as indivisible? Does it work better for a right of access such as *via* than for water rights? Explain.
5. It appears that the water right in this case was created by contract, because Pomponius refers to stipulator and promissor, the parties to a stipulatio. Nonetheless, he proceeds as if it were a servitude. Remember that not everyone who lived under Roman law was a citizen capable of owning land and property rights. What circumstances might justify treating another type of water right as a servitude? To what extent does Pomponius' opinion reflect the assimilation of servitudes to personal rights?
6. The Republican jurist Ofilius considered a case where the plaintiff wanted to stop his neighbor from adding water to the channel. He granted an action only for all the water, that is, not just on the added water, because water cannot be divided (*D.* 43.20.1.17 Ulp. [Ofilius] 70 *ad Ed.*). Does Ofilius' opinion help to clarify what Pomponius means by indivisible? Or does it address a different issue, for example, the physical properties of water or the technology needed to separate the added water? Ofilius' opinion concerned the interdict for Daily and Summer Water, one of the interdicts that protected water rights whether they were personal or praedial. Several cases in the next section relate to this interdict as well as section II.C in chapter 3.

C. *Modus* and Multiple Servitudes

Case 2.18. Conditions and Modus

D. 8.1.4 pr Papinianus libro septimo Quaestionum

Servitutes ipso quidem iure neque ex tempore neque ad tempus neque sub condicione neque ad certam condicionem (verbi gratia " quamdiu volam") constitui possunt: sed tamen si haec adiciantur, pacti vel per doli exceptionem occurretur contra placita servitutem vindicanti: idque et Sabinum respondisse Cassius rettulit et sibi placere.

Papinian in the seventh book of Questions

By the right itself, servitudes can be established neither from one time nor to another time nor on condition nor until a specific condition [is fulfilled] (for example, as long as I like). But if these terms are added, when a person claims a servitude by *vindicatio* he will be faced with a defense of pact or fraud contrary to agreed terms. Cassius reported that Sabinus also gave this response and that he agreed.

1. How long did a servitude last? What does Papinian mean when he writes that a servitude cannot be subject to a condition? In what sense were servitudes unconditional?
2. Papinian introduces the possibility of an agreement between the owner of the servient estate and the owner of the dominant estate on terms limiting the exercise of the servitude. In other cases, these terms are known as a *modus*. Why might the parties agree to a *modus*?
3. Can the right-holder avoid the *modus* by claiming ownership of the servitude? Why not?
4. When a right-holder brought a legal claim for his servitude he used a modified version of *vindicatio*, the action for claiming ownership. When the praetor gave the formula for this action, he could include a defense or *exceptio* which, if proved in the trial, freed the defendant from liability. A defense of fraud concerned on the right-holder's behavior (had he acted in bad faith?) while a defense of pact depended on an agreement (had the right-holder agreed not to sue?). Under what circumstances could the owner of the servient estate use this defense? On claims for servitudes, see Case 2.34.
5. The parties could bring a separate action on the *modus* itself since it was a contract. What issues could be resolved in a lawsuit about modus?

Case 2.19. More Than One at a Time

D. 43.20.4 Iulianus, libro quadragensimo primo Digestum

Lucio Titio ex fonte meo ut aquam duceret, cessi: quaesitum est, an et Maevio cedere possim, ut per eundem aquae ductum aquam ducat: et

> si putaveris posse cedi per eundem aquae ductum duobus, quemadmodum uti debeant. respondit: sicut iter actus via pluribus cedi vel simul vel separatim potest, ita aquae ducendae ius recte cedetur. sed si inter eos, quibus aqua cessa est, non convenit, quemadmodum utantur, non erit iniquum utile iudicium reddi, sicut inter eos, ad quos usus fructus pertinet, utile communi dividundo iudicium reddi plerisque placuit.

Julian in the forty-first book of his Digest

> I have granted to Lucius Titius [a right] to conduct water from my spring. The question is: May I grant also to Maevius [a right] to conduct water along the same water channel? And if you think it is possible for [a right] to be granted along the same water channel to two persons, how should they use it? The jurist replied: Just as a right of way or to drive animals can be granted to several people either together or separately, so the right of channeling water can rightly be established. But if there is no agreement among those to whom water is granted about how they should use it, making available an analogous action will not be unfair, just as many jurists agree that an analogous action for dividing jointly owned property is to be available to those who share a usufruct.

1. Can the owner of the servient estate grant a right of *aquaeductus* on the same channel to two people? What rationale does Julian give to support his answer?
2. Julian quotes the opinion of an unnamed jurist about multiple rights of way on the same land. By introducing this quotation Julian is arguing by analogy. Explain the analogy and evaluate it. Should the same rules govern *aquaeductus* and rights of way? Why or why not?
3. When more than one person had a servitude of *aquaeductus* on the same channel, what issues or conflicts might arise that are not involved when there is only one servitude? How does Julian expect these conflicts to be resolved?
4. When multiple users cannot agree about how to share a common water channel, Julian proposes that they use an analogous action (*actio utilis*) based on the action for dividing jointly owned property (*communi dividundo*). The action for dividing jointly owned property

was a legal procedure that heirs could use to separate their shares in an inheritance, and often usufruct was left as part of an inheritance. Why is the action for dividing joint property also appropriate to servitudes? How robust is Julian's analogy between servitude and usufruct?

Case 2.20. Environmental Constraints

D. 8.3.2.2 Neratius, libro secundo Regularum

Si aquae ductus vel haustus aquae sufficiens est, potest et pluribus per eundem locum concedi, ut et isdem diebus vel horis ducatur.

Neratius in the second book of Rules

If channeling water or drawing water is sufficient, it can be granted to several people across the same place, for example, so that it be conducted during the same days or hours.

1. Can more than one person have a water right to use the same source? Does it matter whether they have *aquaeductus* or *haustus*? Should it matter?
2. What limit does Neratius set on the number of water servitudes on the same source? How could this limit be enforced? What would the parties need to know to observe this limit?
3. The Republican jurist Quintus Mucius considered another kind of environmental constraint when he wrote that it was not possible to grant *aquaeductus* to one person and a right of way to another person on the same place (*D.* 8.3.14 Pompon. 32 *ad Q. Mucium*). Can you reconstruct his argument? Is a legal principle at stake or are practical considerations primary?

Case 2.21. Allocation by Time, Volume, Season (*Modus*)

D. 43.20.5 pr–1 Iulianus, libro quarto ex Minucio

Cum constet non solum temporibus, sed etiam mensuris posse aquam dividi, potest eodem tempore alius cottidianam, alius aestivam aquam ducere, ita ut aestate dividatur inter eos aqua, hieme solus ducat is qui

> cottidianae ius habeat. (1) Inter duos, qui eodem rivo aquam certis horis separatim ducebant, convenit, ut permutatis inter se temporibus aqua uterentur: quaero, cum amplius tempore servitutibus praefinito ita duxissent, ut neuter eorum suo tempore usus esset, num ius utendi amisissent. negavit amisisse.

Julian in the fourth book from Minucius

> Since it is accepted that water can be divided not only by times but also by measures, one person can conduct water daily at the same time [as] another person can conduct water in the summer (i.e., summer water), such that in summer the water is divided between them but in winter only the one with the right to daily water conducts it. 1. It was agreed between two people who used to conduct water from the same watercourse separately at different times to use the water, but exchanging times. I ask whether they lost the right of use because they had conducted water for longer than the statutory period such that neither of them used it at his own time. The jurist said that they had not lost their rights.

1. This case concerns *modus* or terms agreed among parties to a servitude about how to exercise their rights. What terms did the parties agree? Why might water be scheduled differently in summer than in winter?
2. Why does this case come to the jurist's attention? What is the legal problem?
3. What circumstances might have led the two parties to exchange their scheduled times? What does this case suggest about the staff and agricultural practices on the dominant estate?
4. Is Julian's opinion about the exchange of schedule consistent with the other cases on servitudes? Why or why not.
5. Roman irrigation canals were often unimproved, that is, not lined with cement and not fitted with ceramic pipes. The water ran between dirt berms with barriers that could be moved to let the water flow in and out. How easy would it be to implement a schedule for water sharing with this technology? Reconstruct the process in as much detail as you can.

6. We are not well-informed about Roman technology for measuring the volume of flowing water. The flow in Rome's aqueducts was measured in terms of the diameter of pipes (Case 4.11, Study Question 4; and see Front. *Aq.* 64, and 65–73). Julian may have this kind of measurement in mind or alternatively some kind of proxy measurement such as acreage or the size of the pipes (cf. Cases 3.28 and 3.29). In some situations, the Romans allocated water in proportion to the land that was to be irrigated. Which type of measurement would be the easiest to manage? the most fair? Explain.
7. In other historical and modern societies, irrigation communities employ ditch-runners who move from field to field, alerting farmers when their turn at watering has come and ensuring that they observe the limits. Julian seems to assume a much smaller community, just two users, possibly because he writes about a hypothetical situation rather than a real case. How does the number of irrigators affect the implementation of modus?
8. Landowners also scheduled delivery of water; for example, water from the Aqua Crabra (a stream or spring) was delivered to villas near Tusculum at scheduled days and times (Front., *Aq.* 9.5). Roman inscriptions record schedules for water delivery, listing the name of the person with the water right, his allocation, and the schedule for delivery to his land (figures 1 and 2). Two longer inscriptions also document this kind of irrigation community (Cases 3.25 and 3.29). Why would the parties to a servitude set up an inscription like this?

Case 2.22. Watering Animals

D. 43.20.1.18 Ulpianus, libro septuagensimo ad Edictum

Trebatius, cum amplior numerus pecoris ad aquam appelletur, quam debet appelli, posse universum pecus impune prohiberi, quia iunctum pecus ei pecori, cui adpulsus debeatur, totum corrumpat pecoris adpulsum. Marcellus autem ait, si quis ius habens pecoris ad aquam appellendi plura pecora adpulserit, non in omnibus pecoribus eum prohibendum: quod est verum, quia pecora separari possunt.

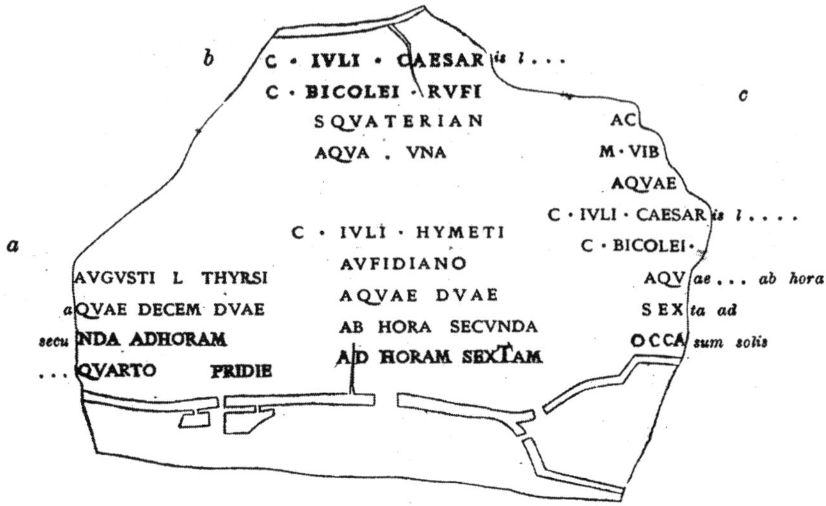

Fig. 1. *Corpus Inscriptionum Latinarum* 6.1261. This fragmentary inscription (now lost) was found in the gardens of S. Maria on the Aventine and is known from a transcription. It depicts water courses and reservoirs; it also records a schedule for delivery amounts, scheduled times, and names of the individuals who received water.

Translation of CIL 6.1261:

To . . . (farm) belonging to Thyrsis, freedman of Augustus / twelve waters (pipes?) / from the second hour to the . . . hour on the fourth day before . . .
To the Squaterian farm belonging to Gaius Bicoleus Rufus, freedman of Gaius Julius Caesar, one water (pipe?)
To the Aufidian (farm) belonging to Gaius Julius Hymetus, two water (pipes?) from the second to the sixth hour
To the Ac . . . (farm) belonging to Marcus Vibius . . . / water (pipes?) / . . . belonging to Gaius Bicoleus Rufus, freedman of Gaius Julius Caesar / water (pipes?) from / the sixth hour to/ sunset

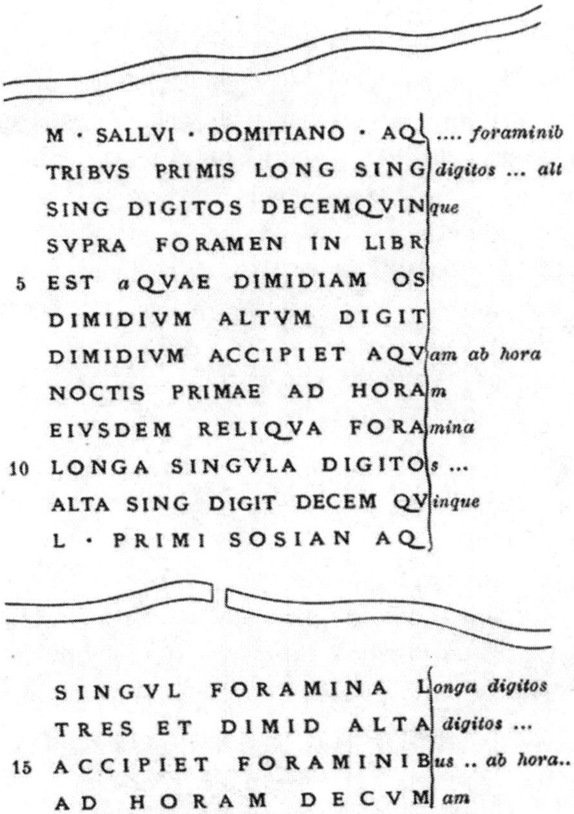

Fig. 2. *Corpus Inscriptionum Latinarum* 14.3676. The inscription is laid out between and below two water channels. It gives the names of the parties to whom water is delivered as well as amounts and times of day for delivery. Amounts are measured in digits, a unit that Frontinus defines as one-sixteenth of a foot and may refer to the dimensions of a reservoir or basin. The schedule is indicated not by a simple interval (e.g., three hours) but by the start and end times: for example, "from the first hour of night to . . ." (lines 7–8) and "to the tenth hour" (line 16), as in the inscription from Lamasba (see Case 3.25).

Translation of CIL 14.3676 (fig. 2):

> To the Domitian farm belonging to Marcus Sal<l>vius water . . . through the first three (taps?) each . . . digits long and fifteen digits . . . / beyond the tap (which?) is level with the water . . . he will receive half the water half . . . (to?) half a digit deep from the first hour of the night to the . . . hour of the same (?day); the remaining taps each . . . digits long and fifteen digits deep . . . water belonging to Lucius Primus Sosianus taps each three digits long and half a digit deep he will receive through taps . . . to the tenth hour.

Ulpian in the seventieth book on the Edict

> Trebatius says that when a greater number of herd animals is driven to water than ought to be, the whole herd may be prevented without punishment, because adding an animal to the herd, which has a right to water, destroys the whole right of driving animals to water. Marcellus however says that if someone with a right of driving animals to water has watered more animals, he is not to be prevented from [watering] all of them, which is correct, because the animals can be separated.

1. This case concerns the servitude for watering animals (*adpulsus*) or, more precisely, a *modus* for this servitude. What terms did the parties agree for the exercise of the servitude? What problem arose in enforcing this modus?
2. Ulpian quotes two jurists' views on the dispute about the *modus*: Trebatius, a Republican jurist and Marcellus, Ulpian's contemporary. How does each jurist resolve the dispute? What arguments might each jurist advance in support of his opinion? Which jurist's opinion makes better law? Explain.
3. Does this case indicate that the law on servitudes changed from the Republic to the Severan era? Why or why not?
4. The jurists' discussion of *modus* demonstrates an awareness of subtractability: the idea that every time one person uses a resource there is less left for the next person. How seriously do the jurists take the problem of subtractability? How good a solution do they propose to the problem with *modus*?

D. Impact on the Servient Estate

Case 2.23. Consent to a Servitude

D. 8.2.5 Ulpianus, libro septimo decimo ad Edictum

> Invitum autem in servitutibus accipere debemus non eum qui contra dicit, sed eum qui non consentit. ideo Pomponius libro quadragensimo et infantem et furiosum invitos recte dici ait: non enim ad factum, sed ad ius servitutis haec verba referuntur.

Ulpian in the seventeenth book on the Edict

> In connection with servitudes, we should understand that a man who speaks against it is not unwilling but one who does not agree. For the same reason Pomponius, in his Fortieth book, says that an infant and a lunatic cannot properly be said to be unwilling: and these words refer not to the fact of the servitude but the right.

1. The owner of the servient estate had to agree to a servitude to his neighbor, but there could be some question about what it meant to consent. How does Ulpian define consent?
2. Ulpian quotes an opinion by Pomponius to support his opinion. What examples does Pomponius introduce? How do they clarify the meaning of consent? What qualities or abilities must a person have in order to be able to give legal consent? Do you think that this jurists' definition of consent is the same as the meaning of consent in a social or business situation? Explain.
3. In what circumstances could there be a dispute about consent? Why might it not be clear whether or not the owner of the servient estate had agreed to the servitude? How helpful would the legal opinions be in resolving such a dispute?
4. What kind of relationship between neighbors do these definitions of consent assume? To what extent does Pomponius take a normative view of neighborly relations? That is, does Pomponius base his opinion on how neighbors ideally should get along or on a more realistic view of actual behavior?
5. The landowner's consent to a servitude remained part of the law through the post-Classical period and was incorporated into the prae-

tor's edict according to an imperial constitution of 223 CE issued by Severus Alexander (*CJ* 3.34.4). How can we explain the persistence of this requirement?

Case 2.24. The Route of aquaeductus

D. 8.3.21 Paulus, libro quinto decimo ad Sabinum

Si mihi concesseris iter aquae per fundum tuum non destinata parte, per quam ducerem, totus fundus tuus serviet.

Paul in the fifteenth book on Sabinus

If you grant me a watercourse across your farm without designating which part of your land I am to conduct water across, your whole farm will be encumbered.

1. When I have a servitude of *aquaeductus*, where on the servient estate can I channel water?
2. What limits does Paul impose on the route of canals for *aquaeductus*? What (and whose) interests do these limits protect?
3. How fair is Paul's rule? Does he adequately balance the rights of the two landowners? Or does he give an advantage to one of them?
4. To what extent does Paul's rule accommodate investment and development of farms?
5. In this case, Paul uses the older expression, *iter aquae* for the servitude of *aquaeductus*, possibly because it appeared in the work of Sabinus which he was interpreting. His usage shows that both terms were still understood in the third century CE, reflecting the conservative nature of legal language. Can you think of any archaic or old-fashioned terms that we still use in contemporary law?

Case 2.25. A Tacit Understanding

D. 8.1.9 Celsus, libro quinto Digestorum

Si cui simplicius via per fundum cuiuspiam cedatur vel relinquatur, in infinito, videlicet per quamlibet eius partem, ire agere licebit, civiliter modo: nam quaedam in sermone tacite excipiuntur. non enim per villam ipsam nec per medias vineas ire agere sinendus est, cum id aeque commode per alteram partem facere possit minore servientis fundi detrimento. verum constitit, ut qua primum viam direxisset, ea demum ire agere deberet nec amplius mutandae eius potestatem haberet: sicuti Sabino quoque videbatur, qui argumento rivi utebatur, quem primo qualibet ducere licuisset, posteaquam ductus esset, transferre non liceret: quod et in via servandum esse verum est.

Celsus in the fifth book of his Digest

If a man is granted or bequeathed a right of way without qualification over some other person's farm, he may walk and drive animals without limit, that is to say, across any part of the estate whatsoever at least according to civil law, because certain things are allowed tacitly in the expression. That is to say he is not allowed to go or drive animals through the farm buildings or in the middle of vineyards, when he could just as conveniently do it across another part with less harm to the servient estate. But once he has established [a servitude], he ought to go or drive where he first directed his path and he ought not to have the power to change it further. Sabinus seemed to think this also, when he used the example of a watercourse, which could be laid out anywhere at first, but after water had been conducted, it should not be moved. It is true that this same rule should be observed for right of way.

1. This case concerns servitude without *modus* or, as Celsus writes, without reservation (*simplicius*). Did this mean that the servitude could be exercised anywhere on the servient estate? What examples does Celsus give of places that are excluded from the servitude? What does he mean when he writes "just as conveniently"? Whose convenience is at stake? Formulate a general principle that unites all his examples.
2. How does Celsus describe the right way to exercise a servitude? His remarks evoke the contrast between the letter and the spirit of the law. Does he prefer that the right-holder follow the letter or the spirit of the law? Explain.
3. What assumptions does Celsus make about the social norms of neighborly behavior? Do you think that law or social morality is a better guide for neighbors' behavior? Why?
4. Celsus cites an analogy used by the jurist Sabinus. Explain the anal-

ogy. How persuasive is this analogy as argument to support Celsus' opinion?

5. Paul considers the same issue, limiting the exercise of a servitude to the parts of the servient estate where there were no buildings, trees, or vines at the time when the servitude was established (*D.* 8.3.22 Paul. 33 *ad Sab.*). How does Paul's rule differ from Celsus' rule? Which rule gives an advantage to the right-holder? Which rule would the owner of the servient estate prefer?
6. In a case about *iter* and *actus*, the jurist Iavolenus advises the parties to work with an arbitrator (*arbiter*) if there is difficulty determining the route of the right of way (*D.* 8.3.13.1 Iavol. 10 *ex Cassio*). What would be the usual way of determining a route? What advantages could arbitration offer?

Case 2.26. Not Doing Anything

D. 8.1.15.1 Pomponius, libro trigensimo tertio ad Sabinum

Servitutium non ea natura est, ut aliquid faciat quis, veluti viridia tollat aut amoeniorem prospectum praestet, aut in hoc ut in suo pingat, sed ut aliquid patiatur aut non faciat.

Pomponius in the thirty-third book on Sabinus

It is not in keeping with the nature of servitudes that anyone should do anything, such as remove bushes or provide a more pleasing view or, as in this case, paint his building, but it is in the nature of servitudes that he allow something or not do something.

Hypothetical fact pattern: *Titius has a servitude for aquaeductus that passes alongside a hedge on Maevius' land. Titius wants Maevius to remove the hedge.*

1. When Pomponius writes about "anyone," who does he have in mind? What is the owner of the servient estate required to do?
2. Apply Pomponius' rule to the hypothetical fact pattern. Can Titius legally compel Maevius to remove the hedge? Why or why not?

3. The details in this case suggest an actual legal dispute about one of the urban servitudes, prospect or the right to a view, in which the right-holder objected to what he saw on the servient estate. What would be a comparable issue for one of the water servitudes (*aquaeductus* or *haustus*)?
4. In another case, Pomponius, with some reluctance, allows a bridge to be built over a canal that itself crosses a bridge (*D.* 43.20.3.5–6 Pompon. 34 *ad Sab.*). Why does he hesitate? How does the servitude limit the rights of the owner of the servient estate?
5. In the servitude for discharge (*stillicidium*), the owner of the servient estate was prohibited from building anything that stopped the water dripping from the eaves, according to Paul (*D.* 8.2.20.6). How does *stillicidium* limit the rights of the owner of the servient estate? Is this same kind of 'doing nothing' that Pomponius has in mind? Explain. For more on *stillicidium*, see Case 1.23.
6. Pomponius' rule seems to minimize the burden on the owner of the servient estate. But even passive tolerance could have a price, as revealed in a rescript of 246 CE (*CJ* 3.34.5). The emperors wrote to the provincial governor instructing him to intervene on behalf of a soldier whose neighbor had built something that interfered with his servitude. The neighbor was to remove the construction and compensate the soldier for damage caused by his interference. What circumstances might lead the owner of a servient estate to build something that interfered with a water channel?

III. Changes and Challenges

A. How Servitudes Are Lost

Case 2.27. Loss by Non-use

Paulus, Sententiae 1.17.1–2

1. Viam iter actum aquae ductum, qui biennio usus non est, amisisse videtur: nec enim ea usucapi possunt, quae non utendo amittuntur.
2. Servitus hauriendae aquae vel ducendae biennio omissa intercidit et biennio usurpata recipitur.

Paul in his first book of Sentences

> A servitude for right of way (*via*) or driving a vehicle (*iter*) or animals (*actus*) or channeling water (*aquaeductus*) which has not been used for two years seems to have been lost: for these [rights] which are lost by not using them cannot be acquired by *usucapio*. 2. A servitude for drawing water (*haustus*) or of channeling water (*aquaeductus*) ceases to exist when it is not used for two years and is recovered if it is wrongly appropriated for two years.

1. How is a servitude lost?
2. How long a period of time must the non-use continue for the right to be lost? The prescribed time seems to have been set by statute, although no direct evidence for the legislation itself survives. Does two years seem like a reasonable standard? Why or why not?
3. Why is a servitude lost when it is not used? What reason does Paul give? What other reasons can you advance to support the rule?
4. Review Case 2.6 and Case 2.11 on *usucapio* then evaluate Paul's explanation for loss by non-use. His reasoning seems a bit circular. Which do you think came first, the ban on usucapio or the rule of loss by non-use? Explain.

Case 2.28. Who Can Exercise a Servitude?

D. 8.6.20 Scaevola, libro primo Regularum

> Usu retinetur servitus, cum ipse cui debetur utitur quive in possessionem eius est aut mercennarius aut hospes aut medicus quive ad visitandum dominum venit vel colonus aut fructuarius

Scaevola in the first book of Rules

> A servitude is maintained by use when the person to whom it is owed exercises it or the person who is in possession of it or a hired laborer or a guest or his doctor or someone who comes to visit the owner, or a tenant or someone with usufruct of the estate.

1. Does the owner of the dominant estate have to use the servitude himself to avoid loss by non-use? Why doesn't it matter who uses the right?

2. Consider the different types of people who can exercise the right. What do they all have in common? How would you name the category to which they all belong?
3. How consistent is the rule in this case with Paul's opinion that a person maintains a servitude only when he believes that he is exercising a right (Case 2.6)? Can the two opinions be reconciled?
4. Romans, especially the elite, usually owned several farms in different places; scattered property holdings is an important strategy for minimizing risk in a preindustrial economy. How does the rule on non-use accommodate this social reality?

Case 2.29. Intervals

D. 8.6.7 Paulus, libro tertio decimo ad Plautium

Si sic constituta sit aqua, ut vel aestate ducatur tantum vel uno mense, quaeritur quemadmodum non utendo amittatur, quia non est continuum tempus, quo cum uti non potest, non sit usus. itaque et si alternis annis vel mensibus quis aquam habeat, duplicato constituto tempore amittitur. idem et de itinere custoditur. si vero alternis diebus aut die toto aut tantum nocte, statuto legibus tempore amittitur, quia una servitus est: nam et si alternis horis vel una hora cottidie servitutem habeat, Servius scribit perdere eum non utendo servitutem, quia id quod habet cottidianum sit.

Paul in the thirteenth book on Plautius

If a right to channel water is established so that it is conducted only in the summer or only in one month, how can it be lost by non-use, since there is no continuous period of time when it could be exercised but was not? Accordingly, if someone has water in alternate years or months, [the right] is lost when twice the prescribed period has elapsed. The same rule is observed for the right to go in a vehicle (*iter*). But if [the right is exercised] on alternate days or all day or only at night, it is lost in the time established by law, because a servitude is continuous. For if he had a servitude for every other hour or for one hour daily, Servius writes that he loses the servitude by not using it [in the time established by law], because the right that he has is daily.

1. How does Paul apply the rule on non-use to different delivery schedules? Why is the prescribed period doubled in some cases? What is the underlying logic to the application of the rule?
2. Why does a *modus* for intermittent use make it difficult to determine whether a servitude has been lost by non-use?
3. What social needs might these types of intermittent use satisfy? Try to imagine what the Romans used these rights for and why the intervals made sense.

Case 2.30. Non-use and Irrigation

Codex Justinianus 3.34.10 Impp. Diocletianus et Maximianus AA. Et CC Nymphidio (294 CE)

> Si tibi servitutem aquae deberi praeses animadverterit nec hactenus non utentem spatio temporis amisisse perspexerit, uti te iure proprio providebit. Nam si hoc minime probetur, loco proprio facto opere dominus fundi continere aquam et facere, quominus ager tuus rigari possit, non prohibetur.

Emperors Diocletian and Maximian Augusti to Nymphidius

> If the governor became aware that a servitude of water was owed to you and he did not determine that you had lost it by not using it for the prescribed period of time, he will see to it that you have your full right. For if this were not deemed correct, then the owner of a farm will not be prevented from retaining water by building something, and making it impossible for your land to be irrigated.

1. This case presents an imperial constitution of the emperors Diocletian and Maximian in which they instruct the governor of a province about the rule on non-use of water rights. Try to reconstruct the situation: Who are the parties? What has caused the conflict? Why might it have been difficult for the governor to apply the rule on non-use in this situation?
2. What rationale do the emperors give for applying the rule on non-use in this case? What policy issues or interests does their decision serve?
3. In 531 CE Justinian extended the period of non-use from two to ten years when the right-holder lived on the land and twenty years when he did not (*CJ* 3.34.13). Why do you think Justinian changed the rule?

What circumstances could cause a right-holder to be away from his land for so long a period of time? Should we assume that only the right-holder could exercise a servitude in post-Classical law? See Case 2.28 for the rule in Classical law.

4. Communication between the emperor and Roman governors gives us a glimpse of how Roman law operated in the provinces beyond Rome. What does this constitution reveal about the competence of Roman officials and about the quality of justice in the provinces?

Case 2.31. A Start and Stop Spring

D. 8.3.34.1 Papinianus, libro septimo Quaestionum

Si fons exaruerit, ex quo ductum aquae habeo isque post constitutum tempus ad suas venas redierit, an aquae ductus amissus erit, quaeritur:

D. 8.3.35 Paulus libro quinto decimo ad Plautium

(35) Et Atilicinus ait Caesarem Statilio Tauro rescripsisse in haec verba: " hi, qui ex fundo Sutrino aquam ducere soliti sunt, adierunt me proposueruntque aquam, qua per aliquot annos usi sunt ex fonte, qui est in fundo Sutrino, ducere non potuisse, quod fons exaruisset, et postea ex eo fonte aquam fluere coepisse: petieruntque a me, ut quod ius non neglegentia aut culpa sua amiserant, sed quia ducere non poterant, his restitueretur. quorum mihi postulatio cum non iniqua visa sit, succurrendum his putavi. itaque quod ius habuerunt tunc, cum primum ea aqua pervenire ad eos non potuit, id eis restitui placet."

Papinian in the seventh book of Questions

If a spring dried up from which I have a right to conduct water and it returned to its streams after the established time period, is my right to conduct water lost?

Paul in the fifteenth book on Plautius

Atilicinus says that Caesar (i.e., the emperor) wrote back to Statilius Taurus in the following words: "These men, who were accustomed to channel water from the Sutrine estate approached me and explained that they had not been able to conduct the water from a spring on the Sutrine estate that they had used for a number of years, because the spring had dried up, and that afterwards the water had begun to flow again from the spring. They asked me to restore their right, because they had lost it not by neglect or fault, but because they were not able to conduct [the water]. I thought that they should be granted relief because their petition did not seem unfair. Therefore it is decided that the right be restored to them which they had at that time when the water first could not come all the way to them.

1. This case reports a rescript from an emperor who is probably be to identified as Augustus, because it mentions Statilius Taurus, a leading general during his reign. The case is unusual for preserving so many details, such as the location, an estate near Sutrium ("the Sutrine estate"), and the name of one of the parties, Statilius Taurus. What caused the legal dispute? Who were the plaintiffs? defendant? What did each party (plaintiff and defendant) claim? Who won?
2. What legal question or problem was at the heart of the dispute? How did Augustus justify his verdict? Is his verdict consistent with other cases on loss by non-use? Does his rescript make the law more fair? easier to apply? Explain.
3. In some respects, this case involves a conflict between the letter and the spirit of the law. That is, should a legal rule be applied strictly on the basis of its wording (a servitude is lost if it is not exercised for two years)? Or should a judge look to the principle behind the rule and test the facts against principle rather than the precise wording of the law? Does Augustus follow the letter or the spirit of the law? Do you agree with his decision? Why or why not?
4. Is the outcome of the case surprising, given the identity of the defendant? Why or why not? Given the hierarchical nature of Roman society, how might we expect social and political connections to affect the quality of justice?

B. Repairs and Management of Watercourses

Case 2.32. Regular Maintenance

D. 8.4.11.1 Pomponius, libro trigensimo tertio ad Sabinum

Si prope tuum fundum ius est mihi aquam rivo ducere, tacita haec iura sequuntur, ut reficere mihi rivum liceat, ut adire, qua proxime possim, ad reficiendum eum ego fabrique mei, item ut spatium relinquat mihi dominus fundi, qua dextra et sinistra ad rivum adeam et quo terram limum lapidem harenam calcem iacere possim.

Pomponius in the thirty-third book on Sabinus

If I have a right to conduct water in a canal near your farm, these rights are also tacitly implied: I am permitted to repair the canal and to approach by the shortest route to repair it, I and my workmen, and also the owner [of the servient] estate should leave me room to go to the canal on the left and the right and pile up dirt, lime, stone, sand, and chalk.

1. This case concerns the right of management, that is, the right to build and repair infrastructure necessary for exercising a right of use. Does the servitude holder need permission from the owner of the servient estate to repair his water channel? Why or why not?
2. Who is responsible for repairing a water channel? Who bears the costs and enjoys the benefits of the repairs?
3. If the right-holder encountered opposition to his repairs, he could sue the owner of the servient estate. Can you explain why? Alternatively, he could ask the praetor to issue an interdict or an order prohibiting interference with repairs to canals (Case 3.26). An interdict was an expedited procedure. Why might a quicker procedure be advantageous especially for water rights?
4. The owner of the servient estate also had legal remedies if he objected to repairs. Ulpian recommended that he get a guarantee from the right-holder for damage to his property, or he could use *vindicatio* to claim that there was no right to repairs at all (*D.* 43.21.3.8–9 Ulp. 71 *ad Ed.*). What would each party have to prove if they disagreed about repairing a watercourse?

Case 2.33. Repair or Improvement?

D. 8.3.15 Pomponius, libro trigensimo primo ad Quintum Mucium

Quintus Mucius scribit, cum iter aquae vel cottidianae vel aestivae vel quae intervalla longiora habeat per alienum fundum erit, licere fistulam suam vel fictilem vel cuiuslibet generis in rivo ponere, quae aquam latius exprimeret, et quod vellet in rivo facere, licere, dum ne domino praedii aquagium deterius faceret.

Pomponius in the thirty-first book on Quintus Mucius

> Quintus Mucius writes that, when [a person has] a right to channel water across another man's estate daily or in summer or over longer intervals of time, he is allowed to lay in the canal his own pipe, either ceramic or of any kind at all, in order to spread the water more widely; and he is allowed to do what he likes in the canal, as long as he does not make the water supply worse for the owner of the servient estate.

1. What changes does Mucius allow the right-holder to make in the infrastructure? Should these changes be allowed as part of the "tacitly implied" right of management described by Pomponius in the preceding case? Why or why not?
2. Would it be more accurate to describe these changes as improvements? How does Mucius limit the changes to the infrastructure? Why might these changes "make the water course less advantageous to the servient owner"?
3. Even after Mucius' opinion, improvements to water channels remained controversial. Servius allowed an above-ground channel to be converted into an underground culvert if it improved conservation and containment of the water (*D.* 43.21.3.pr Ulp. 70 *ad Ed.*). Do you think Servius is thinking in modern terms about conservation? Or does his opinion reflect other concerns, such as farming practices?
4. Labeo and Pomponius also considered the conversion of a canal to an underground channel. Labeo refused the conversion if it made access to water less convenient for the owner of the servient estate, while Pomponius allowed it because the owner of the servient estate was benefiting from the channel more by chance than by right (*D.* 43.21.2 Paul. 66 *ad Ed.*). Which jurist follows Mucius' opinion more closely? What assumptions underlie their opinions? Which rationale do you find most persuasive? Why?

C. Actions for Servitudes

Case 2.34. An Action in rem

Gaius, *Institutiones* 4.3

> In rem actio est, cum aut corporalem rem intendimus nostram esse aut ius aliquod nobis conpetere, uelut utendi aut utendi fruendi, eundi,

agendi aquamue ducendi uel altius tollendi prospiciendiue, aut cum actio ex diuerso aduersario est negatiua.

D. 8.5.2 pr–1 Ulpianus, libro septimo decimo ad Edictum

De seruitutibus in rem actiones competunt nobis ad exemplum earum quae ad usum fructum pertinent, tam confessoria quam negatoria, confessoria ei qui seruitutes sibi competere contendit, negatoria domino qui negat. (1) Haec autem in rem actio confessoria nulli alii quam domino fundi competit: seruitutem enim nemo vindicare potest quam is qui dominium in fundo vicino habet, cui seruitutem dicit deberi.

Gaius in the fourth book of his Institutes

There is an action *in rem* when we claim either that corporeal property is ours or that some right belongs to us, for example, [a right] of use or usufruct or of going on foot, driving animals, conducting water or building higher or prospect; and there is the opposite action (*actio negativa*) for our adversary.

Ulpian in the seventeenth book on the Edict

In the case of servitudes, actions *in rem* lie to us on the analogy of those actions which apply to usufruct, both the *actio confessoria* and the *actio negatoria*, the *actio confessoria* for the one who claims that servitudes belong to him and the *actio negatoria* for an owner who denies them. (1) This *actio confessoria in rem* lies to no one other than the owner of the farm, however. In fact, no one can claim a servitude by *vindicatio* other than the person who has ownership in a neighboring farm that he says is owed a servitude.

1. What kind of action was used for bringing a lawsuit about a servitude? Why is an action *in rem* appropriate for servitudes, according to Gaius? Can you think of other reasons?
2. The action for a servitude was modeled on *vindicatio*, the procedure for claiming ownership (cf. *D.* 8.3.5 pr Ulp. 17 *ad Ed.*). Roman law, like other legal systems, tended to be conservative: rather than inventing a new action, the jurists adapted an existing legal remedy to a new situation. The action had a different name depending on who was the plaintiff. Which action did the owner of the dominant estate use? The owner of the servient estate?

3. What does the owner of the dominant estate have to prove in this action? What does the owner of the servient estate have to prove? The *actio negatoria* is unusual because it requires the plaintiff to prove a negative.
4. The right-holder could bring action not just against the owner of the servient estate but also against anyone who interfered with the exercise of his right (*D.* 8.5.10.1 Ulp. 53 *ad Ed.*). Who else might interfere with a servitude, and why? Do you think the jurists were worried about fraud or is confusion a more likely problem? Explain.
5. An *in rem* action had broader liability than an *in personam* action, and for this reason a plaintiff could win greater compensation when praedial rights were violated. What economic interests were protected by *in rem* actions for servitudes? Why would Romans prefer broader protections for these interests?

Case 2.35. Which Court Hears Claims?

D. 8.3.1.2 Ulpianus, libri secundo Institutum

Traditio plane et patientia servitutium inducet officium praetoris.

Ulpian in the second book of his Institutes

Transfer and sufferance of servitudes will give grounds for the praetor's help.

1. Which magistrate had jurisdiction over legal matters relating to servitudes?
2. What does Ulpian mean by "transfer and sufferance of servitudes"? What issues did these legal proceedings address? Generate a couple of hypotheticals based on the cases preceding this one.
3. The term *traditio* can designate one of the conveyances for transferring ownership (i.e., delivery), but here the word is translated as "transfer," referring to any change of title. Why does it make sense to interpret *traditio* as a nontechnical term in this context?
4. A plaintiff wishing to sue for a servitude would have to present his claim in Rome where the urban praetor held court. How much would this location deter or make it difficult to use the law to either protect

or protest a servitude? Would it be more of a problem for rustic than for urban servitudes? Why?

Case 2.36. Consequences of Litigation

D. 8.5.18 Iulianus, libro sexto ex Minucio

Is, cuius familia vicinum prohibebat aquam ducere, sui potestatem non faciebat, ne secum agi posset: quaerit actor, quid sibi faciendum esset. respondi oportere praetorem causa cognita iubere bona adversarii possideri et non ante inde discedere, quam is actori ius aquae ducendae constituisset et, si quid, quia aquam ducere prohibitus esset, siccitatibus detrimenti cepisset, veluti si prata arboresve exaruisset.

Julian in the sixth book from Minucius

A man, whose slaves prevented his neighbor from conducting water, did not make himself available so that legal action could not be brought against him. The plaintiff asked what he should do. I replied that, after an investigation, the praetor ought to order the defendant's property to be confiscated and not returned until he had established the plaintiff's right of conducting water and made good any loss from droughts, because he had been prevented from conducting water, such as if his meadows or trees had dried up.

1. This case probably reports an actual legal dispute in which Julian advised the plaintiff, but some details have been lost. Reconstruct the situation as far as you can. Which party was the plaintiff? the defendant? What circumstances led to the lawsuit? Who won the case? What sanctions does Julian instruct the praetor to order?
2. What do you think Julian means when he writes that the defendant must "make good any loss"? Is he thinking about payment in kind or a monetary payment? Which would the plaintiff prefer? Why?
3. What were the plaintiff's losses? What examples of loss does Julian give? An irrigated pasture could be a source of profit from haying or livestock. Trees could be fruit orchards or olive plantations; both needed irrigation during rainless summer months, and saplings were irrigated until they had established themselves in the soil. These crops

and livestock were raised for self-sufficiency and for the market. To what extent does market participation make it more likely that a right-holder would bring a lawsuit for a servitude? Explain.

D. Servitudes in the Sale of Land

Case 2.37. Tacit Transfer

D. 41.1.20.1 Ulpianus, libro vicensimo nono ad Sabinum

Quotiens autem dominium transfertur, ad eum qui accipit tale transfertur, quale fuit apud eum qui tradit: si servus fuit fundus, cum servitutibus transit, si liber, uti fuit: et si forte servitutes debebantur fundo qui traditus est, cum iure servitutium debitarum transfertur. si quis igitur fundum dixerit liberum, cum traderet, eum qui servus sit, nihil iuri servitutis fundi detrahit, verumtamen obligat se debebitque praestare quod dixit.

Ulpian in the twenty-ninth book on Sabinus

But whenever ownership is transferred, it is transferred to the buyer in the same condition as it was with the seller. If a farm was servient, it passes with servitudes. If it was unencumbered, it passes as it was. If by chance servitudes were owed to a farm which was transferred, then it is transferred with the right of servitudes that are owed. If therefore someone said that a farm was unencumbered, which was in fact servient when he handed it over, he does not remove the right of servitude from it at all, but in fact he makes an obligation for himself and he will be obliged to make good what he said.

1. The sale of land was an occasion when questions could arise about water rights or servitudes. Ulpian considers three situations: sale of a servient estate, sale of a dominant estate, and a "mistake" about the status of the land. What happens to the servitude in each situation?
2. What are the pros and cons of tacit transfer of servitudes? How else could servitudes be transferred when land is sold?
3. Why might we characterize the third situation as a "mistake"? What is the alternative? Who bears the economic costs of such a mistake?

4. Paul applies the same rule about mistakes to urban servitudes (*D.* 8.4.12 Paul. 15 *ad Sab.*). Would it be easier to make a mistake about an urban or a rural servitude? Explain.
5. The Roman orator Cicero wrote a letter to his brother, Quintus, about an estate that he was planning to sell. He had discussed with their agent the possibility of imposing a servitude on the land; he had also consulted with a contractor about building an aqueduct on the property:

I hear that you now would like to hold onto Boblius' property. You decide what seems best about this. Caesius was saying that once the water is gone and a legal right established and a servitude is imposed on the farm we can still get the price, if we wanted to sell it. I have Mescidius with me. He said that you agreed on three sesterces per foot, and that he measured it on foot at 3,000 paces. It looked like more to me. But I promise that no better expense can be made. I had summoned Cilio from Venafrum but on the very day a tunnel crushed four of his slaves and apprentices at Venafrum. (Cic. *Q.Fr.* 3.1.3)

How did Caesius think the servitude would affect the sale price? Why might Cicero be skeptical of his opinion? How could the cost of building an aqueduct affect a decision about servitudes? Note that the reference to the tunneling accident at Venafrum suggests that there was an aqueduct there before Augustus built the one that is discussed in chapter 4.

6. An imperial constitution of 223 CE applies the rule of tacit transfer to servitudes in the provinces, explaining that the servitude transfers with land if the previous owners were not able to stop its use (*CJ* 3.34.3). Who benefits from this constitution? Why would the seller want to stop the exercise of a servitude?

Case 2.38. Delivery of a Servitude

D. 8.1.20 Iavolenus, libro quinto ex posterioribus Labeonis

Quotiens via aut aliquid ius fundi emeretur, cavendum putat esse Labeo per te non fieri, quo minus eo iure uti possit, quia nulla eiusmodi iuris vacua traditio esset. ego puto usum eius iuris pro traditione possessionis accipiendum esse ideoque et interdicta veluti possessoria constituta sunt.

Iavolenus in the fifth book of his Epitome of Labeo's Posthumous Works

Whenever a right of way or another right belonging to a farm is purchased, Labeo thinks that a guarantee should be given that nothing will be done by you [i.e., the seller] to hinder exercise of the right, because there can be no bare delivery of a right of this sort. I myself think that the exercise of this right should be regarded as delivery of possession and, for this reason, interdicts have been created on the analogy of the possessory interdicts.

1. Why was it not possible to transfer servitudes by delivery (*traditio*)? What does Labeo mean by "bare delivery"? Typically when the buyer takes possession of the object of sale, this delivery confirms the transfer of title. Recall that rustic praedial servitudes and the land to which they were attached was conveyed by *mancipatio* or *in iure cessio* (see Case 2.9).
2. What solution to the problem of delivery does Labeo propose? Similarly Gaius recommended that the seller add a clause to the sale contract specifying the servitudes owed by or to it (*D.* 8.4.3 Gaius, *Book 7 On the Provincial Edict*). Is this a good solution? Or does it raise as many problems as it solves?
3. What different solution to the problem of delivery does Iavolenus propose? Which solution do you think makes better law? Why? Possessory interdicts protected nonowners with an interest in possession of or access to property. Is the right-holder more like a possessor or an owner? Explain.
4. The praetor's edict contained several interdicts that could be used to protect water rights. Review the Study Questions to Cases 2.6, 2.7, 2.17, and 2.32, and make a list of the situations in which interdicts could be used. Why was the interdict needed as an alternative to *vindicatio*? For more on the interdicts relating to water rights, see also chapter 3.

Case 2.39. Sale and Loss by Non-use

D. 8.6.18.1 Paulus, libro quinto decimo ad Sabinum

Tempus, quo non est usus praecedens fundi dominus, cui servitus debetur, imputatur ei, qui in eius loco successit.

Paul in the fifteenth book on Sabinus

The period of time during which the previous owner of a farm did not exercise a servitude owed to it will be counted against the person who succeeds in his place (i.e., his successor in title).

Hypothetical Fact Pattern A
Titius had not used his servitude for eight months when he sold the dominant estate to Seius.

If Seius starts exercising the right as soon as he becomes owner, does he lose the servitude?

Hypothetical Fact Pattern B
Titius had not used his servitude for three years when he sold the dominant estate to Seius.

If Seius starts exercising the right as soon as he becomes owner, does he lose the servitude?

1. The case considers how to apply the rule on loss by non-use when the dominant estate is sold (cf. Case 2.27). Under what circumstances does the new owner lose the servitude? keep it? Use the hypotheticals to explain your answer.
2. Does the rule on non-use give more advantage to buyers or sellers? Why?
3. How does the rule on non-use encourage negotiation between buyers and sellers?
4. How could a buyer or seller be certain whether any servitudes were attached to land and if so of what kind? To what extent does the rule on non-use improve access to information in the real estate market?

Case 2.40. Labeo on Future Servitudes

D. 8.3.10 Paulus, libro quadragensimo nono ad Edictum

> Labeo ait talem servitutem constitui posse, ut aquam quaerere et inventam ducere liceat: nam si liceat nondum aedificato aedificio servitutem constituere, quare non aeque liceat nondum inventa aqua eandem constituere servitutem? et si, ut quaerere liceat, cedere possumus, etiam ut inventa ducatur, cedi potest.

Paul in the forty-ninth book on the Edict

> Labeo holds that a servitude can be established to allow you to search for water and conduct it if it is found. Indeed, if it is permitted to establish a servitude for a building that has not yet been built, why should it not equally be permitted to establish a servitude the same when water has yet to be found? If we can grant a right to search [for water], it is also possible to grant a right to conduct water once found.

1. What is Labeo's position: can a servitude be established when no source of water is known to the parties, or not? Is this opinion consistent with the other rules for servitudes?
2. How did Labeo justify his opinion? Evaluate his analogy between a servitude for water that has not been found and a servitude on a building that has not been built. How robust is it? Explain.
3. Servitudes for water use were especially important for agriculture if not for bare subsistence, certainly for diversification and producing a surplus that could be sold for a profit. How does Labeo's opinion take these economic interests into account?
4. Consider Labeo's opinion in the context of the sale of land. Why would a buyer want to add a clause to the sale contract reserving a future servitude? How would such clause affect the sale price of the land?

CHAPTER 3

Rivers and Seas

In Roman discussions of water rights, rivers raised many of the same legal issues as the sea because their fluid nature resists fixed boundaries. First of all, both were hard to categorize as property because property categories were based on ownership. The only simple case was rivers on private land, which were private and thus subject to the ordinary mechanisms of ownership, such as servitudes. Public rivers were owned by the Roman people or local community, while no one owned the sea. Yet the Romans considered both the sea and public rivers to be free and open for everyone to use. The incongruity between the concept of open access and Roman property institutions led to a great deal of discussion among the jurists in their treatment of rivers and the sea.

To accommodate the open access nature of the sea and public rivers, the jurists took several approaches. In some cases they attempted to define an individual right (*proprium ius*) analogous to an owner's right to use resources on his land. More often they worked with concepts of common use (*communis usus*) or public benefit (*publica utilitas*) to provide a legal basis for rights in the sea and public rivers. Ultimately, the jurists created a new category defined by open access, common property (*res communes*), and assigned to it the air, public rivers, and the sea as well as the sea shore.

The jurists' discussion of open access resources in fact began with the sea shore, which was at first classified as public property. Already in the late Republic, they recognized a potential contradiction between treating the shore as both public and open access. Persistent questions about the use of the shore include how much of the beach was open to all and where did private property begin.

In Roman law, the right to use public rivers and the sea were equivalent to rights of use, similar to servitudes but personal rights and less clearly defined. Everyone could use the sea for fishing, that is, had a right of access to sink a line and a right of withdrawal to take fish. The principle emerges from discussions of who owns the fish and prefigures the later legal concept of first possession. The jurists' discussions of the sea reflect philosophical ideas as well as traditional beliefs about the natural world.

For rivers, shipping and diversion of water posed the most legal challenges. The Romans understood that these two activities could be mutually exclusive, and early in their history they introduced praetorian interdicts to regulate access and withdrawal of water from rivers. They also used interdicts to define a right of management which applied both in the river itself and along its banks. Changes to a riverbank caused by flooding could affect the exercise of these rights, and also seems to have been a favorite topic for the jurists to generate test cases.

The interdict on drains complements the interdicts on diversions as well as the action for warding off rainwater covered in chapter 1. In the Mediterranean climate, removing water could be as important as supplying it. This interdict authorized substantial intrusions on ownership for the sake of public health and safety.

I. Sea and Shore

A. Public and Common to All

Case 3.1. Open Access and First Possessors

D. 41.2.1.1 Paulus, quinquagensimo quarto ad Edictum

Dominiumque rerum ex naturali possessione coepisse Nerva filius ait eiusque rei vestigium remanere in his, quae terra mari caeloque capiuntur: nam haec protinus eorum fiunt, qui primi possessionem eorum adprehenderint. item bello capta et insula in mari enata et gemmae lapilli margaritae in litoribus inventae eius fiunt, qui primus eorum possessionem nanctus est.

Paul in the fifty-fourth book on the Edict

The younger Nerva says that ownership of property begins from natural possession and a trace of this condition remains in things which are captured on land, sea, or air. For these things become property of the people who first take possession of them. Likewise things captured in war, islands arisen in the sea, gemstones and pearls found on the sea shore become the property of the person who first acquires possession of them.

1. The jurists considered the legal status of the sea indirectly when they explained the origin of ownership of things in the sea. Who owned things in the sea, according to Nerva? What kinds of things do you think Nerva had in mind when he wrote "captured on land, sea, or air"?
2. What does Nerva mean by "natural possession"? The jurists understood possession to mean physical control over things that could be protected by legal actions. In this respect, possession was similar to ownership. How does Nerva understand the relationship between natural possession and ownership?
3. How did Paul modify Nerva's rule? What examples does he add to Nerva's category of things captured on land, sea, and air? Should a person be able to acquire ownership of all these kinds of things in the same way? Why or why not?
4. Why might ownership of things in the sea cause controversy? Who owned things before they were caught?
5. Iavolenus wrote that a person who took something from the sea did not acquire ownership of it until its owner considered it lost (*D.* 41.1.58 Iavol. 11 *ex Cass.*). Would Nerva and Paul agree? How easy would it be to implement Iavolenus' rule?
6. Although the Romans do not have an expression equivalent to "open access," the legal category of *res nullius* expresses the core idea. *Res nullius* was property that no one owned but that could be owned by the first person who took physical control over it. The term may not

have been used in Nerva's day; it first appears in the second century CE in Gaius' textbook (*Inst.* 2.9). The idea of the sea as open access can be traced to Plato's *Laws* (7.824b) and in Roman sources to Plautus' play the *Rudens* (lines 696–75) in which a fisherman claims ownership of his catch. The Republican jurist Quintus Mucius seems to have endorsed the idea as well (*D.* 7.4.23 Pompon. 26 *ad Q. Muc.*). Where in Nerva's explanation can you see traces of the concept of *res nullius*?

Case 3.2. Common Use of the Sea

D. 43.8.3 pr–1 Celsus libro tricensimo nono Digestorum

> Litora, in quae populus Romanus imperium habet, populi Romani esse arbitror: (1) Maris communem usum omnibus hominibus, ut aeris, iactasque in id pilas eius esse qui iecerit: sed id concedendum non esse, si deterior litoris marisve usus eo modo futurus sit.

Celsus in the thirty-ninth book of his Digest

> I am of the opinion that the shores, where the Roman people hold power, belong to the Roman people. (1) [and] that all people have common use of the sea, just like the air, and that piles sunk in it (i.e., the sea) belong to the person who laid them. But this is not to be allowed if use of the sea or shore will be made worse in this way.

1. Celsus discusses three categories of property: private, public, and common, and gives examples of things that belong to each category. What are his examples? Can you think of others? Who owns each kind of property? What qualities or principles define each category?
2. Celsus introduced "common use" as a way of thinking about common property. His approach reconciles a paradox in Nerva's view in the preceding case, namely that no one owns the sea and everyone owns it. Is common use limited to fishing, as in the preceding case? What other uses of the sea could be included?
3. What limit does Celsus impose on the use of common property? What does he mean by "the use will be made worse"? Come up with a hypothetical or two that would show what "worse" means.

Case 3.3. Public or Common to All

D. 47.10.13.7 Ulpianus libro quinquagensimo septimo ad Edictum

Si quis me prohibeat in mari piscari vel everriculum (quod graece σαγήνη dicitur) ducere, an iniuriarum iudicio possim eum convenire? sunt qui putent iniuriarum me posse agere: et ita Pomponius et plerique esse huic similem eum, qui in publicum lavare vel in cavea publica sedere vel in quo alio loco agere sedere conversari non patiatur, aut si quis re mea uti me non permittat: nam et hic iniuriarum conveniri potest. conductori autem veteres interdictum dederunt, si forte publice hoc conduxit: nam vis ei prohibenda est, quo minus conductione sua fruatur. si quem tamen ante aedes meas vel ante praetorium meum piscari prohibeam, quid dicendum est? me iniuriarum iudicio teneri an non? et quidem mare commune omnium est et litora, sicuti aer, et est saepissime rescriptum non posse quem piscari prohiberi: sed nec aucupari, nisi quod ingredi quis agrum alienum prohiberi potest. usurpatum tamen et hoc est, tametsi nullo iure, ut quis prohiberi possit ante aedes meas vel praetorium meum piscari: quare si quis prohibeatur, adhuc iniuriarum agi potest. in lacu tamen, qui mei dominii est, utique piscari aliquem prohibere possum.

Ulpian in the fifty-seventh book on the Edict

If someone should prevent me from fishing or towing a dragnet (which is called *sagene* in Greek) in the sea, would I be able to sue him on a charge of outrage? There are some who believe that I can bring a claim for outrage; Pomponius and most [jurists think] that he is like a person who does not allow [me] to bathe in a public bath or sit in a public theater or to walk or sit or do business in any other [public] place, or if someone does not allow me to use my own property. For this man can be charged with outrage. The Republican jurists granted an interdict to a contractor if he had a public contract on the grounds that he was not to be forcibly prohibited from fulfilling his contract. If however I were to prevent someone from fishing in front of my house or villa, what answer should be given? am I to be held liable on a charge of outrage or not? The sea and its shores are certainly common to all, just like the air. It has very often been written in a rescript that fishing or even catching birds cannot be prohibited, except that someone can be prevented from entering another person's land. This has been asserted that even if with no legal right, someone can be prevented from fishing in front of my house or villa. If someone is prevented, he can bring a claim of outrage for this. I can however prevent someone from fishing in a lake which is part of my property.

1. The main focus of this case is on the delict of outrage (*iniuria*), which involved injury to a person's reputation or dignity, and specifically how location defined the claim. Ulpian determines that a person can bring an action for outrage if he is prevented from using public places or his own private property because he has been denied the exercise of his legal rights. His decision depends on his view of access to public places. Reconstruct his position as best you can: what examples of public places does Ulpian consider? How coherent is his categeory of public property? Explain.
2. How does Ulpian's concept of public property compare with that of other jurists in preceding cases? Do his examples clarify the distinction between public and common property? Why or why not?
3. How does private property differ from both public and common property? What is the legal basis for this distinction?
4. To what extent does Ulpian agree with Celsus' view of common use (Case 3.2)?

Case 3.4. Common by Natural Law

D. 1.8.2 pr–1 Marcianus, libro tertio Institutionum

Quaedam naturali iure communia sunt omnium, quaedam universitatis, quaedam nullius, pleraque singulorum, quae variis ex causis cuique adquiruntur. (1) Et quidem naturali iure omnium communia sunt illa: aer, aqua profluens, et mare, et per hoc litora maris.

Marcianus in the third book of Institutes

Some things are common to all by natural law, some things belong to a community, some belong to no one, and most things belong to individuals and they are acquired in various ways for each one. (1) These things also are common to all by natural law: air, running water, the sea and therefore the shores of the sea.

1. What categories of property does Marcian list? How does he distinguish them from each other?
2. Which resources are shared by all people, according to Marcian? Compare the common resources listed by Ulpian and Celsus in the preceding cases. How well does the concept of common use fit Marcian's category of *res communes*?
3. What is meant by "running water"? Why might some jurists have hesitated to include running water among *res communes*? Marcian may mean that water flowing in public rivers was open access, like the sea. Why is it difficult to group public rivers with the air, sea, and sea shore? How can access to each of them be limited? Which one does subtractability affect the most? The problem of open access to public rivers also comes up in the jurists' discussion of the River Interdicts later in this chapter.
4. In his treatise *On Duties,* Cicero describes common property as something that all people have in common and each can share without harm to himself, and he lists running water first among the common goods that all humans share (*Off.* 1.51–52). His discussion prefigures the modern concept of a common pool resource and the related idea of subtractability, that is, the idea that every person's use of a resource subtracts something from the whole, leaving less for others. Where can you see Cicero's ideas in the jurists' treatment of water resources?
5. What legal basis or law does Marcian invoke for his definition of common goods? The Romans appealed to natural law when they sought a principle outside their own legal system and with universal application. Such appeals "naturalize" law by identifying it with a state of nature, for example, the physical environment. What assumptions does Marcian make about the sea and the shore? How does he "naturalize" the sea? How would he define "nature"?
6. Marcian's formulation came at the end of a long juristic discussion of common property and was endorsed by Justinian (*Inst.* 2.1.1). It is still quoted in contemporary scholarship on common pool resources or

the commons. Which jurist's definition of common property do you think most closely corresponds to the modern concept of a commons defined as property that is subtractable and hard to regulate? Explain.

B. Along the Sea Shore

Case 3.5. Where the Waves Play

D. 50.16.96 pr Celsus libro vicensimo quinto Digestorum

Litus est, quousque maximus fluctus a mari pervenit: idque Marcum Tullium aiunt, cum arbiter esset, primum constituisse.

Celsus in the twenty-fifth book of his Digest

There is sea shore as far as the biggest wave reaches from the sea. Marcus Tullius [Cicero] first established this, so they say, when he was an arbiter.

1. The sea and its shore were common property, but there was uncertainty about how much of the beach was open to all. Where does Celsus locate the boundary? Is his view here consistent with Case 3.2?
2. Celsus attributes his definition of the shore to Cicero and reports that Cicero used the definition when serving as mediator in a legal dispute. In his treatise on rhetorical topics, Cicero ascribes a similar definition to his contemporary, the jurist Gaius Aquilius Gallus (*Topica* 32):

And so Aquilius, my friend and colleague, used to define what is "shore" as where the waves play, when he argued about the shores which you wish to be all public, because people were asking to whom they belonged. (*Solebat igitur Aquilius collega et familiaris meus, cum de litoribus ageretur, quae omnia publica esse vultis, quaerentibus eis quos ad id pertinebat, quid esset litus, ita definire, qua fluctus eluderet.*)

What is meant by Aquilius' words, "where the waves play"? Do Aquilius and Cicero agree about where to locate the boundary of open beach? Explain.

3. In modern law, the beach between the low and high tide marks is public or common, and everyone can freely walk or fish along it. Which Roman definition best matches the modern one? Why?

Case 3.6. Who Owns the Shore

D. 41.1.14 pr Neratius libro quinto Membranarum

Quod in litore quis aedificaverit, eius erit: nam litora publica non ita sunt, ut ea, quae in patrimonio sunt populi, sed ut ea, quae primum a natura prodita sunt et in nullius adhuc dominium pervenerunt: nec dissimilis condicio eorum est atque piscium et ferarum, quae simul atque adprehensae sunt, sine dubio eius, in cuius potestatem pervenerunt, dominii fiunt.

Neratius in the fifth book of Parchments

Whatever someone builds on the shore will belong to him. For the shores are not public in the sense that they are part of the people's property but in the sense that they were first created by nature and have not yet come into anyone's property. The legal condition of the shores is not unlike that of fish and wild animals which, as soon as they are caught, without doubt become the property of the person who has legal control over them.

Hypothetical fact pattern: *Lucullus sinks pilings and builds a dining room on the beach in front of his villa.*

1. In the hypothetical, does Lucullus own the dining room? How does Neratius explain the legal basis of his ownership?
2. Neratius suggests that the sea shore is *res nullius*, or property that "has not yet come into anyone's ownership," just like fish in the sea. How convincing is this analogy? Why is a building on the shore a more difficult problem than fish in the sea?
3. According to Neratius, there are two kinds of public property. How does he distinguish them from each other? To which category does he assign the sea? The sea shore?
4. A later jurist, Scaevola, cites an unnamed jurist who allowed construction on the sea shore as long as it did not interfere with public use,

publicus usus (*D.* 43.8.4 Scaev. 5 *Resp.*). Can the concept of public use help to explain Neratius' second kind of public property? If so, how?

Case 3.7. The Shore and the Interdict on Public Places

D. 43.8.2.8 Ulpianus libro sexagensimo octavo ad Edictum

Adversus eum, qui molem in mare proiecit, interdictum utile competit ei, cui forte haec res nocitura sit: si autem nemo damnum sentit, tuendus est is, qui in litore aedificat vel molem in mare iacit.

Ulpian in the sixty-eighth book on the Edict

An analogous interdict is available against a person who built a breakwater in the sea if this could by chance harm the plaintiff. If however no one suffers loss, a person who builds on the shore or piles up a breakwater in the sea is to be protected (by this interdict).

1. Under what circumstances can the interdict on public places prohibit building on the shore? Why might the Romans want to prevent or allow individuals to build on the shore?
2. To what extent is this case consistent with the previous one about building on the shore? Should a breakwater be treated differently than a building on the shore? Why or why not?
3. The praetor could grant an analogous interdict (*interdictum utile*) when the circumstances of the case justified a legal remedy but did not fully match the wording in his edict. The interdict on public places specified that the building take place on public property. Why does the breakwater require an analogous interdict?
4. Review the cases in the first section of this chapter. Which concept—public use, common use, common to all—best fits Ulpian's opinion in this case? Explain.

Case 3.8. Selling the Sea Shore

D. 18.1.51 Paulus, libro vicensimo primo ad Edictum

Litora, quae fundo vendito coniuncta sunt, in modum non computantur, quia nullius sunt, sed iure gentium omnibus vacant: nec viae publicae aut loca religiosa vel sacra. itaque ut proficiant venditori, caveri solet, ut viae, item litora et loca publica in modum cedant.

Paul in the twenty-first book on the Edict

The shores abutting a farm are not counted in its acreage when it is sold because they belong to no one but are free to all according to the law of nations. Nor are public roads or religious or sacred places counted. Consequently, it is customary to add a clause that roads and also the sea and public places come into the acreage in order to benefit the seller.

1. Can the owner of land along the shore sell the beach in front of his lot? Why or why not?
2. Paul describes the shore as belonging to no one or *res nullius* and open to all by the law of nations, *ius gentium*. How consistent is his opinion with that of other jurists? For example, would Paul agree with Nerva that the shore can be owned (Case 3.6)?
3. *Ius gentium* or "the law of nations" refers to custom or to the laws common to most states. Is either one a good basis for the rules limiting access to the sea? Why or why not?
4. Paul compares the shore to public, sacred, and religious property. Religious property (*res religiosae*) meant places of burial where the human remains made the land holy. Sacred property (*res sacrae*) was dedicated to the gods by the Roman people, for example, temples and shrines. Both religious and sacred property were governed by religious law and not by the *ius civile*, that is, it was not possible to own, possess, or sell them. According to Paul, the sea is treated in the same way as these other types of property. Does his view seem correct to you? Why or why not?
5. When the Romans sold land, they often added clauses or conditions to the contracts limiting the liability of buyers or sellers. What conditions does Paul recommend? What economic interests do such conditions protect?

Case 3.9. Access for Fishing

D. 1.8.4 pr Marcianus, libro tertio Institutionum

Nemo igitur ad litus maris accedere prohibetur piscandi causa, dum tamen villis et aedificiis et monumentis abstineatur, quia non sunt iuris gentium sicut et mare: idque et Divus Pius piscatoribus Formianis et Capenatis rescripsit.

Marcian in the third book of his Institutes

> Therefore no one is prohibited from approaching the sea shore to fish as long as he keeps away from villas, buildings, and tombs, because they are not governed by *ius gentium,* as the sea is. The deified Antoninus Pius wrote this in a rescript to the fishermen of Formiae and Capena.

1. In this case Marcian reports a rescript by the emperor Antoninus Pius to the fishermen of Formiae and Capena, two towns on the Italian coast near Rome, where wealthy Romans built elegant villas. Reconstruct the situation as best you can from the details of the case. Who are the parties? What was the cause of their dispute?
2. How did the emperor resolve the dispute? What legal principle does he invoke to support his decision?
3. To what extent is the emperor's decision consistent with the jurists' opinions about the shore in other cases?
4. Why might the fishermen have needed help from the emperor to resolve the problem? Would it matter if these fishermen were well-to-do owners of fishing enterprises and villas, not solitary, humble anglers? Explain.
5. What economic interests does the emperor's rescript protect? The fishermen may have been *publicani,* or tax collectors, who had contracts with the Roman state granting them a right to fish in exchange for payment or tax (cf. Case 3.18). If so, is the state's interest in sea fishing consistent with Marcian's rationale based on *ius gentium*? Why or why not?

Case 3.10. Servitudes and the Sea

D. 8.4.13 pr Ulpianus libro sexto Opinionum

> Venditor fundi Geroniani fundo Botriano, quem retinebat, legem dederat, ne contra eum piscatio thynnaria exerceatur. quamvis mari, quod natura omnibus patet, servitus imponi privata lege non potest, quia tamen bona fides contractus legem servari venditionis exposcit, personae possidentium aut in ius eorum succedentium per stipulationis vel venditionis legem obligantur.

Ulpian in the sixth book of Opinions

The seller of the Geronian Farm added a clause about the Botrian farm, which he kept, to prohibit tuna fishing in front of it. Although a servitude cannot be imposed by private agreement on the sea, because it is open to all by nature, nevertheless the possessors or their successors in this right are bound by the clause in the stipulatio or sale contract, because good faith demands that a contract's clause be observed.

1. This case concerns a seller who owned two nearby farms near the shore. When he sold one of them (Geronian) he included in the sale contract a condition relating to the farm that he did not sell (Botrian). How did that condition limit the use of the farm after the sale? Why might the seller have wanted to control activities on the shore near his farm?
2. Why is it impossible to impose a servitude on the sea according to Ulpian in this case? What other reasons could be adduced to support this opinion?
3. Why does Ulpian think that the condition should be enforced? What other legal opinions does he consider? Which opinion about the condition is more consistent with other cases on the status of the sea?
4. Why might Ulpian have decided that it was more important to enforce the contract than to respect the principle of open access to the sea? Do you agree with him? Why or why not?

II. Rivers

A. River Interdicts

Case 3.11. Prohibitory Interdicts

D. 43.12.1 pr Ulpianus libro sexagensimo octavo ad Edictum

Ait praetor: "ne quid in flumine publico ripave eius facias neve quid in flumine publico neve in ripa eius immittas, quo statio iterve navigio deterior sit fiat."

D. 43.13.1 pr Ulpianus libro sexagensimo octavo ad Edictum

Ait praetor: "in flumine publico inve ripa eius facere aut in id flumen ripamve eius immittere, quo aliter aqua fluat, quam priore aestate fluxit, veto."

D. 43.14.1 pr Ulpianus libro sexagensimo octavo ad Edictum

Praetor ait: "quo minus illi in flumine publico navem ratem agere quove minus per ripam onerare exonerare liceat, vim fieri veto. item ut per lacum fossam stagnum publicum navigare liceat, interdicam."

Ulpian in the sixty-eighth book on the Edict

The praetor says: "You are not to do anything in a public river or on its bank or release anything in a public river or on its bank, so that mooring or passage becomes worse for shipping."

The praetor says: "I forbid [your] doing anything in a public river or on its bank or releasing anything into a public river or on its bank so that the water flows otherwise than it did last summer."

The praetor says: "I prohibit the use of force to prevent sailing a boat or raft in a public river, or loading or unloading along its bank. I will also grant an interdict so that sailing across a public lake, canal, or lagoon is allowed."

1. This case presents the wording of three interdicts on public rivers (see table 3, p. 16). They illustrate the remedy-based nature of Roman law because each one provides a legal action for a specific situation. What does each interdict prohibit? Generate an example for each interdict of a specific activity that it would prohibit.
2. Which interdict or interdicts expressly address shipping goods on rivers? Which interdict or interdicts address transportation more generally?
3. Why does protecting the flow of a river also protect shipping? What other activities could this interdict protect?
4. All three interdicts regulate the water in the river and its banks. Why did the praetor regulate the use of river banks, as well as their water?

The Romans used both boats and rafts for river transport, and they also floated rafts of timber downstream. When traveling upstream, boats were towed by humans or animals. How do the interdicts address these varied means of transportation?

Case 3.12. A Restitutionary Interdict

D. 43.13.1.11–12 Ulpianus libro sexagensimo octavo ad Edictum

Deinde ait praetor: "quod in flumine publico ripave eius factum sive quid in flumen ripamve eius immissum habes, si ob id aliter aqua fluit atque uti priore aestate fluxit, restituas." (12) Hoc interdictum restitutorium proponitur: superius enim prohibitorium est et pertinet ad ea, quae nondum facta sunt. si quid igitur iam factum est, per hoc interdictum restituetur: si quid ne fiat prospicitur, superiore interdicto erit utendum, et si quid post interdictum redditum fuerit factum, coercebitur.

Ulpian in the sixty-eighth book on the Edict

Then the praetor says: "You must restore what you have done in a public river or on its bank or anything you have released into the river or its bank if, for this reason, water flows otherwise than it flowed last summer." (12) This interdict is provided for restitution. For the interdict above is for prohibition and applies to things which have not yet happened. So if anything has been done already, it is made good through this interdict. If the aim is that nothing should happen, the interdict above is to be used, and if anything will be done after the interdict is issued, it will be punished.

1. What is the purpose of a restitutionary interdict? How does Ulpian distinguish restitutionary and prohibitory interdicts?
2. Under what circumstances will the praetor grant a restitutionary interdict? a prohibitory interdict? What must a defendant have done in each case?
3. Could a plaintiff have both a prohibitory and a restitutionary interdict? Explain with a hypothetical situation illustrating your answer.

4. Once the praetor grants this interdict, what was the defendant required to do? What difficulties might a plaintiff encounter in trying to enforce this interdict?
5. What happens if the defendant continues his activity after the interdict is issued? Ulpian's choice of verb (*coercebitur*) points to *coercitio*, the magistrate's legal power to impose summary punishment. Does the threat of summary punishment make the interdict more effective? Why or why not?

Case 3.13. Public and Perennial

D. 43.12.1.1–3 Ulpianus libro sexagensimo octavo ad Edictum

> Flumen a rivo magnitudine discernendum est aut existimatione circumcolentium. (2) Item fluminum quaedam sunt perennia, quaedam torrentia. perenne est, quod semper fluat, ἀέναος, torrens ὁ χειμάρρους: si tamen aliqua aestate exaruerit, quod alioquin perenne fluebat, non ideo minus perenne est. (3) Fluminum quaedam publica sunt, quaedam non. publicum flumen esse Cassius definit, quod perenne sit: haec sententia Cassii, quam et Celsus probat, videtur esse probabilis.

Ulpian in the sixty-eighth book on the Edict

> A river is distinguished from a stream by size or by the opinion of the people living around it. (2) Some rivers are perennial, others are torrents. In Greek, perennial is what is always flowing, "ever-running," a torrent is "winter-flowing." But if a river dried up one summer which otherwise flowed year round, it is no less perennial for this reason. (3) Some rivers are public, some are not. Cassius determined that a river which was perennial, was public; this opinion of Cassius, which Celsus also approves, seems to be justifiable.

1. How did Cassius define a public river? What other ways to define a public river does Ulpian consider? Can you think of other features or factors that could be used to define a public river?
2. What reasons might Ulpian have had for preferring Cassius' definition of a public river? Which definition do you think is the most useful? Why?

3. In the semi-arid regions around the Mediterranean, some rivers (or torrents) had seasonal flow, filling with snow melt in the spring or rainfall in autumn and winter. Which definition of a public river best fits this physical environment? Explain.
4. Extreme climate events, such as drought, could change hydrological patterns. How does Ulpian accommodate extreme weather in defining a public river? How robust is his approach?

Case 3.14. Public or Private?

D. 43.12.1.4 Ulpianus libro sexagensimo octavo ad Edictum

Hoc interdictum ad flumina publica pertinet: si autem flumen privatum sit, cessabit interdictum: nihil enim differt a ceteris locis privatis flumen privatum.

Ulpian in the sixty-eighth book on the Edict

This interdict applies to public rivers. If the river is private, the interdict is inapplicable; for a private river is in no way different from other private places.

1. This case concerns the interdict on rivers. Review the wording of the interdict in Case 3.11. How does Ulpian limit its scope?
2. How is a private river different from a public river in Roman law?
3. Ulpian asserts that a private river is not different from other private property. What does he mean? Do you agree? In what way is a river different from other private property? Is it different from other private water resources such as springs and lakes?
4. Why did the Romans need to define a public river? Why was it not sufficient to say that a river was public if it was not private?
5. What rationale does Ulpian give for excluding private rivers from this interdict? A landowner could use *vindicatio* to defend his right to a private river. Those who could not prove title could use a different interdict, either for retaining possession or to recover possession of property that had been taken by force. What facts would the praetor consider in deciding which remedy was appropriate? How easy would it be to establish these facts in the Roman world?

B. Navigation

Case 3.15. The Interdict on Flow

D. 43.13.1.1–2 Ulpianus libro sexagensimo octavo ad Edictum

> Hoc interdicto prospexit praetor, ne derivationibus minus concessis flumina excrescant vel mutatus alveus vicinis iniuriam aliquam adferat. (2) Pertinet autem ad flumina publica, sive navigabilia sunt sive non sunt.

Ulpian in the sixty-eighth book on the Edict

> By this interdict the praetor has seen to it that rivers not flood when too few diversions have been granted and that changes to the banks do not bring any harm to the neighbors. (2) This interdict applies to public rivers, whether navigable or not.

1. How does Ulpian explain the purpose of this interdict? Review the wording of the interdict on flow in Case 3.11 and evaluate Ulpian's interpretation. Does he change the scope or appliction of the interdict? Explain.
2. What costs of limiting use of the river does Ulpian contemplate? What externalities does he ignore?
3. In this case, the manuscript tradition reports two different verbs: as printed the text indicates "flooding" (*excrescant*) while the alternate reading shows the rivers "drying up" (*exarescant*). Why is "flooding" likely to be the correct reading? Why might the variant "drying up" have been introduced? Some editors who prefer "drying up" delete the word *minus*, so it reads simply "because diversions have been granted." Which circumstance—flooding or drying up—poses greater risks?
4. Why does this interdict apply to both navigable and nonnavigable rivers? According to Labeo the praetor should not allow diversion of navigable rivers and their tributaries, which may or may not be navigable (*D.* 39.3.10.2 Ulp. 53 *ad Ed.*). To what extent does Ulpian agree with Labeo? Which jurist's opinion do you prefer, and why?
5. In the Republican era, Rome hired contractors to clear brush growing over public rivers or the towpaths along the banks, and one of the earliest praetorian formulas was for an action against a contractor who failed to clear the brush (Gel. 11.17.2). Cleaning a river could involve

considerable cost, as shown in a imperial constitution of Theodosius and Valentinian (*CTh* 14.27.2) concerning the Nile at Alexandria. The emperors allowed the city to spend four hundred gold coins, which had been earmarked for river clearing, for ships for the emperor instead. Why did the state have an interest in maintaining access to rivers for boat traffic?

Case 3.16. Last Summer's Flow

D. 43.13.1.8 Ulpianus libro sexagensimo octavo ad Edictum

Is autem hoc interdicto tenetur, qui aliter fecit fluere, quam priore aestate fluxit. et idcirco aiunt praetorem priorem aestatem comprehendisse, quia semper certior est naturalis cursus fluminum aestate potius quam hieme. nec ad instantem aestatem, sed ad priorem interdictum hoc refertur, quia illius aestatis fluxus indubitatior est. aestas ad aequinoctium autumnale refertur. et si forte aestate interdicetur, proxima superior aestas erit intuenda: si vero hieme, tunc non proxima hieme aestas, sed superior erit inspicienda.

Ulpian in the sixty-eighth book on the Edict

By this interdict a person is liable who causes a river to flow otherwise than it flowed last summer. They say that the praetor included last summer for this reason, because a river's natural current is always more certain in summer than winter. This interdict refers not to the summer that is just starting but to the previous summer, because that summer's flow is less open to doubt. It counts as summer until the autumn equinox. If by chance the interdict is issued in the summer, the most recent summer before is to be considered: but if in winter, not the summer immediately preceding but the one before that is to be considered.

1. What standard does the interdict establish for determining a river's flow? How does Ulpian interpret that standard?
2. What does the praetor need to know in order to decide whether to grant the plaintiff relief with this interdict? How does he determine whether the defendant's actions have in fact changed the flow of the river?

3. What policy aims might have motivated this interdict? How compatible are these aims?
4. The Romans recognized four seasons as we do, but Ulpian proceeds as if there were just two seasons, winter and summer. In a case on the interdicts on daily and summer water, he defines summer and winter as the periods between the autumnal and vernal equinoxes (*D.* 43.20.1.32 Ulp. 70 *ad Ed.*). Why is this two-season year useful for implementing the interdict on flow? The legal definition of seasons draws our attention to the arbitrariness of the calendar and to the different ways that humans define the seasons. For example, when the Romans wrote calendars for farming, they defined the seasons in terms of tasks appropriate to the time of year, for example, sowing wheat in autumn and harvesting it in late spring, pruning vines in early spring, and mending broken tools during the winter. Or recall the seasonal weather patterns in the Mediterranean, where most rain falls during the winter and summers are typically dry. Which definition of the seasons makes most sense for the interdicts, and why? What problems could arise when people use different seasonal systems?

Case 3.17. Rivers and Roads

D. 43.14.1 1 Ulpianus libro sexagensimo octavo ad Edictum

> Hoc interdicto prospicitur, ne quis flumine publico navigare prohibeatur: sicuti enim ei, qui via publica uti prohibeatur, interdictum supra propositum est, ita hoc quoque proponendum praetor putavit.

Ulpian in the sixty-eighth book on the Edict

> By this interdict it is provided that no one be prevented from sailing on a public river. Just as an interdict was provided above for a person who is prevented from using a public road, so the praetor thought that this interdict also ought to be provided.

1. The case concerns the interdict on navigating in a public river (Case 3.11). How does Ulpian explain its purpose?
2. Ulpian compares public roads and public rivers. How robust is his analogy? In another case, he explains that there is common use of pub-

lic rivers, roads, and the sea shore (*fluminum publicorum communis est usus, sicuti viarum publicarum et litorum, D.* 39.2.24 pr Ulp. 81 *ad Ed.*). Does the concept of common use strengthen Ulpian's analogy? Why or why not? Compare common use of the sea and sea shore in the cases on the sea.

3. In the Roman world river shipping was often less expensive and more reliable than land transport. How do the interdicts respond to this economic constraint?

Case 3.18. Lakes and Lagoons

D. 43.14.1.7 Ulpianus libro sexagensimo octavo ad Edictum

> Publicano plane, qui lacum vel stagnum conduxit, si piscari prohibeatur, utile interdictum competere Sabinus consentit: et ita Labeo. ergo et si a municipibus conductum habeat, aequissimum erit ob vectigalis favorem interdicto eum tueri.

Ulpian in the sixty-eighth book on the Edict

> If a contractor who has a lease on a lake or lagoon is prevented from fishing, Sabinus agrees that an analogous interdict is available, and Labeo also thinks so. Therefore if it is contracted by the townspeople, it will be most fair for him to be protected by the interdict for the sake of taxes.

1. The case concerns the interdict on navigating a public river. Why did Sabinus and Labeo determine that the interdict did not apply but instead granted an analogous interdict? Review Case 3.7 for the analogous interdict. How does Ulpian justify the analogous interdict?
2. The interdict on navigating a public river was also extended to protect watering animals in a public river or on its banks (*D.* 43.14.1.8–9 Ulp. 68 *ad Ed.*). How can you explain this extension? To what extent is this broadening of the interdict consistent with its original aims?
3. The contractor in this case is a tax collector (*publicanus*) who has a contract with a town to collect taxes levied on the catch of fish from a lake or a coastal lagoon. In general, interdicts were available to all citizens who wanted to protect their use of public or common property.

Why is the tax collector a special case? Is this opinion consistent with other applications of the river interdicts? Why or why not?

4. Fishing on public rivers came in for special consideration in another case where Papinian allowed the possibility of exclusive rights to use a public river, or a canal diverted from it for a person who fished there for many years (*D.* 41.3.45 pr Papin. 10 *Resp.*). As Papinian notes, this opinion is an exception to the general rule that *usucapio* or *praescriptio* did not apply to public property. To add to the confusion, the fisherman acquired his right by long use, just as if it were a praedial servitude (a private property right): recall that the jurists recognized long or customary water use as a legal right (see Case 2.12). How can we account for these different legal views on the use of public rivers? The problem illustrates the incomplete systematization of Roman law and its flexibility for addressing varied social and economic needs. At what point, though, do you think the concept of a public river becomes so attenuated that it is no longer useful? When does a public river become private?

C. Irrigation

Case 3.19. Daily and Summer Water

D. 43.20.1 pr Ulpianus libro septuagensimo ad Edictum

Ait praetor: "uti hoc anno aquam, qua de agitur, non vi non clam non precario ab illo duxisti, quo minus ita ducas, vim fieri veto."

Ulpian in the seventieth book on the Edict

The praetor says: "I forbid the use of force to prevent you from drawing from him the water at issue, which you have not conducted this year by force or stealth or favor."

1. This case presents the wording of the Interdict on Daily and Summer Water. What is the purpose of this interdict? What does a plaintiff have to prove in order to convince the praetor to issue this interdict? Note: the interdict refers to the plaintiff as "him."
2. Explain the difference between force, stealth, and favor? Favor (*pre-*

carium) is a legal term here that refers to legally authorized possession of property that lasts only as long as the owner wishes; it could be revoked at any time. Which condition would be the most difficult to prove?

3. This interdict applied to both public rivers and private water sources governed by servitudes (*D.* 43.20.1.7 Ulp. 70 *ad Ed.*). Does it make sense to protect both kinds of water rights with the same legal remedy? Why or why not?
4. When an individual had a servitude to use private water, he could use a claim for ownership (*vindicatio*) to protect his right (Case 2.34, cf. Case 2.28). Why might an interdict be needed for private water as well?
5. In post-Classical law, a similar interdict was introduced to protect diversion of water from reservoirs (*D.* 43.20.1.38–44 Ulp. 70 *ad Ed.*), possibly influenced by the law on civic aqueducts (see Case 4.12). Would it be more difficult to protect access to water from natural sources than man-made reservoirs? Why or why not?

Case 3.20. Rivals

D. 43.20.1.26 Ulpianus libro septuagensimo ad Edictum

Si inter rivales, id est qui per eundem rivum aquam ducunt, sit contentio de aquae usu, utroque suum usum esse contendente, duplex interdictum utrique competit.

Ulpian in the seventieth book on the Edict

If there is conflict about the use of water between rivals, that is, those who draw water through the same canal, each claiming his own use [of water], a double interdict lies for both of them.

1. If two people disagree about how to share a canal, can they both use the interdict on daily and summer water? What would be the outcome of such a double interdict? Is it a good solution to their problem?
2. Each party in this case claims his own use (*suum usum*). The expression suggests a right of use, either a servitude or a personal right to channel water. Why do they assert use rather than ownership? Review Cases 2.19, 2.20, 2.21, and 2.29, and explain how this case takes into account the law of servitudes.

3. What alternative remedy was available? Why might the interdict be the better choice? Explain.
4. The Latin word for two people sharing a canal is "rival" (*rivalis*), and the word also has the same connotation as in English. What does this usage reveal about the nature of water-sharing arrangements?

Case 3.21. Two Kinds of Water

D. 43.20.1.3 Ulpianus, libro septuagensimo ad Edictum

Duo autem genera sunt aquarum: est cottidiana, est et aestiva. cottidiana ab aestiva usu differt non iure. cottidiana ea est, quae duci adsidue solet vel aestivo tempore vel hiberno, etiamsi aliquando ducta non est: ea quoque dicitur cottidiana, cuius servitus intermissione temporis divisa est. aestiva autem ea est, qua aestate sola uti expedit, sicuti dicimus vestimenta aestiva, saltus aestivos, castra aestiva, quibus interdum etiam hieme, plerumque autem aestate utamur. ego puto probandum ex proposito utentis et ex natura locorum aquam aestivam a cottidiana discerni: nam si sit ea aqua, quae perpetuo duci possit, ego tamen aestate sola ea utar, dicendum est hanc aquam esse aestivam: rursum si ea sit aqua, quae non nisi aestate duci possit, aestiva dicetur: et si ea sint loca, quae natura non admittant aquam nisi aestate, dicendum erit recte aestivam dici.

Ulpian in the seventieth book on the Edict

There are however two kinds of water: there is daily and also summer water. Daily water differs from summer water in use not in right. Daily water is water that is usually conducted continuously in either summertime or wintertime, even if it is at times not conducted. Water is also called daily when its servitude is divided by an interval of time. But summer water is water that is expedient to use only in summer, just as we speak of summer clothes, summer pastures, summer camps, which we sometimes use in winter, too, but mostly in summer. I think that distinguishing summer water from daily water should be determined by the intention of the person using it and by the nature of the place. For if there were water that I use only in summer, although it can always be conducted, it should be called summer water. Then again if there were water that could not be conducted except in summer, it should be called summer water. But if there are places that do not allow water by nature except in summer, it will rightly be called summer water.

1. Review the wording of the interdict on daily and summer water (Case 3.19). Does it mention either "daily" or "summer" water? How does Ulpian explain this omission?
2. Why was it necessary to specify that the interdict could apply to both daily and summer water?
3. How does Ulpian define daily water? summer water? How well do his analogies support his definitions? What use of the water most likely caused the Romans to create the category of summer water?
4. An earlier jurist Neratius considered four factors defining daily and summer water:

   - legal right: does the person have a right to draw water only in the summer?
   - intention: does the person plan to draw off water only in the summer?
   - nature of the water: does the water flow only in summer?
   - use of the water: is the water useful only in the summer?

   Neratius had determined that "summer" should be defined on the basis of its nature and use (*D.* 43.20.6 Nerat. 3. *Membr.*). Does Ulpian agree? Which jurist gives more weight to environmental factors? Which jurist's definition is better, and why?

Case 3.22. Assignment of Rights

D. 43.20.1.44 Ulpianus, libro septuagensimo ad Edictum

Meminisse autem debemus in hoc interdicto totam quaestionem finiri adsignationis: non enim praeparat hoc interdictum causam, ut superiora interdicta, nec ad possessionem temporariam pertinet, sed aut habet ius adsignatum sibi aut non habet, et interdictum totum finitur.

Ulpian in the seventieth book on the Edict

We should however remember that the entire question of assignment is resolved with this interdict. For this interdict does not prepare a claim, as the interdicts above, nor does it pertain to temporary possession. But either he has a right assigned to him or not, and the whole interdict is resolved.

1. What question was answered when the praetor issued an interdict on daily and summer water? How is this interdict different from other interdicts, for example, a possessory interdict which assigns possession to one party, thus assigning the roles of plaintiff and defendant?
2. How does this interdict achieve a speedy resolution to a dispute over water rights? Why would speed be advantageous in this situation? Can you think of any potential drawbacks to praetor's deciding the case in a single hearing?
3. Through the interdicts, the praetor was responsible for the law on water resources of all kinds, natural and man-made, private and public. The earliest evidence comes from a second-century BCE inscription that records a praetor's interdict on water in northern Campania (*CIL* 10.8236). While the praetor assigned water rights by interdict, it is unlikely that there was a consistent system of administrative grants for access to public rivers like the one for civic aqueducts; the praetor also played a role in supervising city aqueducts (see Cases 4.23, 4.24, 4.35). How good a tool were the interdicts for regulating water rights?
4. Romans generally assumed that public waters—rivers, lakes, springs—were open access or free for all to use, but they were usually managed as common pool resources are today. How compatible are rights assigned by the praetor with protecting open access? How effectively could this interdict manage access and subtractability? Review the cases at the beginning of this chapter on the jurists' classification of water: how did the jurists' theoretical ideas about common property inform their interpretation of the interdicts?

Case 3.23. The Uses of Diverted Water

D. 43.20.1.11–12 Ulpianus, libro septuagensimo ad Edictum

Illud quaeritur, utrum ea tantum aqua his interdictis contineatur, quae ad agrum irrigandum pertinet, an vero omnis, etiam ea, quae ad usum quoque et commodum nostrum. et hoc iure utimur, ut haec quoque continineatur. propter quod etiam si in urbana praedia quis aquam ducere velit, hoc interdictum locum habere potest.

Ulpian in the seventieth book on the Edict

It is asked whether only water which is directed at irrigating a field is covered by these interdicts, or whether all water is covered, even water which is directed at our use and benefit. We apply this law to also cover this water. For this reason this interdict can have a place even if someone wishes to conduct water onto urban estates.

1. What activities did the interdict on daily and summer water originally protect? How does Ulpian expand its scope?
2. What does Ulpian mean by "our use and convenience"? Compare the expression, "common use" which he used to explain access to the sea, sea shore, and public rivers (Case 3.3). Are the terms equivalent? Why or why not?
3. Pomponius writes that the interdict protects water drawn off "not only for irrigation, but for herd animals or amenity" (*D.* 43.20.3 pr Pompon. 34 *ad Sab.*). Does Pomponius change the interdict's scope more or less than Ulpian does? Explain.
4. Civic aqueducts often served both urban populations and rural areas along their routes to town. This case envisions a similar situation for diversions from rivers. What conflicts might arise in these situations? Would differences in social and political power generate more dispute in urban than rural areas? Explain.
5. In another case, Labeo argued that the interdict protected the diversion of hot water as well as cold, even though the interdict originally applied to cold water:

> Labeo also writes that even though the praetor means cold water in this interdict, interdicts are still not to be refused for hot waters, as there is a necessary use of these waters too. For sometimes hot water is cooled and provides supply for irrigating fields. The same thing happens in these cases as happens in certain places where water is needed to irrigate the fields, even though it is hot, for example, at Hierapolis. It is well known that fields are irrigated with hot water in the land of the Hierapolitans in Asia. (*D.* 43.20.1.13 Ulp. 70 *ad Ed.*)

Is the protection of hot water closer to the original aims of the interdict than diversion to urban places? Labeo also argued that the action for warding off rainwater should apply to hot water (Case 1.2, Study Question 7). How might his opinions respond to the needs of people living across the Roman Empire?

Case 3.24. Proportional Allocation

D. 8.3.17 Papirius Iustus, libro primo de Constitutionibus

Imperatores Antoninus et Verus Augusti rescripserunt aquam de flumine publico pro modo possessionum ad irrigandos agros dividi oportere, nisi proprio iure quis plus sibi datum ostenderit. item rescripserunt aquam ita demum permitti duci, si sine iniuria alterius id fiat.

Papirius Iustus, in the first book on Constitutions

The Emperors Antoninus Augustus and Verus Augustus wrote in a rescript that water from a public river for irrigating the fields ought to be divided in proportion to the size of land holdings, unless someone could show that more was given to him by an individual right. They further wrote that conducting water is allowed only if it is done without harm to another.

1. Reconstruct the conflict that led to the emperors' rescript. Who are the parties? What caused their dispute?
2. How did the emperors Marcus Aurelius and Lucius Verus resolve the dispute? What limits did they impose on individual irrigators?
3. What kinds of harm could diversions cause for "neighbors" sharing a public river? What incentives could motivate neighbors either to prevent or to inflict harm on their neighbors by diverting water?
4. Why is proportional allocation a good solution to scarce water supply? What circumstances might make it a less attractive solution?
5. It is not clear what the emperor meant by an individual right (*proprio iure*). It cannot refer to a servitude because no servitude was needed to divert a public river (see Case 3.4), but is probably best interpreted as an administrative grant of some kind, possibly by praetorian interdict (cf. Case 3.22). How can a system of individual grants be reconciled with proportional allocation of water? with open access?

6. A common resource such as a public river was subject to subtractability, that is, every person's use decreased the water for others. Where can you find evidence for subtractability in this case? How well does proportional allocation answer the challenge of subtractability?
7. Why might the emperors have taken an interest in this case? Agriculture was the largest sector of the Roman economy, and the Roman state collected taxes in the form of crops, primarily grain but also olive oil, which was used to feed the city of Rome and the Roman army. How could a local dispute over water rights have a ripple effect across the empire?

Case 3.25. An Irrigation Community in North Africa

Corpus Inscriptionum Latinarum 8.18587 = 4440 preamble and lines 1–16

Imp(eratore) Caes(are) M(arco) Aurelio Inv(i)cto Pio Felice Aug(usto) amplissimo [sacerdote Dei Invicti Solis Elagabali, quaesita re per et .....] / Valentinum, quibus ea res delegata est ex decreto ordinis et colonor[um Lamasbensium, aquarum quae dari] / solitae sunt, constitit ita debere aquam decurrere si quando fo[ns decurrit, ut monstrat forma infra scripta, aquae decur] / rentis quae propterea distributa interim non est, quoniam tempora [iniqua id prohibuerunt—]

Scalai ex d(ie) septimo Kal(endas) Octobr(es) primo mane/ quo Claudiana descendit ad matrice(m) riganda(m) h(ora) u(na):

Mattius Fortis 100 k(apita) ex h(ora) (prima) d(iei) (septimi) Kal(endas) Octobr(es) in h(oram) (quintam dimidiam) d(iei) eiusdem p(ro) p(arte) s(ua) h(orae) (quattuor et) s(emis)
Flavius Adiutor Vet(eranus) 350 k(apita) ex h(ora) (quinta dimidia) d(iei) (septimi) Kal(endas) Octobr(es) in h(oram) (decem dimidiam) d(iei) eiusdem p(ro) p(arte) s(ua) h(orae) (quinque)
Her(edes) Apulei Faustini 117 k(apita) ex h(ora) (decima dimidia) d(iei) (septimi) Kal(endas) Octobr(es) in h(oram) (duodecimam) d(iei) eiusdem p(ro) p(arte) s(ua) h(ora una et) s(emis)
Apuleus Rogatianus 110 k(apita) ex h(ora) (duodecima) d(iei) (septimi) Kal(endas) Octobr(es) in h(oram) (unam demidiam) noctis eiusd(em)

p(ro) p(arte) s(ua) h(ora una et) s(emis)
Apuleius Africanus 110 k(apita) ex h(ora) (una demidia) noctis (septimi) Kal(endas) Octobres in h(oram) (tertiam) noctis eius(dem) d(iei) p(ro) p(arte) s(ua) h(ora una et) s(emis)
Apuleius Processus 120 k(apita) ex h(ora) (tertia) noc(tis) (septimi) Kal(endas) Octob(res) in h(oram) (sextam) noc(tis) eiusdem p(ro) p(arte) s(ua) h(orae quattuor)
Her(edes) Aeli Chrysae 500 k(apita) ex h(ora) (sexta) noc(tis) (septimi) Kal(endas) Octob(res) in h(oram) (unam demidiam) (sexti) Kal(endas) Octo(bres) p(ro) p(arte) s(ua) h(orae septem et) s(emis)

Lamasba Irrigation Decree

When the emperor Caesar Marcus Aurelius Unconquered, Pious, Blessed, Augustus most reverent [priest of the Unconquered Sun God, when the situation had been investigated by both . . . and] Valentinius, to whom had been referred, according to the decree of the senators and [colonists of Lamasba, the question about the waters which were given] customarily, it was decided that the water ought to flow down whenever the spring [flowed down just as the chart inscribed below directs, and of the flowing water] which is not assigned in the interval, [since inequal times prohibit it . . .]

The "ladders" from September 25 the first hours in the early morning when the [aqua] Claudiana flows down to the registered land that is to be irrigated:

Mattius Fortis 100 kapita from the first hour of the day September 25 to hour five and a half of the same day, four and a half hours for his share
Flavius Adiutor Veteranus 350 kapita, from hour five and a half of the day September 25 to the hour ten and a half of the same day, five hours for his share
Heirs of Apulieus Faustinus 117 kapita, from the tenth and a half hour of the day September 25 to the twelfth hour of the same day, one and a half hours for their share.
Apuleus Rogatianus 110 kapita from the twelfth hour of the day September 25 to the hour one and a half of the same night, an hour and a half for his share

Apuleius Africanus 110 kapita from hour one and a half of the night of September 25 to the third hour of the same night, an hour and a half for his share
Apuleius Processus 120 kapita from the third hour of the night of September 25 to the sixth hour of the same night, four [*sic*] hours for his share
Heirs of Aeliua Chrysa 500 kapita, from sixth hour of the night of September 25 to hour one and a half of September 26, seven and a half hours for their share

1. The Lamasba Irrigation decree is slightly out of place in this chapter because it concerns not a river or the sea, but the Aqua Claudiana, a seasonal stream or wadi near a Roman colony in North Africa (see the introduction and Shaw 1982). Nevertheless it appears here because it documents an irrigation community similar to the one addressed in the rescript in the preceding case and to the one in Spain presented in the next section of this chapter (Case 3.29). This decree is recorded in an inscription that constitutes all we know of a dispute in this irrigation community. The first part of this case presents the preamble of the decree which dates the text to the reign of the emperor Elagabalus (218–222 CE) and provides some context. The Roman authorities were involved in settling the dispute along with a local committee headed by Valentinius and another person, whose name is not preserved. Why might the Roman authorities have become involved in this irrigation dispute?
2. The second part of this case presents the beginning of the register of water allocations and an introductory sentence about ladders which should probably be interpreted as sluices or barriers of some kind used to divert water into individual plots. The Aqua Claudiana has been identified with a spring near Lamasba; its waters were probably collected in two reservoirs or basins from which water was distributed by gravity flow to individual parcels. What information does the introductory sentence present? Why did the community begin irrigating in September?
3. What do the entries reveal about the allocation of water and the assignment of water rights in this irrigation community? When and

how was water distributed? Reconstruct the system as best you can. Was water scarce and in high demand? How can you tell? The inscription presents no word for water rights and no other legal terms to help determine what kind of rights the landowners had. It is likely that the inscription affirms local law or customary arrangements for water sharing, although Roman servitudes could be a model (see Cases 2.18–2.22).

4. In each entry, the letter "K" describes the amount of irrigated land acreage in terms of the number of trees grown on it (mostly olive, fig, vine, but also almond and fruit trees). Why are trees an appropriate proxy for the size of individual parcels of land? Is the water allocated consistently? That is, does each irrigator receive the same amount of water per "k"? How can we explain the allocation of water?
5. Several of the individuals share a family name, Apuleus (or Apuleius; the spelling varies in the inscription), which suggests that some members of the irrigation community belonged to the same family. How could kinship complicate things in an irrigation community?

Case 3.26. Water Quality

D. 43.20.1.27 Ulpianus, libro septuagensimo ad Edictum

Labeo putat per hoc interdictum prohiberi quem, ne quid in illo fundo faciat fodiat serat succidat putet aedificet, quare ex re ea aqua, quam ille hoc anno per fundum tuum sine vitio duxit, inquinetur vitietur corrumpatur deteriorve fiat: et similiter de aestiva aqua debere interdici ait.

Ulpian in the seventieth book on the Edict

Labeo thinks that by this interdict a person is prohibited from doing, digging, sowing, cutting down, pruning, [and] building anything on that farm, that would cause the water, which he conducted in this year across your farm without harm, to be polluted, spoiled, fouled, or made worse. And he says that a similar interdict is due for summer water.

1. How does Labeo interpret the wording of the interdict on daily and summer water (cf. Case 3.19)? How does he change its scope?
2. Why might Labeo's expansion of the interdict be controversial? How could it be justified?

3. Labeo's opinion addressed daily water but Ulpian applied it also to summer water. Should both daily and summer water be protected from pollution in the same way? Why or why not?
4. Polluting the water in the city aqueducts was punished with a fine, according to a senate decree of 116 BCE (Front. *Aq.* 97, Case 4.20). Which legal remedy—fine or interdict—do you think would be more effective in maintaining water quality? Explain.

D. Maintenance

Case 3.27. Canals

D. 43.21.4 Venuleius libro primo interdictorum

De rivis reficiendis ita interdicetur, ut non quaeratur, an aquam ducere actori liceret: non enim tam necessariam refectionem itinerum quam rivorum esse, quando non refectis rivis omnis usus aquae auferretur et homines siti necarentur. et sane aqua pervenire nisi refecto rivo non potest: at non refecto itinere difficultas tantum eundi agendique fieret, quae temporibus aestivis levior esset.

Venuleius in the first book on Interdicts

An interdict will be granted for the repair of canals without inquiring whether the plaintiff was allowed to conduct water. For the repair of roads is not as necessary as repair of canals since, if canals were not repaired, all use of the water would be lost and people would die of thirst. For clearly water cannot arrive unless the canal is repaired. But if a road is not repaired there could be difficulty in walking and driving, which would be less onerous in summertime.

1. The interdict on canals protected their cleaning and repair (*D.* 43. 21.1 pr Ulp. 70 *ad Ed.*). What rationale does Venuleius give for this interdict? How compelling is his rationale? Compare Case 3.17.
2. The interdict on canals applied whether they ran on public or private land (*D.* 43. 21.1 pr Ulp. 70 *ad Ed.*). Can you explain why?
3. To what extent does the interdict on canals address the same issues as the interdict on daily and summer water? Consider the various uses of water as well as rural and urban settings.

Case 3.28. Springs

D. 43.22.1.7–9 Ulpianus libro septuagensimo ad Edictum

Hoc interdictum eandem habet utilitatem, quam habet interdictum de rivis reficiendis: nisi enim purgare et reficere fontem licuerit, nullus usus eius erit. (8) Purgandus autem et reficiendus est ad aquam coercendam, ut uti quis aqua possit, dummodo non aliter utatur, quam sic uti hoc anno usus est. (9) Coercere aquam est continere sic, ne diffluat, ne dilabatur, dummodo non permittatur cui novas quaerere vel aperire: hic enim innovat aliquid praeter id, quam praecedenti anno usus est.

Ulpian in the seventieth book on the Edict

This interdict has the same application as the interdict on repairing canals. For unless cleaning and repairing a spring is permitted, it will not be possible to use it. (8) A spring must be cleaned and repaired in order to contain the water so that someone can use the water, provided that he does not use it otherwise than he used it in this year. (9) To contain water means to keep it from flowing or slipping away, provided that seeking or opening new sources is not allowed; for this accomplishes something new and beyond the use in the previous year.

1. What is the purpose of the interdict on springs? Why was it difficult to keep private water infrastructure in good working order?
2. Why are repairs more likely to cause conflict than cleaning? How robust are Ulpian's definitions of "repair" and "contain"? How effective is his approach to resolving disputes about repairs?
3. When the Romans drew water from a spring they often improved it by building a basin to collect the water or a channel to contain it. In contrast, many irrigation canals were dirt-walled ditches. Do these practical considerations justify different protections for canals and springs? Why or why not?
4. Ulpian writes that this interdict has the same benefit as the interdict on canals. Do you agree with Ulpian? What benefit or application does each type of hydraulic infrastructure serve?
5. Who was responsible for repairs and cleaning of canals? When an individual had a servitude to channel or draw water from a spring, he

also had a right to repair the infrastructure (see Cases 2.32 and 2.33). Why was the interdict on springs also needed?

Case 3.29. An Irrigation Community in Spain

lex rivi Hiberiensis 3a-3b-3c (col. 1.27–38 and 42–46)

> Rivos quibus utentur communiter purgent re/feciant ita ut qua fine quisque aquam habet / usque eo operas praestet; perfectis rivis, [a]b ea / mole quo quisque aquam derivat ad proxuma[m] / molem purgare anno bis cum ei magistrati pa/gi diem dixerint denuntiaverint; id adsidue / fieri debeat quod ipsius dolo malo non fiat.
>
> [3b] Item si quis canalem aut pontem positum habet, / tamquam moles observatur et eum locum is /tueri et purgare debebit et quantum ab ea re / rivus impeditus erit quominus aqua iusta per/fluat . . .
>
> [3c] . . . ab rivo Hiberiensi ex ea die /quae pa[g]anis placuerit aquam avertant operasque ad / imam sortem aquationis avertant operasque ad / eum rivum reficiendum purgandumque ex idi/bus Iulis inducant.

The Ebro irrigation decree, para. 3a

> [The irrigators] should clean and repair the canals which they use in common in this way: each person is responsible for the works up to where he has access to water. Where canals have been built, each person [is to clean] from the dam where he diverts water to the next dam, twice a year when the village officials have named the day and sent notice. Whatever would be malice not to have done should be done diligently. [3b] And likewise if anyone has a conduit or bridge installed, he will need to take care of this place and clean it just as a dam is cared for, and as much as the canal is blocked so that lawful water does not flow through . . . [3c] from the day which the irrigators have agreed on, they should divert the water from the Ebro canal and turn the works away at the last water turn and put in place the works for repair and cleaning after the fifteenth of July.

1. This case comes from the *lex rivi Hiberiensis* (*lrH*), an inscription recording the bylaws of an irrigation community in Spain. The decree

is named for a canal that carried water from the Ebro river, and then the irrigators diverted water from this main canal onto their land with diversion dams or barriers. Who was responsible for cleaning and repairing the canal? How were their duties assigned? Is it an equitable arrangement? Why or why not?

2. The *lrH* mentions of a right to water (*ius aquae*, see Study Question 5 below), but as in the Lamasba inscription, there are too few details to determine the legal nature of the right. It is likely that the Ebro irrigators relied on local law or custom, but again Roman servitudes could provide a model. This passage in this case assigns to the irrigators the right of management, that is, they are legally authorized to repair and maintain the portion of the canal from which they divert water. But the expression sounds more like a duty than a privilege: can you find words or phrases that impose a duty? Should maintenance be considered more of a duty than a right? Explain.
3. When do the irrigators perform repairs and maintenance? How can we explain the logic behind the schedule?
4. In another passage of the bylaws, the village officials (*magistri pagi*) are instructed to enforce the rules on maintenance and the contribution of money for repairs:

> and if anyone does not furnish anything that is ordered or required of him or makes a delay or acts slowly or does not pay his money on the due date, for every violation he must pay twenty-five denarii into the accounts controlled by the village official. (*lrH* col. 1.6–15)

The fine imposed by the *lrH* (twenty-five denarii = one hundred sesterces) was equivalent to the monthly pay of a city scribe, a low-level administrative job. How effective would this fine have been in ensuring compliance with the law? What incentives could motivate an irrigator to perform maintenance on the canal? Which was more likely to motivate the irrigators to perform annual maintenance, the positive incentives or the threatened penalty?

5. The irrigators met in an assembly to decide about the rules for their community, to determine the allocation of water, and to organize

repairs. Each man had a right to speak in proportion to his water right (*sententia dum proportione quan/tum quique aquae ius habent sententiam dicant, lrH* para. 1a, col. 1.7). It is likely that water was allocated in proportion to acreage or the size of the farm. Is proportional allocation of water more fair than proportional voting in the assembly? Why or why not? Compare the kinds of proportional allocation in the Ebro community with that of the Lamasba community.

6. Did the irrigators have the legal power to alienate or transfer ownership of their water rights? What evidence does the degree present to support your answer?
7. Can this decree be interpreted as assigning rights of withdrawal, even though it uses no legal terms for water rights? Why or why not?

E. Drains and Sanitation

Case 3.30. Drains

D. 43.23.1 pr Ulpianus libro septuagensimo primo ad Edictum

Praetor ait: "quo minus illi cloacam quae ex aedibus eius in tuas pertinet, qua de agitur, purgare reficere liceat, vim fieri veto. damni infecti, quod operis vitio factum sit, caveri iubebo."

D. 43.23.1.15 Ulpianus libro septuagensimo primo ad Edictum

Deinde ait praetor: "quod in cloaca publica factum sive ea immissum habes, quo usus eius deterior sit fiat, restituas. item ne quid fiat immittaturve, interdicam."

Ulpian in the seventy-first book on the Edict

The praetor says: "I forbid the use of force to prevent him cleaning and repairing the drain at issue which extends from his house to yours. I will order him to give a guarantee for damage which is caused by a fault in the work."

Ulpian in the seventy-first book on the Edict

Then the praetor says: "You are to make good what you have done or released in a public drain that makes its function worse; and by interdict I prohibit that anything to be done or released."

1. This case presents both the prohibitory and the restitutionary interdicts on drains. What is the purpose of each interdict?
2. Reconstruct the kinds of situations that the interdicts address. Who wants to repair the drain, the plaintiff or the defendant? Draw a picture of the drain and the two properties.
2. A drain could be either a hollowed-out place where waste collected or it could be fitted with pipes (*D.* 43.23.1.4, 6 Ulp. 71 *ad Ed.*). What particular risks or challenges does each type of drain present?
3. How does the praetor expect the defendant to protect his property? The praetor refers to a *cautio* or guarantee against anticipated damage, that was used when one plans to engage in work that could harm the other's property. This *cautio* was a formal promise which gave rise to a legal claim if damage occurred. How adequate is this protection? How does it to compare to the protection of the interdict?
4. Review Cases 1.4, 1.7, and 1.14, which consider the possibility of a *cautio* for anticipated damage as an alternative to the action for warding off rainwater. To what extent does the interdict on drains address the same problems as the action on warding off rainwater? How are the legal remedies different?
5. What does the restitutionary interdict require of the defendant? Who pays the cost of restitution?
6. In the extract following the restitutionary interdict, Ulpian explains that the interdict prohibits doing or releasing anything that makes the use of a public drain worse (*D.* 43.23.1.16 Ulp 71 *ad Ed.*). Review the restitutionary part of the interdict on flow (Case 3.12). Compare their language and aims. How can you explain the similarities and differences?
7. The restitutionary interdict on drains applied also to public drains but the prohibitory interdict applied only to private property (*D.* 43.23.1.4 Ulp 71 *ad Ed.*). How can we account for the different scope of these two interdicts?

Case 3.31. Health and Safety

D. 43.23.1.2, 7 Ulpianus libro septuagensimo primo ad Edictum

Curavit autem praetor per haec interdicta, ut cloacae et purgentur et reficiantur, quorum utrumque et ad salubritatem civitatium et ad tutelam pertinet: nam et caelum pestilens et ruinas minantur immunditiae cloacarum, si non reficiantur. . . . (7) Quia autem cloacarum refectio et purgatio ad publicam utilitatem spectare videtur, idcirco placuit non esse in interdicto addendum "quod non vi non clam non precario ab illo usus," ut, etiamsi quis talem usum habuerit, tamen non prohibeatur volens cloacam reficere vel purgare.

Ulpian in the seventy-first book on the Edict

Through these interdicts, however, the praetor provided that drains be cleaned and repaired, and both of these relate to the citizens' health and safety. For filthy drains threaten to cause foul air and collapse, if they are not kept in good repair. . . . (7) But because the repair and cleaning of drains seems to aim at public benefit, it was decided that this clause should not be added to the interdict, "that he did not use it by force or stealth or favor," so that even if someone made such a use (i.e., of a drain), he still would not be prevented from cleaning and repairing a drain if he wished.

1. What rationale does Ulpian give for the interdict on drains? How persuasive is his argument? What other arguments could be made to support this interdict?
2. What limiting phrase has the praetor omitted from the interdicts on drains? Compare the wording of the other interdicts. What are the consequences of the omission? How does Ulpian explain the change? Do you find his rationale persuasive? Why or why not?
3. In another case, Ulpian writes that the interdict on drains may be brought against owners of not only adjacent houses but also more distant properties (*D.* 43.23.1.11 Ulp. 71 *ad Ed.*). How far does the right extend: one house over? a block away? farther? How could this extensive intrusion be justified?
4. A jurist of the Augustan era, Fabius Mela, writes that this interdict allows a person to enter his neighbor's house and take up the paving stones so as to clean the drain (*D.* 43.23.1.12 Ulp. 71 *ad Ed.*). What justifies such an intrusion on private property? Why might a neighbor agree to the repairs?

Case 3.32. Construction of a New Drain

D. 43.23.2 Venuleius libro primo de interdictis

> Quamquam de reficienda cloaca, non etiam de nova facienda hoc interdicto comprehendatur, tamen aeque interdicendum Labeo ait, ne facienti cloacam vis fiat, quia eadem utilitas sit: praetorem enim sic interdixisse, ne vis fieret, quo minus cloacam in publico facere liceret: idque Ofilio et Trebatio placuisse. ipse dicendum ait, ut ne factam cloacam purgare et restituere permittendum sit per interdictum, novam vero facere is demum concedere debeat, cui viarum publicarum cura sit.

Venuleius, from the first book on interdicts

> Although repairing a drain but not building a new drain is included in this interdict, nevertheless, Labeo said that there should also be an interdict preventing the use of force against someone building a drain because there is the same benefit. For the praetor has issued an interdict that force not be used to deny permission to build a drain in a public place, and Ofilius and Trebatius approved. Labeo himself says that it should be stated that cleaning and repairing an existing drain are to be permitted by interdict, but that the person in charge of public roads ought to give permission for building a new drain.

1. Could the interdict on drains be used to protect the construction of a new drain on private property? in a public place? What conflicts of interest are likely to arise around the construction of a new drain? How does the interdict address them?
2. Presumably the person who built a drain on public land was acting on his own behalf not as a city contractor. Try to reconstruct the situation: what was the source of the water? Did the drain cross public land or discharge the water onto it? How can you justify allowing private construction on public land? In another case, Labeo explains that a private drain could be connected to a public drain (*D.* 43.23.1.9 Ulp. [Labeo] 71 *ad Ed.*).
3. The Romans were aware that drains could damage public property. The general interdict on public places could be used to restrain a landowner whose drains emptied onto a public road and made it impass-

able (*D.* 43.8.2.26 Ulp. 68 *ad Ed.*). How did the Romans balance one landowner's need to remove waste water with the rights of his fellow citizens to enjoy public places? What are the trade-offs between public and private interests in this situation? How would you balance them?

4. In ancient Rome, the Senate contracted out the construction of public works like drains to private construction companies. The first emperor, Augustus, created a new city official to coordinate new projects as well as maintenance of public roads, the *curator viarum* (compare *the curator aquarum* in Case 4.8). Labeo refers to this official when he distinguishes the praetorian interdict on drains from regulation of public drains. In other words, two different authorities controlled drains in the city. What are the likely consequences of this division of labor? What evidence is there that the Romans viewed it as a problem and took steps to mitigate the difficulties? Which institution—praetorian interdict or city administration—do you think would do a better job of managing drains? Why?

Case 3.33. Drainage Ditches

Corpus Inscriptionum Latinarum 1^2.5 ch. 104

Qui limites decumaniqu<e> intra fines c(oloniae) G(enetivae) deducti factique erunt, quaecumqu(e) fossae limitales in eo agro erunt, / qui iussu C. Caesaris dict(atoris) imp(eratoris) et lege Antoniana senat(us) que / c(onsultis) ple(bi)que sc(it is) ager datus atsignatus erit, ne quis limites / decumanosque opsaeptos neve quit immolitum neve / quit ibi opsaeptum habeto, neve eos arato, neve e<a>s fossas / opturato neve opsaepito, quo minus suo itinere aqua / ire fluere possit. Si quis atversus ea quit fecerit, is in / res sing(ulas), quotienscumq(ue) fecerit, (sestertium) (mille) c(olonis) c(oloniae) G(enetivae) I(uliae) d(are) d(amnas) esto, / eiusq(ue) pecun(iae) cui volet petitio p(ersecutio)q(ue) esto.

Charter of the Colony Iulia Genetiva, Ch. 104

Whatever boundary lanes and main roads have been laid out and built within the territory of the colony Genetiva and whatever boundary ditches there will be on the land given and assigned by order of Gaius Caesar, dictator [and] imperator, and by the lex Antonia and by senate decrees and by plebiscites: no one shall keep them fenced in or have anything built or enclosed on them nor shall anyone plough them or close or seal off ditches to stop water flowing and going along its way. If anyone does anything contrary to this law, he is to give as penalty for every violation one thousand sesterces to the colonists of the colony Iulia Genetiva, and a claim and legal action for this fine belongs to whoever wishes to pursue it.

1. This case comes from the charter of the Roman colony, Urso, founded in Spain for Caesar's veterans (see the introduction for background on this law). Typically in rural land drainage ditches (*fossae limitales*) ran along roads between parcels of land that were assigned to colonists. These ditches were public property, which the community was authorized to regulate. Summarize in your own words the legal rules on drainage ditches in this colony. What do these rules aim to accomplish?
2. Who benefits from this regulation on ditches? What kinds of activities might cause blocked ditches?
3. In some places ditches served for both drainage and irrigation. To what extent are these purposes complementary? How well do the rules in this charter take into account both activities?
4. The Urso charter addresses ditches in rural areas, whereas the interdict on drains seems aimed at urban contexts. Should the legal rules be different in these two locations? Why or why not?
5. Is the Urso regulation likely to be more effective at ensuring the water flow than the *lrH* (Case 3.29)? Why or why not? (Recall that the *lrH* set the penalty for failure to clean the canals at twenty-five denarii = one hundred sesterces). How does this compare with the penalty in the Urso charter? How can we account for the difference? What other incentives or deterrents are at work in both situations?

III. River Banks

Case 3.34. What Is a River Bank?

D. 43.12.1.5 Ulpianus libro sexagensimo octavo ad Edictum

Ripa autem ita recte definietur id, quod flumen continet naturalem rigorem cursus sui tenens: ceterum si quando vel imbribus vel mari vel qua alia ratione ad tempus excrevit, ripas non mutat: nemo denique dixit Nilum, qui incremento suo Aegyptum operit, ripas suas mutare vel ampliare. nam cum ad perpetuam sui mensuram redierit, ripae alvei eius muniendae sunt. si tamen naturaliter creverit, ut perpetuum incrementum nanctus sit, vel alio flumine admixto vel qua alia ratione, dubio procul dicendum est ripas quoque eum mutasse, quemadmodum si alveo mutato alia coepit currere.

Ulpian in the sixty-eighth book on the Edict

A bank will be correctly defined as what holds a river when it keeps its natural course; but if it ever grows larger for a time from rain showers or the sea or some other reason, it does not change its banks. After all no one said that the Nile, which covers Egypt with its flood, changes or widens its banks. For when it returns to its permanent size, the banks of its bed have to be shored up. If however a river swelled from natural causes so that it gained a permanent increase, or if another river was mixed in or for some other reason, doubtless it must be said that it has also changed its banks, just as if it began to flow in a different way after the river bed had changed.

1. How does Ulpian define a river bank? Would it be more accurate to say that he defines the riverbed? Explain.
2. What criteria does Ulpian use to determine if the change to a river's course is temporary or permanent? In the Mediterranean, some rivers run all year (perennial) while others are seasonal torrents fed by snowmelt in spring and heavy rains in fall and winter (cf. Case 3.13). How well do his criteria match the environment in which Roman law operated?
3. Ulpian cites the Nile as an example to support his criteria. How good an example is it? Why would Ulpian choose the Nile as an example? What does his choice reveal about the nature of juristic thought?

Case 3.35. Alluvio

D. 41.1.7.1 Gaius libro secundo Rerum Cottidianarum sive Aureorum

Praeterea quod per alluvionem agro nostro flumen adicit, iure gentium nobis adquiritur. per alluvionem autem id videtur adici, quod ita paulatim adicitur, ut intellegere non possimus, quantum quoquo momento temporis adiciatur.

Gaius in the second book of Common Matters or Golden Rules

Furthermore what the river adds to our field by alluvion becomes ours by the law of nations. This land seems to be added by alluvion which is added so gradually that we cannot perceive how much is added at any point in time.

1. The Roman word *alluvio* is similar to the modern legal term "alluvion," which refers to the increase in land from the deposit of soil by natural action of a stream, river, or the sea (not to be confused with alluvium or the land itself that is deposited). How does Gaius define alluvion? Why does he specify gradual accretion? What other circumstances could cause change to a river's bank?
2. Who owns land created by alluvion? Do you agree with Gaius' answer to this question? Why or why not?
3. What is the legal basis for owing land added by alluvion? In Roman law, individuals owned structures that they built on the sea shore by the law of nations (*ius gentium*) while the shore itself was public or open to all (Cases 3.2, 3.3, 3.4). Are riverbanks more like the sea shore or the structures on it? Can you reconstruct Ulpian's reasons for treating them this way?

Case 3.36. Washed Away by Flooding

D. 41.1.7.2 Gaius libro secundo Rerum Cottidianarum sive Aureorum

Quod si vis fluminis partem aliquam ex tuo praedio detraxerit et meo praedio attulerit, palam est eam tuam permanere. plane si longiore tempore fundo meo haeserit arboresque, quas secum traxerit, in meum fundum radices egerint, ex eo tempore videtur meo fundo adquisita esse.

Gaius in the second book of Common Matters or Golden Rules

But if the force of the river detached some part of your estate and carried it to mine, it obviously remains yours. Of course, if it adhered to my land for a rather long time and the trees which it dragged with it grew roots into my farm, from that time it seems to be added to my farm.

1. In what sense does the land washed away remain yours? When does land washed away become mine?
2. What are the practical implications of Gaius' opinion? In other words, why would you want to retain ownership of land that had washed away? How could you exercise rights as owner over land separated from the riverbank?
3. In Roman law there were several legal mechanisms for acquiring ownership. The property's owner could transfer title to a new owner using a legal conveyance such as *mancipatio*. When property was unowned or its owner unknown, it was possible to acquire ownership by taking and holding possession for a period of time through *usucapio*. When something was attached to land, it became the property of the landowner by *accessio*. In addition, Roman law endorsed the first taker principle for ownership of things without an owner (*res nullius*): for example, whoever captured a wild animal or a natural resource became its owner through *occupatio*. Which legal mechanism best fits Gaius' view of the ownership of alluvial land?
4. Why is land washed away treated differently from land added by alluvion (Case 3.35)?
5. Celsus extends Gaius' rule to land washed away from a public river that fronts my land (*D.* 41.1.30.1 Pomponius 34 ad Sab.). Why is this case more difficult? Review the cases on river interdicts and public rivers as you consider this question.

Case 3.37. New Islands

D. 41.1.7.4 Gaius libro secundo Rerum Cottidianarum sive Aureorum

Quod si uno latere perruperit flumen et alia parte novo rivo fluere coeperit, deinde infra novus iste rivus in veterem se converterit, ager, qui a duobus rivis comprehensus in formam insulae redactus est, eius est scilicet, cuius et fuit.

Gaius in the second book of Common Matters or Golden Rules

Now if a river broke through on one side and begin to flow in a new channel in a different place, and then farther downstream this new channel turned back into the old channel, the land which is surrounded by both channels and transformed into an island of course belongs to the person to whom it belonged before.

1. When a river changes course creating a new island, who owns it? Is the answer as obvious ("of course . . .") as it seems to Gaius? Explain.
2. Try to draw before and after pictures of the situation described by Gaius. Does it matter how far downstream the river returns to its former bed or how big the new island is? Why or why not?
3. Does the same legal rule apply to a new island as to land added by alluvion or land washed away in the preceding cases? Should the same principle apply? Why or why not?

Case 3.38. River Changes Course Twice

D. 41.1.7.5 Gaius libro secundo Rerum Cottidianarum sive Aureorum

Quod si toto naturali alveo relicto flumen alias fluere coeperit, prior quidem alveus eorum est, qui prope ripam praedia possident, pro modo scilicet latitudinis cuiusque praedii, quae latitudo prope ripam sit: novus autem alveus eius iuris esse incipit, cuius et ipsum flumen, id est publicus iuris gentium. quod si post aliquod temporis ad priorem alveum reversum fuerit et flumen, rursus novus alveus eorum esse incipit, qui prope ripam eius praedia possident. cuius tamen totum agrum novus alveus occupaverit, licet ad priorem alveum reversum fuerit flumen, non tamen is, cuius is ager fuerat, stricta ratione quicquam in eo alveo habere potest, quia et ille ager qui fuerat desiit esse amissa propria forma et, quia vicinum praedium nullum habet, non potest ratione vicinitatis ullam partem in eo alveo habere: sed vix est, ut id optineat.

Gaius in the second book of Common Matters or Golden Rules

But if a river left its natural bed entirely and began to flow in another place, its former bed belongs to those who have estates near the bank, in proportion to the each estate's length, that is, the length along the bank. The new bed, however, begins to have the legal status of the river itself, that is, it is public by the law of nations. But if after some time the river returns to its former bed, the new bed belongs again to those who have estates near the bank. The owner whose land the new bed has totally filled, can have nothing in this bed by strict interpretation, even though the river has returned to its former bed, because that land which had been his, ceased to exist when it lost its own form, and he is not able to have any part in this bed by reason of proximity because he has no adjacent land. But it is hardly likely that this argument would win in court.

1. Gaius contemplates two situations in which a public river changes its course. Describe them, identifying what is the same and different about them.
2. In both situations, what effect does the change of the river's course have on the legal status of the land around it? Who owns the new banks? Who owns the new river bed?
3. Although it is not clear until the second sentence, the case concerns a public river. Is Gaius' view in this case consistent with his rule on land washed away, which Celsus applied to public rivers (Case 3.36, Study Question 5)? Should the two situations be treated the same way? Explain.
4. When private land is flooded, the legal effects are different, according to Gaius, because "flooding does not change the form of the farm and for this reason, when the water recedes, it clearly still belongs to the same person who owned it before" (*D.* 41.1.7.6 Gaius 2 *Rerum Cott.*). Do you agree? Why or why not? Why do public and private rivers have different effects on riverine land rights?
5. At the end of the case, Gaius observes that his argument is not likely to win in court but rather follows the legal principles to the logical extreme. What rules of ownership does his argument illustrate? What other factors could (or should) a court take into account when making a judgment about changing river banks?

Case 3.39. Mooring and Freight

D. 1.8.5 pr Gaius libro secundo Rerum Cottidianarum sive Aureorum

Riparum usus publicus est iure gentium sicut ipsius fluminis. itaque navem ad eas appellere, funes ex arboribus ibi natis religare, retia siccare et ex mare reducere, onus aliquid in his reponere cuilibet liberum est, sicuti per ipsum flumen navigare. sed proprietas illorum est, quorum praediis haerent: qua de causa arbores quoque in his natae eorundem sunt.

Gaius in the second book of Common Matters or Golden Rules

There is public use of river banks, just as of the river itself, according to the law of nations. Thus it is free to anyone at all to land a boat on the banks or to tie ropes to trees rooted there, or to dry nets or draw them up from the sea, or to unload some freight on them, just as sailing the river itself. But their ownership stays with those whose estates border them. For this reason trees rooted in them also belong to the same people.

1. What activities does Gaius allow in and around public rivers? Why might trees growing on the bank pose special problems?
2. What legal basis does Gaius give for open access to river banks?
3. In this case, Gaius deals with some of the same issues as in the river interdicts (cf. Cases 3.11-3.18). To what extent is Gaius' view of riverbanks consistent with the interdicts?
4. Why does Gaius invoke *ius gentium* when the interdict already protects these activities? Or in what circumstances would the interdict apply? When might the *ius gentium* be a better legal standard?

Case 3.40. The Interdict on Shoring Up Banks

D. 43.15.1 pr–4 Ulpianus libro sexagensimo octavo ad Edictum

Praetor ait: "quo minus illi in flumine publico ripave eius opus facere ripae agrive qui circa ripam est tuendi causa liceat, dum ne ob id navigatio deterior fiat, si tibi damni infecti in annos decem viri boni arbitratu vel cautum vel satisdatum est aut per illum non stat, quo minus viri boni arbitratu caveatur vel satisdetur, vim fieri veto." . . . (4) Dabitur autem satis vicinis: sed et his, qui trans flumen possidebunt.

Ulpian in the sixty-eighth book on the Edict

The praetor says: "I forbid the use of force to prevent you from doing work in a public river or on its bank to protect the bank or a field that is near the bank, as long as sailing is not made worse because of it, [and]

if a guarantee or security by the good man standard is given to you for threatened damage for ten years or if it is not his fault that no guarantee or security is given." . . . (4) Security will be given to the neighbors, and also those who have land across the river.

1. What is the purpose of the interdict on shoring up banks? What kinds of damage could be caused by building up the banks of a river?
2. Why would a landowner want to build up the banks of a river along the edge of his property? What circumstances would lead a landowner to seek the interdict on shoring up banks?
3. How is the protection of this interdict limited? Construct a hypothetical case to test this limit.
4. The interdict applies unless the parties have already made other arrangements to protect themselves. For example, a person who builds up his banks can give a guarantee or security to his neighbor that his work will not damage their land or that he will compensate them for any damage caused by his work. When the parties negotiate for themselves about reinforcing river banks, the law privileges that private arrangement. What are the benefits of such neighborly negotiation? In what circumstances would an interdict be a better solution?

Case 3.41. A Defense for the Interdict on Flow

D. 43.13.1.6–7 Ulpianus libro sexagensimo octavo ad Edictum

Sunt qui putent excipiendum hoc interdicto "quod eius ripae muniendae causa non fiet," scilicet ut, si quid fiat, quo aliter aqua fluat, si tamen muniendae ripae causa fiat, interdicto locus non sit. sed nec hoc quibusdam placet: neque enim ripae cum incommodo accolentium muniendae sunt. hoc tamen iure utimur, ut praetor ex causa aestimet, an hanc exceptionem dare debeat: plerumque enim utilitas suadet exceptionem istam dari. (7) Sed et si alia utilitas vertatur eius, qui quid in flumine publico fecit (pone enim grande damnum flumen ei dare solitum, praedia eius depopulari), si forte aggeres vel quam aliam munitionem adhibuit, ut agrum suum tueretur eaque res cursum fluminis ad aliquid immutavit, cur ei non consulatur? plerosque scio prorsus flumina avertisse alveosque mutasse, dum praediis suis consulunt. oportet enim in huiusmodi rebus utilitatem et tutelam facientis spectari, sine iniuria utique accolarum.

Ulpian from the sixty-eighth book on the Edict

There are some jurists who think that there should be a defense to this interdict as follows, "that it was not done to build up the banks," as if there was no place for the interdict, if something were done that made the water flow a different way, if in fact it were done to shore up the bank. But others do not agree on this because river banks are not to be shored up with harm to people living nearby. We use the legal principle that the praetor evaluates from the situation whether he should grant a defense. Most of the time, the benefit convinces that the defense is to be granted. (7) But if some other benefit is involved for the person who did something in a public river (for example, because the river usually caused him significant loss or made his land uninhabitable), if perhaps he built dams or some other embankment to protect his field, and this situation changed the course of the river to some extent, why should his interest not be considered? I know that many people have diverted rivers and changed their beds, while looking after their estates. In circumstances of this sort it is right to look to the benefit and protection of the person taking action, of course, without injury to the neighbors.

1. This case considers a possible defense against the interdict on flow. In Roman litigation, there were standard defense clauses that the praetor could include (or not) in the formula as he saw fit. What is the defense?
2. Did all jurists agree that building up the banks could be a defense against the interdict on flow? Why might this defense have been controversial?
3. Why does Ulpian think that this defense should be allowed? What does Ulpian mean by "benefit" and "harm"? Does he refer to economic benefits only? Explain.
4. Does the defense to the interdict on flow provide the same legal protection as the interdict on shoring up the bank? Are the two legal remedies consistent or contradictory? Are the jurists just being sloppy,

or does the contradiction arise from the remedy-based approach of Roman law?

Case 3.42. Fouling the Water

Codex Theodosianus 7.1.13 Impp. Gratianus, Valentinianus, Theodosius Augusti Richomeri Com(iti) et Magistro utriusque mil(itiae)

> Cum supra virentes fluminum ripas omnis legionum multitudo consistit, id provida auctoritate decernimus, ut nullus omnino immundo fimo sordidatis fluentis commune poculum polluat neve abluendo equorum sudore deproperus publicos oculos nudatus incestet atque ita et turbido potum caeno misceat et confundat aspectum, sed procul a cunctorum obtutibus in inferioribus partibus fluviorum, id est infra tentoria vagos natatus animalium, prouti libitum videtur, exerceat. Sublimis igitur m(agnificentia) t(ua) id sollicitudinis studio et admonitionis praecepto faciet custodiri, ut unusquisque tribunus agnoscat gravi se subdendum esse supplicio, in cuius parte neglectum probabitur quod agnoscit imperatum.

Emperors Gratian, Valentinian, Theodosius to Richomer, lord and master of both armies, 391 CE

> We decree with our provident authority that, when the whole multitude of the legions settles on the verdant river banks, no one at all in clothes soiled with filthy excrement should defile the common cup of flowing water nor should a naked person in quickly washing away the horses' sweat offend the public view or mix the drink with muddy muck and disfigure its appearance, but he should let the animals loose to swim far from the gaze of all in the lower parts of rivers, that is below the tents, as far as it seems pleasing. Your sublime magnificence will with eager care and instructive correction take care that each and every tribune knows that he will have to undergo severe punishment if an order which he knows, will be found to have been neglected on his part.

1. How does this constitution regulate the use of river banks?
2. Is there any penalty imposed for violating this law? How will it be enforced?

3. What concerns seem to motivate the emperors? What uses of the river are protected?
4. How does this constitution compare with earlier laws on river banks? How can we explain the differences?

CHAPTER 4

Aqueducts

Civic aqueducts harnessed technology and nature to supply public amenities such as basins and baths in cities around the Roman Empire. The infrastructure and the water itself were public property, although the city's ownership was usually assumed rather than expressed. In a few cases, public ownership is signaled by the phrase *ius potestasque*, "right and power," and not by *dominium*, the usual term for ownership in Roman law. Yet, to some extent, Roman law treated public and private aqueducts in the same way, because in both cases the owner controlled rights of access, withdrawal, exclusion, management, and alienation.

A civic aqueduct delivered water on an open access basis to all residents through continuously running public fountains. The state—Rome or the local city that built the aqueduct—authorized access and withdrawals to individuals through administrative procedures. In Republican Rome, the Senate authorized grants for private delivery to houses and land in and around the city, while in provincial cities the local assembly had this power. Later emperors dispensed this benefit in important cities such as Rome, Antioch, and Constantinople. These grants provided rights of use, like servitudes, but they were personal rights that ended with the holder's tenure of the property. The city retained ownership of the water, and in the beginning these grants were nontransferable, but later they could be transferred to the new owner when the land was sold or inherited. Although policing was uneven, the city exercised a right of exclusion for private delivery.

Repairs and maintenance (the right of management) were organized in various ways. At Rome the emperor owned slave crews made up of skilled workers who repaired the aqueducts and played a role in administering private grants. Smaller cities may have followed Rome's model for infrastructure in urban space, but along the rural route of the aqueduct landowners were often responsible for repair and clearing of the channel. The financing varied, too. Some costs were shifted to the landowners who performed repairs as a kind of civic liturgy or tax. The imperial treasury paid for maintenance and in some cases supplemented with earmarked taxes or user fees, although the ideology of water as a free imperial beneficence persisted through the late Empire.

A civic aqueduct was embedded in the social and political life of the city it served. Emperors and local elites often sponsored civic aqueducts, improving welfare for urban residents and at the same time burnishing their own reputations. They also controlled grants for private delivery, which could recognize social status or political service.

The most comprehensive information about Roman aqueducts, their law and everything else, is Frontinus' *De Aquaeductu Urbis Romae*. Consequently, many cases in this chapter come from this treatise, and there is a summary of the laws presented by Frontinus in the introduction to this book. This chapter also includes legal texts and inscriptions about civic aqueducts which offer comparative evidence, some earlier than Frontinus—for example, the inscriptions from Urso and Venafrum.

Note: The cases in this chapter are organized by topic, as in other chapters, but the nature of the sources calls for some special treatment. Within each topic the evidence is presented in mostly chronological order. Cases drawn from Frontinus appear in his order of presentation so that they can be considered in context. The decree on the aqueduct for Venafrum, which addresses many of the topics, is presented in a separate section at the end of the chapter so that it can be read as a whole or assigned with cases on relevant topics.

I. Public Supply and Private Delivery

A. Building an Aqueduct

Case 4.1. Public Works in the Republic

Frontinus, De aquaeductu urbis Romae 5.1–3 and 6.1–4

[5] M. Valerio Maximo P. Decio Mure consulibus, anno post initium Samnitici belli tricesimo, aqua Appia in urbem inducta est ab Appio Claudio censore, cui postea Caeco fuit cognomen. [idem eo anno] et viam Appiam [a porta] Capena usque ad urbem Capuam muniendam curavit. (2) Collegam habuit C. Plautium, cui ob inquisitas eius aquae venas Venocis cognomen datum est. (3) Sed quia is intra annum et sex menses, deceptus a collega tamquam idem facturo, abdicavit se censura, nomen aquae ad Appii tantum honorem pertinuit, qui multis tergiversationibus extraxisse censuram traditur, donec et viam et huius aquae ductum consummaret.

[6] Post annos quadraginta quam Appia perducta est, anno ab urbe condita quadringentesimo octogesimo uno M'. Curius Dentatus, qui censuram cum Lucio Papirio Cursore gessit, Anionis qui nunc Vetus dicitur aquam perducendam in urbem ex manubiis de Pyrrho captis locavit, Spurio Carvilio Lucio Papirio consulibus iterum. (2) Post biennium deinde actum est in senatu de consummando eius aquae opere referente . . . . (3) Tum ex senatus consulto duumviri aquae perducendae creati sunt Curius, qui eam locaverat et Fulvius Flaccus. (4) Curius intra quintum diem quam erat duumvirum creatus decessit; gloria perductae pertinuit ad Fulvium.

Frontinus, On the Water-Management of the City of Rome 5–6

[5] In the consulship of Marcus Valerius Maximus and Publius Decius Mus [312 BCE], thirty years after the beginning of the Samnite War, the Aqua Appia was brought into the City by the censor Appius Claudius (later called "the Blind"). In that year the same man also had charge of constructing the Appian Road from Porta Capena as far as the city of Capua. (2) Appius' colleague in the censorship was Gaius Plautius, called Venox for having discovered the veins of this water. (3) But Plau-

tius resigned from the censorship before the eighteen months' term had elapsed, deceived by Appius who pretended he would do likewise, and so the name of the aqueduct fell to the credit of Appius alone. Indeed, Appius is reported to have extended his censorship by many subterfuges, until he could complete both the road and the aqueduct.

[6] Forty years after Appia was introduced, in the four-hundred-eighty-first year from the founding of the City, Manius Curius Dentatus, who held the censorship with Lucius Papirius Cursor, contracted to bring into the City the Anio aqueduct (now called Anio Vetus). He did so with his personal share of booty captured from Pyrrhus. This was in the second consulship of Spurius Carvilius and Lucius Papirius [272 BCE]. (2) Two years later the question of completing the aqueduct was deliberated in the Senate . . . (3) Then by senatorial resolution Curius, who had let the original contract, and Fulvius Flaccus were appointed as a special two-man board to bring in the water. (4) Within five days of his appointment Curius died; thus the honor of bringing it fell to Fulvius.

1. This case describes the administration of Rome's aqueducts in the Republic. Which magistrates were responsible for building the aqueducts? What happened when construction continued after the magistrate's term ended? Rome's magistrates contracted with private construction companies to do the work. When the Romans built aqueducts in the provinces, sometimes the army did the construction since it had both the man power and the technical expertise in its military engineers.
2. How did the Romans finance construction of Rome's aqueducts? The Senate controlled the state treasury and authorized expenditures on public works. What other sources of funding were used to build aqueducts? Rome's military conquest of Italy, and later lands around the Mediterranean, generated an influx of wealth both for individuals and the state. Why would an individual choose to spend his own riches on building an aqueduct for the city? Compare also Frontinus' account of the construction of Rome's third aqueduct, the Marcia (Front. *Aq.* 7).
3. To what extent was the construction of aqueducts politicized? In the Republic, different men were elected to public office every year, creating multiple opportunities for building an aqueduct. In the empire, emperors sponsored new aqueducts to provide benefits to Rome's residents and also to express their own power. How do the different forms

of government (republic and empire) affect the politics of aqueduct construction?

Case 4.2. Acquiring Land for Rome's Aqueducts

Frontinus, De Aquaeductu urbis Romae 128.1–2

Posset hoc S. C. aequissimum videri, etiam si ex re tantum publicae utilitatis ea spatia vindicarentur. Multo magis autem maiores nostri admirabili aequitate ne ea quidem eripuerunt privatis quae ad modum publicum pertinebant, sed cum aquas perducerent, si difficilior possessor in parte vendunda fuerat, pro toto agro pecuniam intulerunt et post determinata necessaria loca rursus eum agrum vendiderunt, ut in suis finibus proprium ius res publica privatique haberent. (2) Plerique tamen non contenti occupasse fines ipsis ductibus manus adtulerunt per suffossa latera passim cursus aquarum tam ei qui ius aquarum impetratum habent, quam ei qui quantulicumque beneficii occasione ad expugnandos rivos abutuntur.

Frontinus, On the water-management of the city of Rome 128.1

This senatorial resolution would seem to be entirely just, even if these spaces were reclaimed by reason of usefulness to the state alone. Its fairness is all the more apparent in light of the fact that our forefathers, with remarkable equity, did not seize from private parties even those lands which were of necessary interest to the state; but when they were bringing in waters, if a landholder was recalcitrant about selling a part of his property, they paid for the whole, and then after fixing boundaries for the land that was needed they sold the property in their turn, it having been clearly established that the state as well as private parties, each within respective boundaries, should have full and absolute right. (2) But many, not content to have encroached beyond the boundaries, have laid hands upon the conduits themselves. By penetrating the side walls here and there . . . no less those who have a granted right of water, than those who take advantage of the slightest opportunity for an imperial favor to get control of the channels.

1. In this case Frontinus comments on one of the senate decrees of 11 BCE, which authorized a clearway around the aqueducts' route outside the city (Case 4.22). It appears here because he focuses on prac-

tices of the Republic, but it should also be studied with the imperial decrees. How did Rome acquire land for its aqueducts? Reconstruct the process as best you can. What problems does Frontinus anticipate?

2. Does Frontinus describe past or current practices? What motives might Frontinus have had for highlighting the practices of "our forefathers"?
3. Were Rome's aqueducts built on private or public property? What details of the case allow you to answer the question? Compare the purchase of land for a private aqueduct (Case 2.2, Study Question #4).
4. In his account of the construction of the aqueducts, Frontinus mentions the sources of several of Rome's aqueducts (*Aq.* 5–14), including the Tepula which drew water from a spring on Lucullus' property. He also notes that some people believed the spring was located on land belonging to the town of Tusculum, which would make it public property (*Aq.* 8). Why did he include this alternate explanation? How does it square with the principles articulated in this case?
5. This passage is invoked as evidence that Roman law had a concept of eminent domain—that is, the state's power to take private property and convert it to public use. How well did the Romans protect landowners when the state took private property? How good a model does Rome offer to modern communities facing the same issues?
6. What problems arose when a city aqueduct crossed private property? Why does Frontinus mentions landowners both with and without private delivery? He uses the phrase "right to the waters" (*ius aquarum*) for private delivery, although this does not appear to have become a standard term for either personal or praedial servitudes. Compare *ius aquae* in Cases 3.29 and 4.28.

Case 4.3. Land for an Aqueduct in Spain

Corpus Inscriptionum Latinarum 1^3.2951a lines 1–14
(*Tabula Contrebiensis*)

Senatus Contrebie[n]sis quei tum aderunt iudices sunto. Sei par[ret ag]rum quem Salluienses / [ab Sosinest]ane[is] emerunt rivi faciendi aquaive ducendae causa qua de re agitur Sosinestanos / [iure suo Sa]lluiensibus vendidisse inviteis Allavonensibus; tum sei ita [p]arret eei iudices iudicent / eum agrum qua de re agitur Sosinestanos Salluiensibus iure suo vendidisse; sei non parr[e]t iudicent / iur[e] suo non vendidi[sse.] /

Eidem quei supra scriptei [sunt] iudices sunto. Sei Sosinestana ceivitas esset, tum, qua Salluiensis / novissume publice depalarunt qua de re agitur, sei [i]ntra eos palos Salluiensis rivom per agrum / publicum Sosinestanorum iure suo facere licere[t] aut sei per agrum preivatum Sosinestanorum / qua rivom fieri oporteret rivom iure suo Salluie[n] sibus facere liceret dum quanti is a[ger] aestumatu[s] / esset, qua rivos duceretur, Salluienses pequniam solverent, tum, sei ita [p]arret, eei iudices iudicent/ Salluiensibus rivom iure suo facere licer[e]; sei non parret iudicent iure suo facere non licere. / Sei iudicarent Salluiensibus rivom facere licere, tum quos magistratus Contrebiensis quinque / ex senatu suo dederit eorum arbitratu pro agro preivato q[u]a rivos ducetur Salluienses / publice pequniam solvonto. Iudicium addeixit C. Valerius C.f. Flaccus imperator.

Decree of Contrebia (*Tabula Contrebiensis*)

Let those of Contrebia's Senate, who will be present at that time, be judges. If it seems right that the Sosinestani by their own right sold the land at issue, which the Salluienses purchased from the Sosinestani in order to make a canal or conduct water, although the Allavonenses were unwilling, and if it so appears let these judges judge that the Sosinestani by their own right have sold the land at issue to the Salluienses; if it does not so appear, let them judge that they did not sell it by their right.

Let the same men who are written above be judges. On the assumption that there was in fact a city of the Sosinestani, then, if it would be permissible for the Salluienses by their own right to make a canal between the stakes where the Salluienses have recently placed stakes as a matter of public business; or if it would be permissible for the Salluienses by their own right to make a canal through public land of the Sosinestani or through private land of the Sosinestani where it should be made, provided that the Salluienses pay money, as much as the land is worth where the canal would be led, then if it so appears let the judges judge that it is permissible for the Salluienses to do this by their own right; if it does not so appear, let them judge that it is not permissible for them to do it by their own right.

If they judge that it is permissible for the Salluienses to build a canal, then let the Salluienses pay the money at public expense for the private land where the canal will be led in accordance with the arbitration of five men whom the magistrate of Contrebia shall appoint from their Senate. Gaius Valerius Flaccus, son of Gaius, imperator, assigned jurisdiction.

1. This case presents a decree inscribed on a bronze tablet authorizing an agreement between two communities in Roman Spain, the Salluienses and the Sosinestani, about the purchase of land for a public canal or aqueduct. They negotiated terms with the help of the Roman governor, Gaius Valerius Flaccus, in 89 BCE. Two other communities are involved, the Allavonenses, who objected to the sale, and Contrebia, whose town council served as arbitrators. This inscription documents civic aqueducts and the adaptation of Roman law in the provinces. These circumstances account for some unusual features of the legal language, notably the use of a legal fiction to allow these non-Roman communities to use Roman law to articulate their agreement. The law operates as if Roman civic communities were involved ("on the assumption that there was in fact a city of the Sosinestani"). The Salluienses and the Sosinestani can arrange to purchase land, as if they were using the Roman form of sale (*emptio venditio*), and the land becomes public like other state-owned land. The language of the decree is highly formal and thus a little difficult to interpret, but try to reconstruct the situation as best you can. Why did the Salluienses need to purchase land from the Sosinestani for their aqueduct?
2. In a sale, the parties must agree on the object of sale and its price. How did the Salluienses designate the land for the aqueduct? What do they mean when they agree that the Salluienses will pay "as much as the land is worth"?
3. How do you know that the canal was a public work? What was the legal status of the land before and after the sale?
4. Although this inscription involves non-Roman communities and provincial land, it may represent the usual procedure that Roman cities and towns followed to acquire land for public aqueducts. To

what extent is the process at Contrebia consistent with what Frontinus describes for Rome?

5. At the end of the agreement, there is a list of local officials who approved the agreement, not included in the case. What purpose is served by listing these names? How does it contribute to the legal force of the document?

Case 4.4. Another Aqueduct in Spain (Urso)

Corpus Inscriptionum Latinarum 1^2.5 ch. 99

quae aquae publicae in oppido colon(iae) Gen(etiuae)/ adducentur, IIuir(i) qui tum erunt ad decuriones, / cum duae partes aderunt, referto, per quos agros / aquam ducere liceat. qua p<ar>s maior decurion(um), / qui tum aderunt, duci decreuerint, dum ne / per it aedificium, quot non eius rei causa factum / sit, aqua ducatur, per eos agros aquam ducere / i(us) p(otestas)que esto; neue quis facito, quo minus ita / aqua ducatur.

Charter of the Colony Iulia Genetiva, Ch. 99

Whatever public waters are conducted into the town of the colony Genitiva, the duumviri who will be in office at that time will consult the decurions, when two-thirds are present, across which fields it may be allowed to conduct water. [When] the majority of decurions, who will be present, shall have decreed that water is to be conducted, as long as it does not go through a structure which has not been built for this purpose, there will be right and power to conduct water across those fields; nor shall anyone act to prevent the water being conducted in this way.

1. This case presents one of two chapters on aqueducts from the municipal law from Urso (cf. Case 4.10). Who had legal authority over the aqueduct that brought water to Urso? What legal powers do these officials have?
2. Why is a quorum of two-thirds of the assemblymen required for a vote on decisions about the aqueduct? What specific decision about the aqueduct does this case report? What problems does the decree anticipate in implementing this decision? How do the problems compare with the dispute over Salluienses' aqueduct (Case 4.3)?
3. It appears that a route has been planned for the aqueduct and con-

struction awaits approval from the city. What restrictions does the law impose on the aqueduct's route? Why is the route of the aqueduct restricted in this way?

4. Compare the rules for building an aqueduct at Urso with the process at Rome, as described by Frontinus (Cases 4.1 and 4.2). The municipal law makes explicit the magistrate's legal powers which are assumed by Frontinus; indeed the municipal law creates those legal powers. Are landowners equally protected in both places? Was the process as politicized in cities and towns like Urso as it was in Rome? Why or why not?

Case 4.5. The Sources of Constantinople's Aqueduct

Codex Justinianus 11.43.9 Zeno A. Sporacio

Diligenter investigari decernimus, qui publici ab initio fontes vel, cum essent ab initio privati, postquam publice usum praebuerunt, ad privatorum usum conversi sunt, sive sacris apicibus per subreptionem impetratis, ac multo amplius si auctoritate illicita nec appetito colore sacri oraculi huiusmodi aliquid pertemptatum fuisse dignoscitur, ut ius suum regiae civitati restituatur et, quod publicum fuerit aliquando, minime sit privatum, sed ad communes usus recurrat: sacris oraculis vel pragmaticis sanctionibus adversus commoditatem urbis quibusdam impertitis iure cassandis nec longi temporis praescriptione ad circumscribenda civitatis iura profutura.

Emperor Zeno to Sporacius, between 476 and 491 CE

We decree that there is to be a thorough investigation of the springs which were public from the beginning or, although at first private, after they provided public use, were converted back for the use of private individuals, whether something was attempted by acquiring sacred letters in secret or much more openly by unlawful authority and without even a pretext of seeking a sacred decree of this sort, so that its own law is restored to this royal city and so that what was once public be not private at all but revert to common uses. Any sacred decrees or civil penalties bestowed against the city's benefit are to be legally void nor is long possession to avail for restricting the city's rights.

1. In the past, who owned the springs that fed Constantinople's aqueducts? How does Zeno change the legal status of these springs? Reconstruct the events that led to this imperial constitution.
2. How does Zeno justify his law? How persuasive is his rationale?
3. What response does the emperor anticipate to this constitution? How else might those people who owned private springs have reacted to this law?
4. Compare this constitution from the end of the fifth century CE with earlier laws on acquiring land for civic aqueducts. How can we explain both similarities and differences?
5. In describing the construction of the Aqua Julia, Frontinus writes that it did not take water from the Aqua Crabra, a stream or spring in Tusculum near Rome. Instead Agrippa, Augustus' deputy, who was in charge of construction, chose to leave the water for the landowners living near it in Tusculum (Front. *Aq.* 9.4–7). Frontinus also reports that Agrippa restored the Crabra to the residents of Tusculum, after city officials had diverted it to cover their own fraudulent sale of city water. Why did Zeno take such a different decision about the springs supplying Constantinople's aqueducts? Can both policies be justified? Explain.

B. A Public Amenity

Case 4.6. Public and Private in the Republic

Frontinus, De Aquaeductu urbis Romae 94–95

Sequitur ut indicemus quod ius ducendae tuendaeque sit aquae, quorum alterum ad cohibendos intra modum impetrati beneficii privatos, alterum ad ipsorum ductuum pertinet tutelam. (2) In quibus dum altius repeto leges de singulis aquis latas, quaedam apud veteres aliter observata inveni. (3) Apud quos omnis aqua in usus publicos erogabatur et cautum ita fuit: "Ne quis privatus aliam aquam ducat, quam quae ex lacu humum accidit" (haec enim sunt verba legis) id est quae ex lacu abundavit; eam nos caducam vocamus. (4) Et haec ipsa non in alium usum quam in balnearum aut fullonicarum dabatur, eratque vectigalis, statuta mercede quae in publicum penderetur. (5) Aliquid et in domos principum civitatis dabatur, concedentibus reliquis. [95] Ad quem autem magistratum ius dandae vendendaeve aquae pertinuerit, in eis ipsis legibus variatur. (2) Interdum enim ab aedilibus, interdum a censoribus permissum invenio; sed apparet, quotiens in re publica censores erant, ab illis potissimum petitum, cum ei non erant, aedilium eam potestatem fuisse. (3) Ex quo manifestum est quanto potior cura maioribus communium utilitatium quam privatarum voluptatium fuerit, cum etiam ea aqua quam privati ducebant ad usum publicum pertineret.

Frontinus, On the water-management of the city of Rome 94–95

Next we are to indicate what is the legal basis upon which water is to be drawn and its supply is to be safeguarded; the former concerns the limiting of private parties to the quantity of their official grants, the latter the maintenance of the conduits themselves. (2) Investigating more distantly into those regulations established with regard to individual persons, I discover that some matters were handled differently in the times of our ancestors. (3) In their days, all water was delivered for public uses, and it was stipulated as follows: "No private person is to draw water other than that which falls from a basin to the ground" (these are the exact words of the regulation), meaning that overflow from the basins which we now call "lapsed water." (4) Even this water was not granted for use other than by baths or fullers' establishments, and it was subject to a fee, the amount of which was legally fixed, to be paid into the public treasury. (5) Some water was granted for delivery into the homes of leading men of the state, with the consent of the others.

(95) There is no consistency in the statutes themselves about which public officials had the right of granting or selling water. (2) At some times I find that permission was given by aediles, at other times by censors. But apparently whenever there were censors in office, as a rule they dealt with such requests; when there were no censors, the similar power fell upon the aediles. (3) From this it is plain how much more our predecessors cared for benefits to the community than for private pleasures, since even that water drawn by private parties was related to public usefulness.

1. In this case, Frontinus summarizes Republican laws on private delivery of the aqueducts' water. Formulate the legal rules in your own words. Which component rights are regulated (access, withdrawal, exclusion, management, alienation)?
2. Who was responsible for regulating the aqueducts during the Republic? The Romans elected aediles annually and censors every five years: how do these electoral practices help to explain the lack of consistency noted by Frontinus? What are the pros and cons of having two different officials in charge of the aqueducts?
3. Frontinus uses a standard legal expression, "granting and selling," to refer to a lease or a fee for use and not to actual sale, because the city retained ownership of the water (for similar language, see Case 4.33). Why were fees imposed on some deliveries but not others? Who collected them?
4. The term *aqua caduca*, "lapsed water," refers to overflow from public reservoirs and fountains, as defined by Frontinus (Case 4.14; see also Cases 4.10 and 4.33). How easy would it be to capture overflow from a basin? Why were individual withdrawals allowed only from overflow water?
5. Why were fees imposed on some businesses? Who collected them? These were not user fees, but revenue from the fees probably went toward the cost of maintenance and repair of the aqueducts, although there were other types of financing (see Cases 4.25 and 4.26).
6. How does Frontinus characterize the aims of Republican laws on the aqueducts? How effectively would these limits achieve the law's aims? Compare the meaning of "public" in this case with its use by the jurists in discussions of public rivers (e.g., Cases 3.1–4). To what extent did emperors, jurists, and administrators share a unified approach to water resources?
7. According to Frontinus, how did the Roman state's policy on the allocation of water from the aqueducts differ in the Republic and the Empire? Frontinus' presentation may be influenced by nostalgia. Is there any evidence in this case that the Republican system was not as ideal as Frontinus implies? In the cases that follow, be on the lookout for gaps between actual practices and the normative rules of law.

Case 4.7. The lex Rivalicia

Festus 458L

> *Sifus / [dicitur in legibus publi]c̲is ipsis, id quod Graece / [σίφων uocatur, et in le]ge riualicia sic est / [scriptum, quam de usu aqu]ae populum Ser. Sulpi/[cius—- rogauit : mon]tani paganiue si/[fis—-]o̲ ; donec eam inter se / [—-]s iudicatio esto.*

Sextus Pompeius Festus, Excerpts from Verrius Flaccus, On the Meaning of Words

> "Siphon"—the word that is called σίφων in Greek—is used in public laws and it is written this way in the lex Rivalicia that Servius Sulpicius proposed to the people about the use of water: "montani and pagani" for the siphons shall . . . as long as this [law] among them . . . there will be power of granting judgment.

1. The *lex Rivalicia,* the law on streams or canals, is known only from this brief mention in an ancient definition of the word siphon, *sifus,* from Festus' lexicon, written in the second century CE but derived from the work of an Augustan grammarian Verrius Flaccus. The law itself dates to the Republican era, either the second or first century BCE depending on whether we identify its proposer, Servius Sulpicius, as the consul of 144 BCE or the consul of 50 BCE; (the latter was the jurist, Servius). Its date may be earlier if the *rivi* are natural streams rather than an aqueduct. What does Festus reveal about the *lex Rivalicia*? Reconstruct the law as best you can from the details in the case.
2. *Montani* and *pagani* were officials associated with Rome's neighborhoods or wards who had roles in finance and the census. The *lex Rivalicia* apparently gave them legal authority, *iudicatio,* over the use of public water conducted by siphon. What other duties or powers do you think they had? Consider the rights in the environmental bundle: access, withdrawal, exclusion, management, alienation.
3. No archaeological remains of siphons of Republican date have been found, although Trajan's aqueduct used one to bring water to his baths (see Bruun 1991, 135). What particular problems of regulation does a siphon pose?

Case 4.8. The Imperial Water Commissioner

Frontinus, De Aquaeductu urbis Romae 100–101

"Quod Q. Aelius Tubero Paulus Fabius Maximus cos. V. F. de eis qui curatores aquarum publicarum ex consensu senatus a Caesare Augusto nominati essent ornandis, D. E. R. Q. F. P. D. E. R. I. C. placere huic ordini, eos qui aquis publicis praeessent, cum eius rei causa extra urbem essent, lictores binos et servos publicos ternos, architectos singulos et scribas, librarios, accensos praeconesque totidem habere, quot habent ei per quos frumentum plebei datur. Cum autem in urbe eiusdem rei causa aliquid agerent, ceteris apparitoribus eisdem praeterquam lictoribus uti. Utique quibus apparitoribus ex hoc senatus consulto curatoribus aquarum uti liceret, eos diebus decem proximis, quibus senatus consultum factum esset, ad aerarium deferrent; quique ita delati essent, eis praetores aerarii mercedem cibaria, quanta praefecti frumento dando dare deferreque solent, annua darent et adtribuerent; eisque eas pecunias sine fraude sua capere liceret. Utique tabulas, chartas ceteraque quae eius curationis causa opus essent eis curatoribus Q. Aelius Paulus Fabius cos. ambo alterve, si eis videbitur, adhibitis praetoribus qui aerario praesint, praebenda locent. (101) "Itemque cum viarum curatores frumentique parte quarta anni publico fungantur ministerio, ut curatores aquarum iudiciis vacent privatis publicisque." Apparitores et ministeria, quamvis perseveret adhuc aerarium in eos erogare, tamen esse curatorum videntur desisse inertia ac segnitia non agentium officium. Egressis autem urbem dumtaxat agendae rei causa senatus praesto esse lictores iusserat. Nobis circumeuntibus rivos fides nostra et auctoritas a principe data pro lictoribus erit.

Frontinus, On the water-management of the city of Rome 100–101.1

Whereas the consuls Quintus Aelius Tubero and Paulus Fabius Maximus brought forth the subject of furnishing with personnel and supplies the commissioners of public waters who had been named by Caesar Augustus with the consent of the Senate, and inquired of the Senate as to what action might be pleasing on the subject, the senators resolved as follows: it is approved by this body that those who are in charge of public waters, when they are outside the city by reason of their official duties, shall have two lictors, three public slaves, and one architect, as well as the same number of clerks, copyists, assistants, and criers as have those who distribute grain to the plebs. (2) But when they do business within the city by reason of the same official duties, they shall have use of all the same attendants excepting the lictors. (3) And, further, that the water commissioners shall put on record in the state treasury within ten days from the passage of this senatorial resolution a list of those attendants allowed for their use by the terms of this senatorial resolution; and the praetors of the treasury shall grant and disburse on an annual basis to those who are so reported payment and remuneration to the extent that those in charge of distributing grain are accustomed to give and authorize for their personnel; and they shall be allowed to receive these monies without risk of punishment to themselves; (4) and, further, that the consuls Quintus Aelius Tubero and Paulus Fabius, either both together or singly as they see fit, calling upon the praetors in charge of the treasury, shall arrange by contract to supply tablets, paper, and whatever else the commissioners may find necessary for their administrative tasks. (101) And furthermore, in as much as the commissioners of roads and those in charge of grain perform their public service for a fourth part of the year, it is approved that the water commissioners be excused from judicial duties either private or public.

1. In 11 BCE, the Senate issued six decrees relating to the aqueducts; the other decrees are presented in Cases 4.9, 4.12, 4.13, 4.21, 4.22). Each decree opens with the year (identified by the names of the consuls in office) and a formulaic description of the legislative process; then follows the law itself. What provisions did the Senate enact in this decree?
2. In the early years of Augustus' reign, M. Vipsanius Agrippa administered the aqueducts starting in 33 BCE when he served as aedile. Agrippa was a powerful general and supporter of Augustus who chose him as successor in power, though Agrippa did not live long enough to succeed Augustus. After Agrippa's death, Augustus created the post of water commissioner, modeled on his administration and on preexisting city officials that managed the grain supply and the roads.
3. Who belonged to the regular staff of the water commissioner? What

does the staff reveal about the water commissioner's job? Lictors were official bodyguards who accompanied Roman magistrates with *imperium* or executive power. Why might the water commissioner need bodyguards?

4. How was the office of the water commissioner funded? Why is the commissioner required to record the names of his attendants with the treasury?
5. What provisions for office supplies did the Senate make? Why were these supplies needed?
6. What reward or compensation does the water commissioner receive for his service? There were four grain prefects every year, each serving for one quarter of the year, and at least two road commissioners, but only one water commissioner. The wording of the decree suggests that the release from judicial duty was proportional to the term of service.

Case 4.9. The Fountains of Rome

Frontinus, De Aquaeductu urbis Romae 104

"Quod Q. Aelius Tubero Paulus Fabius Maximus cos. V. F. de numero publicorum salientium qui in urbe essent intraque aedificia urbi coniuncta, quos M. Agrippa fecisset, Q. F. P. D. E. R. I. C. neque augeri placere nec minui numerum publicorum salientium, quos nunc esse rettulerunt ei, quibus negotium a senatu est imperatum ut inspicerent aquas publicas inirentque numerum salientium publicorum.(2) Itemque placere curatores aquarum, quos Caesar Augustus ex senatus auctoritate nominavit, dare operam uti salientes publici quam adsiduissime interdiu et noctu aquam in usum populi funderent." In hoc senatus consulto crediderim adnotandum quod senatus tam augeri quam minui salientium publicorum numerum vetuerit. Itemque placere curatores, quos Caesar Augustus ex senatus auctoritate nominavit, dare operam uti salientes publici quam adsiduissime interdiu et noctu aquam in usum populi funderent.

Frontinus, On the water-management of the city of Rome 104

Whereas the consuls Quintus Aelius Tubero and Paulus Fabius Maximus brought forth the subject of the number of public fountains established by Marcus Agrippa, both in the city and within the built-up area adjacent to the city, and inquired of the Senate as to what action might be pleasing concerning the subject, the senators resolved as follows: it is approved that there be neither increase nor decrease in that number of public fountains which are now in existence, as reported by those persons who are commissioned by the Senate with the task of inspecting the public waters and of returning an inventory of the number of public fountains; (2) and, furthermore, it is approved that the water commissioners whom Caesar Augustus has appointed with the authority of the Senate are to devote their attention that public fountains pour forth water for use of the populace with all possible regularity both in daytime and at night. (Front. *Aq.* 104)

1. This case presents the second of the senate decrees of 11 BCE. What is the purpose of this decree? In your own words, state the topics it addressed. What larger policy goals could this decree advance?
2. What responsibilities did the water commissioner have over fountains? Why was the water commissioner required to make an inventory of fountains? How might the inventory help him to fulfill his duties?
3. After quoting the decree, Frontinus explains that the Senate prohibited any change in the number of public fountains because the water supply "seemed inadequate for more widespread delivery" (*Aq.* 104.4). What other considerations might have motivated the Senate?
4. In introducing this decree Frontinus explains the water commissioner's role in enforcing the law and his duty "to ensure that water flows without interruption both day and night" (*Aq.* 103.4). Do the rules on fountains present a good strategy for achieving this goal? Why or why not?

II. Private Delivery

Case 4.10. Private Delivery at Urso

Corpus Inscriptionum Latinarum 1^2.5 ch. 100

si quis colon(us) aquam in priuatum caducam du/cere uolet isque at IIuir(um) adierit postulabit/ <q>ue, uti ad decurion(es) referat, tum is IIuir, a quo/ ita postulatum erit, ad decuriones, cum non mi/nus (quadraginta) aderunt, referto. si decuriones, m(aior) p(ars) qui / tum atfuerint, aquam caducam in priuatum duci / censuerint, ita ea aqua utatur, quo<t> sine priua/ti{m} iniuria fiat, i(us) potest(as)que e(sto).

Charter of the Colony Iulia Genetiva, Chapter 100

If any member of the colony wishes to conduct lapsed water onto a private place and he shall approach the duumvir and ask that he refer the request to the decurions, then the duumvir (whom he petitioned) shall refer the question to the decurions when not less than forty will be present. If the majority of decurions, who will be present at that time, recommend that lapsed water is to be conducted onto private property, he will have right and power to use water so that it is done without harm to private interest.

1. Before working through this case, review Case 4.6 and the Republican law on private delivery from Rome's aqueducts. Compare the laws in Urso and Rome. Are the rules the same? Do they have the same aims? Which system is more likely to achieve its aims? Why?
2. Who controlled individual rights of withdrawal from Urso's aqueduct? In a provincial city or colony, the *duumvir* was like a mayor and the decurions were like town councilors or senators in Rome, and their assembly was like the Senate. What procedure did the decurions' assembly follow in arranging rights of withdrawal? Why does the charter require a two-thirds quorum?
3. The city's legal authority is formulated as "right and power" (*ius potestasque*). Describe the scope of this legal power as precisely as you can.
4. What water can be allocated for individual rights of withdrawal? The Latin term, *aqua caduca*, "lapsed water" probably refers to overflow water from public basins, as it does in Frontinus' treatise on Rome's aqueducts (Cases 4.6 and 4.14).
5. How does the process for arranging rights of withdrawal limit water use at Urso? Consider the impact on supply to private individuals and to public basins in town.

Case 4.11. Caesar's Benefit

Frontinus, De Aquaeductu urbis Romae 105

Qui aquam in usus privatos deducere volet, impetrare eam debebit et a principe epistulam ad curatorem adferre; curator deinde beneficio Caesaris praestare maturitatem et procuratorem eiusdem officii libertum Caesaris protinus scribere. (2) Procuratorem autem primus Ti. Claudius videtur admovisse, postquam Anionem Novum et Claudiam induxit. (3) Quid contineat epistula, vilicis quoque fieri notum debet, ne quando neglegentiam aut fraudem suam ignorantiae colore defendant. (4) Procurator calicem eius moduli, qui fuerit impetratus, adhibitis libratoribus signari cogitet, diligenter intendat mensurarum quas supra diximus modum et positionis notitiam habeat, ne sit in arbitrio libratorum, interdum maioris luminis, interdum minoris pro gratia personarum calicem probare. (5) Sed nec statim ab hoc liberum subiciendi qualemcumque plumbeam fistulam permittatur arbitrium, verum eiusdem luminis quo calix signatus est per pedes quinquaginta, sicut senatus consulto quod subiectum est cavetur.

Frontinus, On the water-management of the city of Rome 105

Anyone who wishes to draw water for private use must follow a procedure of making official application and delivering in person to the commissioner a written authorization from the emperor. The commissioner must thereupon give timely consideration to the grant issued by Caesar and forward it in writing to the appropriate imperial deputy (a freedman of Caesar). (2) Tiberius Claudius seems first to have created this post of imperial deputy, after he brought in Anio Novus and Claudia. (3) The contents of the imperial document ought also to be made known to foremen of the work-crews, that they may not use ignorance as a plea to excuse negligence or fraud on their own part. (4) The imperial deputy, calling upon the levelers, is to provide for stamping a calix of the size specified in the grant, with precise attention to the quantity as represented by the measurements we have spoken of earlier, and he is to be aware of the setting, so that it is not left to the decision of the levelers to approve a calix sometimes larger in aperture, sometimes smaller, in relation to the influence of the parties involved. (5) Neither is it to be left completely to option as to the size of lead pipe which is directly attached: this must conform to the size stamped on the calix for a distance of fifty feet, as stipulated in the following senatorial resolution.

1. How did a person acquire an imperial grant to withdraw water from one of Rome's aqueducts? Outline the administrative process: How many steps were there? Which officials were involved? Was there a fee?
2. What purposes did this process serve? Did it promote fairness or accountability? Explain.
3. Why might Claudius have assigned a new imperial deputy to administer these grants after two new aqueducts (the Anio Novus and the Claudia) went online? Do the layers of administration guarantee accountability? Why or why not?
4. The Romans may not have had the technology to measure volume of flowing water, and if they did there is little evidence. How did they get around this technological limitation? In another passage, Frontinus explains the standard pipe sizes measured in inches or digits or *quinariae* (the unit he prefers; *Aq.* 23–26). The calix was a fitting that was installed either in the pipe or in the delivery tank to regulate the size of the opening. It was made of bronze rather than lead because it was more difficult to bend, according to Frontinus (*Aq.* 36.3–5). Why does Frontinus include this technical specification?
5. In another passage Frontinus comments on grants for private delivery, writing that "it goes without saying that granted water is not to be drawn for use elsewhere than on the property for which it was granted, or from a delivery-tank other than that designated in the written authorization of the emperor; but this is also forbidden by imperial regulations" (*Aq.* 109.6). Does it go without saying, as Frontinus writes? Why or why not? What does his comment reveal about the demand for water and the scope of abuse in the aqueduct system?
6. What is the biggest challenge to implementing this policy? Consider the problems that Frontinus mentions as well as others that you can anticipate.

Case 4.12. Pipes to Private Property

Frontinus, De Aquaeductu urbis Romae 106.1–2

> "Quod Q. Aelius Tubero Paulus Fabius Maximus cos. V. F. quosdam privatos ex rivis publicis aquam ducere, Q. D. E. R. F. P. D. E. R. I. C. ne cui privato aquam ducere ex rivis publicis liceret, utique omnes ei quibus aquae ducendae ius esset datum ex castellis ducerent, animadverterentque curatores aquarum, quibus locis intra urbem apte castella privati facere possent, ex quibus aquam ducerent quam ex castello communi accepissent a curatoribus aquarum. Neve cui eorum quibus aqua daretur publica ius esset, intra quinquaginta pedes eius castelli, ex quo aquam ducerent, laxiorem fistulam subicere quam quinariam."

Frontinus, On the water-management of the city of Rome 106.1–2

> Whereas the consuls Quintus Aelius Tubero and Paulus Fabius Maximus brought forth the subject that certain private parties draw water directly from public channels, and inquired of the Senate as to what action might be pleasing on this subject, concerning the subject the senators resolved as follows: it is not to be allowed for any private party to draw water from public channels, and all persons to whom has been granted the right to draw water are to draw it from delivery-tanks; and the water commissioners are to determine at what locations within and without the city private parties may suitably construct such delivery-tanks, from which they are to draw water which, with approval of the water commissioners, they, in common with other parties, have received from a primary delivery-tank, (2) and no one of those to whom public water is granted is to have the right to attach a pipe larger than five-quarter digits in diameter within a space of fifty feet from that delivery-tank from which they are to draw the water.

1. This case presents the third of the senate decrees of 11 BCE. How does it limit access to and withdrawal of water from Rome's aqueducts?
2. What technology does this senate decree use to regulate private delivery from the aqueducts? Review the rules on the calix in the preceding case. Evaluate how effective overall Roman technological solutions were for limiting access and withdrawals from the aqueducts.
3. After quoting this law, Frontinus presents a rationale for it:

In this senatorial resolution it is worthy of note that permission is for water to be drawn only from a delivery-tank, so that neither the channels nor public pipes may be damaged by numerous tappings. (Front. *Aq.* 106.3)

What purpose or purposes does Frontinus ascribe to the Senate? What other policies might it serve?

4. Compare the law on infrastructure for private delivery at Rome, Urso, and Venafrum (Cases 4.10 and 4.33). Which rules do you think would be most effective, and why?
5. Frontinus urges future water commissioners to be "specially watchful to counter various and shifting forms of fraud" in overseeing both public fountains and private grants (Aq. 103.4). What forms of fraud could be used to get around the limits in this senatus consultum?
6. Similar rules appear in Ulpian's commentary on the edict (*D.* 43.20.1.39–43 Ulp. 70 *ad Ed.*) and in imperial constitutions (*CTh* 15.2.5–6; *CJ* 11.43.3 pr–1). Why were these problems so persistent?

Case 4.13. Transferability

Frontinus, De Aquaeductu urbis Romae 108

"Quod Q. Aelius Tubero Paulus Fabius Maximus cos. V. F. constitui oportere, quo iure extra intraque urbem ducerent aquas, quibus adtributae essent, Q. D. E. R. F. P. D. E. R. I. C. uti usque eo maneret adtributio aquarum, exceptis quae in usum balinearum essent datae aut Augusti nomine, quoad eidem domini possiderent id solum, in quod accepissent aquam."

Frontinus, On the water-management of the city of Rome 108

Whereas the consuls Quintus Aelius Tubero and Paulus Fabius Maximus brought forth the subject that it was necessary to determine by what right those persons to whom waters had been allotted might draw such waters within and without the city, and inquired of the Senate as to what action might be pleasing on the subject, concerning the subject the senators resolved as follows: that the allotment of waters, excepting those granted for use of bathing establishments or in consequence of a servitude for hauling up water, shall remain in force only so long as the same proprietors continue to occupy the property for which they have received the water.

1. This case presents the fourth of the senate decrees of 11 BCE. What rules does this decree introduce? How long does an imperial grant of water rights remain in effect? What circumstances might make it difficult to enforce this rule?
2. What exceptions are made to the prohibition on transferability? How can these exceptions be justified?
3. Frontinus introduces this decree by explaining that in the past, grants to baths were perpetual (*Aq.* 107.1–3). Is it just a matter of tradition, or were other interests at stake?
4. After quoting this senate decree, Frontinus explains how it was to be implemented:

> As soon as the right to any water becomes vacant, this fact is reported and entered in the records, which are examined in order that from vacant water-rights grants may be made to applicants. (2) It was customary for the water staff to cut off such waters immediately, so that between grants they might sell water either to the occupants of the property or indeed to other parties. (3) But a more considerate policy has appealed to our emperor: so that properties may not suddenly be deprived entirely of water, he bestows a grace-period of thirty days, within which the interested parties <may make whatever arrangements are needed>. (*Aq.* 109.1–3)

   Who was responsible for implementing the Senate decree? How and why does practice depart from the words of the statute? In the next paragraph, Frontinus explains that, when several people jointly had private delivery, their right continued as long as one of them survived (*Aq.* 109.4–5). What special complications does a group or partnership present?
5. There is other evidence that the rule in this case was not hard and fast. Frontinus himself notes that in his day water rights were regularly renewed when a new owner takes possession (*nunc omnis aquae*

cum possessore instauratur beneficium, Aq. 107.3). In the Severan era Ulpian reports that a new owner could petition to continue private delivery; this was not special treatment but simply lawful, according to Ulpian (*nec est hoc beneficium, sed iniuria, si quis forte non impetraverit, D.* 43.20.1.43 Ulp. 70 *ad Ed.*). How can we account for these varied rules and practices? What does the variety reveal about the Roman legal system in general? Was change and flexibility a good thing? Why or why not?

Case 4.14. Aqua Caduca ("Lapsed Water")

Frontinus, De Aquaeductu urbis Romae 111

"Caducam neminem volo ducere nisi qui meo beneficio aut priorum principum habent. (2) Nam necesse est ex castellis aliquam partem aquae effluere, cum hoc pertineat non solum ad urbis nostrae salubritatem, sed etiam ad utilitatem cloacarum abluendarum."

Frontinus, On the water-management of the city of Rome 111

I wish no one to draw "lapsed" water except those who have grants to do so issued by myself or by former emperors. (2) For a certain amount of overflow from the delivery-tanks is needed, this being not only conducive to the wholesomeness of our city but also useful for flushing the sewers.

1. This case reports an undated emperor's decree on *aqua caduca* or lapsed water. How does he limit the use of lapsed water?
2. What rationale does the emperor give for this rule? What is meant by "the wholesomeness of our city"?
3. Does this decree limit private grants more than Republican laws did? Explain.
4. Frontinus introduces this decree with remarks on "lapsed" water:

Also subject to grants are those waters which are called "lapsed" [that is, overflow from delivery tanks or emissions from pipes], (2) although such grants are customarily given very sparingly by the rulers. Yet these offer opportunity for fraud on the part of the water men; and how much care should be devoted to preventing such fraud will be clear from a section of the imperial regulations which I quote below. (Front. *Aq.* 110.1–2)

How does Frontinus define "lapsed" water? The Latin word for "emissions," *manationes*, normally means "leaks" (which were repaired quickly), but in this passage it refers to a regulated discharge made directly from the pipes (Rodgers 2004, 230).

5. Compare Frontinus' definition of "lapsed" water with usage in earlier laws (Cases 4.6 and 4.10). Does the meaning change in the imperial era? Why is it hard to know exactly what *aqua caduca* meant?

Case 4.15. Delivery from Hadrian's Aqueduct in Constantinople

Codex Justinianus 11.43.6 pr Impp. Theodosius et Valentinianus AA. Cyro pp

> Omnis servitus aquarum aquaeductus Hadriani sive domorum sive possessionum sive suburbanorum sive balneorum vel per divinos adfatus intimatos in quolibet iudicio vel per usurpationem impertitos penitus exprobretur: maluimus etenim praedictum aquaeductum nostri palatii publicarum thermarum ac nymphaeorum commoditatibus inservire. Et decernimus hanc dispositionem modis omnibus in posterum servari, nemini licentia tribuenda ab eodem aquaeductu precibus oblatis usum aquae petere vel eum audere perforare: scientibus his, qui qualibet ratione putaverint ad huiusmodi molimen accedere, vel officio, si ausum fuerit instruere vel minus instructis precibus parere, centena pondo auri multae nomine fiscalibus rationibus se esse illaturos.

Emperors Theodosius and Valentinian to Cyrus, Praetorian Prefect, 440 CE?

> Every servitude for waters from Hadrian's aqueduct should be condemned completely whether it belongs to houses or plots of land or suburban villas or baths, whether they were acquired through divine declarations issued in any court or through usurpation. For we prefer that the aforementioned aqueduct serve the interests of our palace, public baths, and fountains. We also decree that this arrangement be observed in all respects in the future, and no one is to be granted

permission to seek the use of water from this same aqueduct by offering petitions or to venture to make a hole in it. Those who intend to attempt a contrivance of this sort by any means, or an office, if it dared to draw up a petition or to obey petitions that are not even drawn up, know that they will pay one hundred pounds of gold as a fine to the treasury's accounts.

1. This constitution refers to imperial grants to withdraw water from Hadrian's aqueduct at Constantinople. Consequently, when it refers to servitudes it means personal rights and not praedial servitudes (see Cases 2.1 and 2.8). What change do the emperors make in these grants? How do they justify this change?
2. What penalty do the emperors establish for violations of this constitution? What does the penalty reveal about the social and economic profile of likely offenders? To help in answering, review the information about economic status in Case 4.20, Study Question 4.
3. What difficulties in enforcing this rule do the emperors anticipate? How do the emperors address these challenges? How effective do you think their strategies would be in enforcing the law? Explain.
4. For what purposes do the emperors want to use the water from Hadrian's aqueduct? Try to reconstruct the rationale for this policy. What interests or needs does it serve?
5. Compare the aims of these emperors with the aims of earlier laws on Rome's aqueducts. Have imperial priorities changed? Or are these emperors simply less shy about asserting their priorities?

Case 4.16. Allocation by Rank

Codex Theodosianus 15.2.3 Impp. Gratianus, Valentinianus et Theodosius aaa. Clearcho praefecto Urbi

> Summas quidem domus, si lavacris lautioribus praesententur, binas non amplius aquae uncias aut, si hoc amplius exegerit ratio dignitatis, supra ternas neutiquam possidere, mediocres vero et inferioris meriti domus singulis et semis contentas esse decernimus, si tamen huiuscemodi balneas easdem habere claruerit. Ceteros vero, qui mansionem spatio angustiore sustentant, ad mediae unciae usum tantum gaudere

praecipimus neque obreptionem cuiquam patere, ita ut quod tibi paret officium sex librarum auri multa feriatur, nisi prodiderit usurpantes et is qui fefellit careat impetrato.

Emperors Gratian, Valentinian, Theodosius to Clearchus, city prefect, 382 CE

We decree that even the best houses, if they are furnished with rather lavish baths, are to have no more than two inches of water or, if their status rightly demands more than this, by no means more than three inches, but modest houses of lesser worth are to be satisfied with one and a half inches, but only if it is clear that they have the same kind of baths. We instruct the rest who keep dwellings of smaller size to enjoy the use of only half an inch of water and not to allow anyone secret theft. It is so ordered that a fine of six pounds of gold will be imposed on the office that answers to you, if it fails to hand over those taking water unlawfully, and a person who deceitfully acquires water shall lose it.

1. How did the emperors limit private delivery to houses in Constantinople? What factors determined the allocation of water?
2. For Roman elites, a house was a symbol of status and identity. How did private delivery contribute to a house's display of status? What kinds of status (economic? political? social?) does private delivery represent for the householders of Constantinople? Do the emperors seem more concerned with display or the water supply? Explain.
3. How did the emperors measure the allocation of water? The measurements in inches probably refer to the diameter of the pipe which serves as proxy for the volume of water (for the units of measurement at Rome, see Case 4.11, Study Question 4).
4. Compare the system of private delivery at Constantinople and at Rome. Which system is more efficient? more fair? Are the systems different or does this constitution simply make explicit principles that are assumed in Rome? Use your knowledge of Roman society and water rights to outline a position.

Case 4.17. Record-Keeping at Antioch

Codex Theodosianus 15.2.2 Imppp. Valentinianus, Valens et Gratianus aaa. Fortunatiano comiti rerum privatarum

> Aquaeductus, qui dafnensi palatio usum aquae praestat, quorundam aviditate tenuatur adpositis maioribus fistulis, quam ex imperiali largitate meruerunt. Consensu igitur omnium in tribus locis conceptacula reparentur et singulorum nomina modusque servandus tabulis adscribatur, et si ultra licitum aliquem usurpasse constiterit, per singulos obolos librae unius auri dispendiis ingravetur. Et si sacri tenore rescripti aliqui certum modum aquae meruisse noscetur, non prius eidem accipiendi potestas aliquatenus tribuatur, nisi adito rectore ex ipso conceptaculo quantitatem quam meruit possit adipisci.

Emperors Valentinian, Valens, and Gratian to Fortunatianus, Count of the private estates, 369 CE

> The aqueduct that provides water supply to the Daphne palace is diminished by the greed of certain people because they have inserted larger pipes than they obtained through imperial generosity. By agreement of all, the basins are to be repaired in three places, and the names of individuals and their reserved allocation are to be recorded on tablets. If it is found that anyone has taken more than allowed, a fine of one pound of gold shall be imposed for each obol in excess. Also if it is learned that someone has acquired a certain allocation of water according to the intent of a sacred rescript, he will not have legal power to receive however much is awarded until it is determined through the governor that the amount granted can be taken from that particular reservoir.

1. This constitution outlines procedures for imperial grants from the aqueduct that served the imperial palace at Antioch. Formulate the legal rules in your own words. Which component right or rights does it address? The size of water pipes at Antioch seem to have been measured in units based on the diameter of the obol, a Greek coin, instead of the Roman units (see Cases 4.11 and 4.16).
2. What mechanisms for enforcing imperial grants of private delivery is proposed in this constitution? What problems with enforcement does

the constitution anticipate? What other problems might come up?
3. How was the fine calculated? Was it a fair penalty? Why or why not?
4. What policy goals does this constitution aim to accomplish? How successful do you think it was in achieving those goals? Explain.

Case 4.18. Fraudulent Grants

Codex Justinianus 11.43.5 Impp. Theodosius, Valentinianus AA. Cyro pp.

> Si quis per divinam liberalitatem meruerit ius aquae, non viris clarissimis rectoribus provinciarum, sed tuae praecellentissimae sedi caelestes apices intimare debebit: condemnatione contra illum qui preces moderatoribus insinuare conatur quinquaginta librarum auri et contra universos administratores qui rescriptum per subreptionem elicitum suscipere moliuntur proponenda, apparitoribus nihilo minus eorundem virorum clarissimorum provinciae moderatorum animadversionibus pro vigore tui culminis subiugandis: et amplissima tua sede dispositura, quid in publicis thermis, quid in nympheis pro abundantia civium convenit deputari, quid his personis, quibus nostra perennitas indulsit, ex aqua superflua debeat impertiri.

Emperors Theodosius and Valentinian, Augusti, to Cyrus, Praetorian Prefect, 440 CE

> If someone will have acquired a right to water through our divine generosity, he will have to address heavenly letters not to the governors of the province, most illustrious men, but to your most exalted seat. A fine of fifty pounds of gold is imposed on the condemnation of a person who attempts to present petitions to governors and against all officials who contrive to recognize a rescript acquired in secret. There are to be no less penalties for the ministers of these same illustrious provincial governors in accordance with the strength of your power. As your most fulsome seat will order, what ought to be assigned to the public baths and fountains for the citizens' supply and what to be taken from the overflow for individuals whom our eternal power has favored.

1. What problem with individual rights of withdrawal does this constitution address? Reconstruct the situation as best you can. Why is private delivery a concern for the emperors?
2. Who should control individual rights of withdrawal from Rome's aqueducts, according to these emperors? Who is in fact controlling (or trying to control) the process?
3. What incentive do the emperors put in place for enforcing this constitution? Do you think this constitution is likely to succeed in its aims? Why or why not?
4. In the early sixth century CE, the emperor Anastasius cites this constitution in a decree of his own that asserted the emperor's control over private delivery:

> We affirm the divine arrangement [made] by the emperor Theodosius of famed memory, about those who wish water to be provided to them from public aqueducts or springs, enacted in this law that it remain in its firmness, in order that no one be allowed to draw off water from a public aqueduct or spring either in this most holy city or in the provinces without divine letters acquired in the accustomed way from the sacred office of correspondence or issued or to be issued in the court of your highness or others whom it concerns; whoever violate our orders or allow them to be violated are to be struck with a fine of ten pounds of gold and other most serious displeasure. (*CJ* 11.43.11)

   What problems with Constantinople's water supply does Anastasius address? How do his problems compare with this case? or the problems described by Frontinus in the late first century CE?
4. Compare private delivery in three imperial cities, Rome, Antioch, and Constantinople. Which city has the best laws, and why? Be sure to explain what you mean by "best."

III. Protecting the Water Supply

A. Rome and Italy

Case 4.19. Repairs and Maintenance

Frontinus, De Aquaeductu urbis Romae 96, 97.4

Tutelam autem singularum aquarum locari solitam invenio positamque redemptoribus necessitatem certum numerum circa ductus extra urbem, certum in urbe servorum opificum habendi, et quidem ita ut nomina quoque eorum, quos habituri essent in ministerio per quasque regiones, in tabulas publicas deferrent; eorumque operum probandorum curam fuisse penes censores aliquando et aediles, interdum etiam quaestoribus eam provinciam obvenisse, ut apparet ex S. C. quod factum est C. Licinio et Q. Fabio cos. . . . (97.4) Mancipi etiam si clam eo quem adversus legem fecisset, multa dicebatur.

Frontinus, On the water-management of the city of Rome 96 and 97.4

The maintenance of the individual aqueducts, I find, was customarily awarded by contract. The contractors were required to have a fixed number of slave workmen here and there along the conduits outside the City and a fixed number within the City; the requirement even included that they register in the public records the names of those whom they were to employ and in what localities they were to be assigned. Responsibility for final inspection of the contractors' work lay with censors, sometimes with aediles; occasionally this duty even fell upon quaestors, as we see in a senatorial resolution passed in the consulship of Gaius Licinius and Quintus Fabius . . . (97.4) For a contractor, too, a fine was imposed, even if it was established that someone had broken the law without his knowledge.

1. In this case Frontinus describes administrative practice and summarizes part of the senate decree of 116 BCE (see the next case for the rest). The Senate made law on the aqueducts as part of its power over the treasury and public works (cf. Polybius, *Histories* 6.11.13, 17). How were repairs and maintenance organized in the Republican era? What

roles did Rome's magistrates play in the process? Was it the same as the construction of aqueducts?

2. What mechanisms ensured accountability in repairs and maintenance? How effective were these measures likely to be in keeping the aqueducts in good working order?
3. What policy goals do these laws address? What challenges does the decree anticipate to achieving these goals?
4. In the empire, there were two slave crews—one owned by the state and the other by the emperor—that repaired Rome's aqueducts, and the water commissioner was responsible for maintenance (Front. *Aq.* 116–18). Financing for repairs came from the public treasury (*aerarium*) and the imperial treasury (*fiscus*) as well as from rents on public places and possibly also user fees for private delivery (see Case 4.6; see also Vitr. *Arch.* 8.6.2). Which system—imperial or republican—do you think would be more effective at keeping the aqueducts in good repair, and why? Can you explain why Frontinus does not report any laws governing the imperial system?
5. Compare the treatment of repairs and maintenance of private hydraulic infrastructure. When an individual had a servitude to channel or draw water from a spring, he also had a right to repair the infrastructure (see Cases 2.32 and 2.33). The interdicts on canals and springs also protected repairs to private hydraulic infrastructure (Cases 3.27 and 3.28). Do you think it was more difficult to protect public or private aqueducts from damage? Why?

Case 4.20. Restrictions on Use

Frontinus, De Aquaeductu urbis Romae 97

Quanto opere autem curae fuerit ne quis violare ductus aquamve non concessam derivare auderet, cum ex multis apparere potest, tum et ex hoc quod Circus Maximus ne diebus quidem ludorum circensium nisi aedilium aut censorum permissu inrigabatur, (2) quod durasse etiam postquam res ad curatores transiit sub Augusto, apud Ateium Capitonem legimus. (3) Agri vero, qui aqua publica contra legem essent inrigati, publicabantur. (4) Mancipi etiam si clam eo quem adversus legem fecisset, multa dicebatur. (5) In eisdem legibus adiectum est ita: "Ne quis aquam oletato dolo malo, ubi publice saliet. Si quis oletarit, sestertiorum decem milium multa esto." (6) Cuius rei causa aediles curules iubebantur per vicos singulos ex eis qui in unoquoque vico habitarent praediave haberent binos praeficere, quorum arbitratu aqua in publico saliret.

Frontinus, On the water-management of the city of Rome 97.1–6

The special care taken that no one should venture to damage the conduits or to draw water which had not been granted can be shown by one out of many possible examples. The Circus Maximus was not watered, even on the days when games were held there, without the express permission of aediles or censors; (2) and we read in the writings of Ateius Capito that this regulation remained in effect even after the institution of water commissioners under Augustus. (3) Indeed, properties which had been irrigated with public water against the law were confiscated. (4) For a contractor, too, a fine was imposed, even if it was established that someone had broken the law without his knowledge. (5) In the same regulations this clause was added: "No one with wrongful deceit is to defile with excrement water which issues for public use. If any person should so defile it, the fine is to be 10,000 sesterces." (6) For this reason curule aediles were instructed to appoint two men for each district, out of those who lived there or owned property in that district; these men were to have judicial authority over water which issued for public use.

1. In this case Frontinus summarizes the remaining provisions of the senate decree of 116 BCE. What limits on access and withdrawal of water from the aqueducts did the law impose? How are these provisions related to the ones in the previous case?
2. Which officials were responsible for implementing this law? Would neighborhood deputies be more effective than a citywide magistrate such as the curule aedile or censor? Why or why not? The officials in the case might be the same as the *montani* and *pagani* mentioned in the *lex Rivalicia* (Case 4.7). Review Cases 4.1, 4.6, and 4.19, and compile a job description for the Republican magistrates responsible for the aqueducts.
3. Does the decree punish all pollution of city water? How easy would it be to prove that a person had polluted the water wrongfully? What

does this legal rule reveal about the usual disposal of waste in ancient Rome?

4. What penalties were imposed for violations of this law? How effectively did this law deter abuse of the city water supply? In the second century CE, the annual wage of a soldier in Rome's legions was raised to 1,200 sesterces, while wealthy Romans in the top two census classes possessed property of at least 400,000 sesterces. Is the fine fair? Would it deter either group? Why or why not?
5. There is little evidence for enforcement of laws on the aqueducts beyond a report that the censors of 184 BCE took steps to cut off illegal taps on the aqueducts outside the city (Livy, *History of Rome,* 39.44.4). How well would this senate decree have addressed the situation in 184 BCE? Why was it difficult to police the aqueducts? Would it be more difficult in urban or rural areas? The problem was persistent, as Frontinus' treatise shows: compare also an imperial constitution which expressly reinforces penalty for illegal irrigation (*CTh* 15.2.7 = *CJ* 11.34.4, 397 CE).
6. How long did the senate decree of 116 BCE remain in force? What evidence does Frontinus present that helps to answer this question? Ateius Capito was a jurist who also had a political career serving as consul suffect in 5 CE and as curator aquarum in 13 CE. Frontinus cites his work only twice but he probably used other legal sources as well.
7. According to Frontinus, why did the Senate pass this law? Review Case 4.6 (on private delivery) and outline the policy issues that the Republican laws address. Are the laws adequate to achieve these goals? Why or why not?

Case 4.21. Materials for Maintenance of Rome's Aqueducts

Frontinus, De Aquaeductu urbis Romae 125

Quod Q. Aelius Tubero Paulus Fabius Maximus cos. V. F. de rivis, specibus, fornicibus, aquae Iuliae, Marciae, Appiae, Tepulae, Anienis reficiendis, Q. D. E. R. F. P. D. E. R. I. C. uti cum ei rivi, specus, fornices, quos Augustus Caesar se refecturum impensa sua pollicitus senatui est, reficerentur, ex agris privatorum terra, limus, lapides, testa, harena, ligna ceteraque quibus ad eam rem opus esset, unde quaeque eorum proxime sine iniuria privatorum tolli, sumi, portari possint, viri boni arbitratu aestimata darentur, tollerentur, sumerentur, exportarentur; et ad eas res omnes exportandas earumque rerum reficiendarum causa, quotiens opus esset, per agros privatorum sine iniuria eorum itinera, actus paterent, darentur.

Frontinus, On the water-management of the city of Rome 125

Whereas the consuls Quintus Aelius Tubero and Paulus Fabius Maximus brought forth the subject of repairing the channels, tunnels, and arches which convey the water of Julia, Marcia, Appia, Tepula, and Anio, and inquired of the Senate as to what action might be pleasing on the subject, concerning the subject the senators resolved as follows: that when the repairs are made to the channels, tunnels, and arches, which Caesar Augustus promised the Senate that he would repair from his private funds, the earth, mud, stone, potsherds, sand, wood, and whatever else is required for the purpose shall be granted, taken, removed, carried out from the property of private persons, each of these materials being taken, removed, carried out from a location as convenient as possible and without injury to private persons, the value of the same having been determined by appraisal of some honorable person; and that through the property of private persons without injury to those parties rights of walking and driving be permitted and granted as often as needed for transporting all the said materials in connection with repairs of the said structures.

1. The case presents the fifth of the senate decrees of 11 BCE. What are its main provisions?
2. Who pays for repairs to the aqueducts? Who provides materials for these repairs? According to Frontinus, the cost of repairs was paid by the state treasury and subsidized by user fees paid to the city for water (Front. *Aq.* 116–19). Are the costs allocated fairly? Why or why not?
3. Frontinus introduces this senate decree with some background on the policy that motivated it:

(4) Furthermore, inasmuch as most of the conduits had been laid out through the property of private persons and it was foreseen that there

might in future be difficulty in gathering necessary materials unless this process was somehow accommodated by a legal formality; in order, too, that contractors might not be prohibited by landholders from having access to channels which needed repairs, there was enacted the following senatorial resolution.

What problems does the senate decree attempt to solve? Why was a "legal formality" needed to arrange materials and access for repairs?

4. How does this decree protect private property during routine maintenance? Are these protections adequate? Why or why not?

Case 4.22. Clearway

Frontinus, De Aquaeductu urbis Romae 127

"Quod Q. Aelius Tubero Paulus Fabius Maximus cos. V. F. aquarum, quae in urbem venirent, itinera occupari monumentis et aedificiis et arboribus conseri, Q. F. P. D. E. R. I. C. cum ad reficiendos rivos specusque per quae opera publica corrumpantur, placere circa fontes et fornices et muros utraque ex parte quinos denos pedes patere, et circa rivos qui sub terra essent et specus intra urbem et urbi continentia aedificia utraque ex parte quinos pedes vacuos relinqui ita ut neque monumentum in eis locis neque aedificium post hoc tempus ponere neque conserere arbores liceret, sique nunc essent arbores intra id spatium, exciderentur praeterquam si quae villae continentes et inclusae aedificiis essent. (2) Si quis adversus ea commiserit, in singulas res poena HS dena milia essent, ex quibus pars dimidia praemium accusatori daretur, cuius opera maxime convictus esset qui adversus hoc S. C. commisisset, pars autem dimidia in aerarium redigeretur. (3) Deque ea re iudicarent cognoscerentque curatores aquarum."

Frontinus, On the water-management of the city of Rome 127

Whereas the consuls Quintus Aelius Tubero and Paulus Fabius Maximus brought forth the subject that the rights of way for aqueducts coming into the city are being occupied by monuments and buildings and are being planted up with trees, and inquired of the Senate as to what action might be pleasing, concerning the subject the senators resolved as follows: inasmuch as for repairs to channels and tunnels

<obstructions must be removed> by which public structures are damaged, it is approved that there be a clearing of fifteen feet on either side of springs, arches, and walls, and that a space of five feet on either side be left vacant around the channels which are below ground and around tunnels within the city and within the built-up areas contiguous to the city, and in these places it shall after this time be permitted to locate neither monument nor building nor to plant trees; and if there now exist any trees within the said space, they are to be cut down, excepting those which may be connected with a country residence and enclosed by buildings. (2) If anyone shall act contrary to these provisions, the penalty for each such offense shall be 10,000 sesterces, the half of which shall be given as a reward to the accuser by whose effort most of all condemnation shall have been secured for the person who acted contrary to this senatorial resolution, the other half shall be deposited in the state treasury; (3) and in such case the water commissioners shall conduct a trial and take cognizance. (Front. *Aq.* 127.1–3)

1. This case presents the sixth and last of the senate decrees of 11 BC. How does this decree protect the infrastructure of the aqueducts?
2. What changes to the clearway does this senate decree authorize? Why is the clearway a different size around underground channels than aboveground structures? Why is there an exception for some trees? Is this a reasonable exception? Why or why not.
3. How easy would it be to enforce this decree? Imagine how the water commissioner would go about enforcing its provisions. What difficulties might he encounter?
4. What penalty does the decree set for violations? Is this penalty fair? likely to deter violations? Before you answer, review the information about economic status in Case 4.20, Study Question 4.
5. Who has jurisdiction in trials relating to this decree? What issues or claims could this trial decide? Come up with at least two hypothetical disputes about enforcing this law.
6. In introducing this senate decree, Frontinus describes potential causes of damage to the aqueducts:

Not infrequently, however, damages are occasioned by wrongful behavior on the part of landholders, who cause injury to the channels in a variety of ways. (2) For one thing, they occupy with buildings or trees the spaces alongside the aqueducts which are to be left vacant in accordance with a senatorial resolution. (3) Trees are more harmful, for their roots dislodge the vaulted coverings and sides of the conduits. (4) For another thing, they lay out neighborhood roads and country paths over the aqueduct structures themselves. (5) Finally, they deny access for maintenance. (6) Against all these offenses provision was made in the following senatorial resolution. (Front. *Aq.* 126)

What features of the landscape pose risks to the aqueducts? Which ones would be the most difficult to remedy, and why? Based on this passage, what sort of zoning regulations did the Romans have in areas near the city?

7. Review the six senate decrees of 11 BCE and evaluate the aims and likely effectiveness of this program of legislation (see Cases 4.8, 4.9, 4.12, 4.13, and 4.21).

Case 4.23. Damage to the Conduits (lex Quinctia)

Frontinus, De Aquaeductu urbis Romae 129.1–6

T. Quinctus Crispinus consul [d S.S.] populum iure rogavit populusque iure scivit in foro pro rostris aedis divi Iulii p. K. Iulias. (2) Tribus Sergia principium fuit. (3) Pro tribu Sex. Vibidius L. f. Virro primus scivit. (4) Quicumque post hanc legem rogatam rivos specus fornices fistulas tubulos castella lacus aquarum publicarum quae ad urbem Romam ducuntur ducentur sciens dolo malo foraverit ruperit foranda rumpendave curaverit peiorave fecerit, quo minus eae aquae earumve quae aqua in urbem Romam ire cadere fluere pervenire duci possit quove minus in urbe Roma et in eis locis qua aedificia urbi continentia sunt erunt, in iis hortis praediis locis quorum hortorum praediorum locorum dominis possessoribusve V(su) F(ructuariis) aqua data adtributa est erit, saliat distribuatur dividatur in castella lacus immittatur, is populo Romano HS centum milia dare damnas esto. (6) Et qui D. M. qui eorum ita fecerit, id omne sarcire, reficere, restituere, aedificare, ponere et celere demolire damnas esto sine dolo malo atque omnia ita ut quicumque curator aquarum est, erit, si curator aquarum nemo erit, tum is praetor qui inter cives et peregrinos ius dicet, multa, pignoribus cogito, coercito, eique curatori aut si curator non erit, tum ei praetori eo nomine cogendi, coercendi, multae dicendae sive pignoris capiendi ius potestasque esto. Si quid eorum servus fecerit, dominus eius HS centum milia populo Romano D. D. E. Et qui D. M. qui eorum ita fecerit, id omne sarcire, reficere, restituere, aedificare, ponere et celere demolire damnas esto sine dolo malo atque omnia ita ut quicumque curator aquarum est, erit, si curator aquarum nemo erit, tum is praetor qui inter cives et peregrinos ius dicet, multa, pignoribus cogito, coercito, eique curatori aut si curator non erit, tum ei praetori eo nomine cogendi, coercendi, multae dicendae sive pignoris capiendi ius potestasque esto. Si quid eorum servus fecerit, dominus eius HS centum milia populo Romano D. D. E.

Frontinus, On the Water Management of the City of Rome 129.1–6

The consul Titus Quinctius Crispinus, on the advice of the Senate, duly put the question to the people, and the people as a body duly voted approval in the forum, before the rostra of the temple of the deified Julius, on the thirtieth day of June. (2) The tribe Sergia was the first to vote (3) and for this tribe Sextus Vigidius Virro, son of Lucius, cast the first vote. (4) Whoever, after the passage of this statute, shall knowingly with wrongful deceit pierce, break, cause to have pierced or broken, or damage the channels, tunnels, arches, pipes, tubes, delivery-tanks, or basins of those public waters which are conveyed or will hereafter be conveyed into the city of Rome, whereby the said waters or any of them may be unable to go, fall, flow, reach, or be conveyed, or whereby the same may be hindered from issuing, being distributed, divided, discharged into delivery-tanks or basins within the city of Rome and in those places which are now or will hereafter be built-up areas contiguous to the city, in those estates, properties, and places to the proprietors, holders, usufructuaries of which estates, properties, and places water has been or will hereafter be granted or assigned: that person shall be condemned to pay to the people of Rome a fine of 100,000 sesterces; (5) and, moreover, whoever without wrongful deceit shall have done any one of these things, he shall be condemned to repair, remake, restore, rebuild, or replace what he has damaged, to destroy or demolish what he has built and to perform all such requirements and in such manner as will think right whoever is or shall be water commissioner or, if there is no water commissioner, then that praetor who administers justice between citizens and foreigners, either of which officials shall compel and administer by fine or pledges; and on that account the said commissioner or, if there is no commissioner, then the said praetor shall have the right and power of compulsion, administration, of imposing a fine or collecting a pledge. (6) If a slave shall have done any one of these things, his master shall be condemned to pay to the Roman people 100,000 sesterces.

1. This case presents the first six sections of the lex Quinctia (9 BCE), named for the consul who proposed it. The lists—of parts of the aqueduct and verbs for damage—are characteristic of the formal language of Roman statutes, but they are also important for conveying the scope of the law. Which parts of the aqueduct are specifically protected? What kinds of damage does the law prohibit? Why are some kinds of damage not punished?
2. The decree describes a standard for evaluating a defendant's action: "knowingly and with wrongful deceit." Define this standard in your own words. How does the standard limit the application of this law? Should the law be limited in this way? Why or why not?
3. What penalties does the law establish for damage to the aqueduct?
4. How does the law deal with damage caused by a slave? Why does the law penalize the master and not the slave?
5. What reasons or rationale does the law give for its provisions? Compare the expression of policy in the municipal law from Urso (Cases 4.4, 4.10). How can you account for the differences and similarities?
6. What mechanisms were used to enforce this law? Which official or magistrate had jurisdiction? Why might it be difficult to enforce this law? The Ebro Irrigation Decree (Case 3.29) likewise authorized magistrates to impose fines and collect pledges as they enforced the law. To what extend do both water systems pose the same challenges to enforcement?

Case 4.24. Additional Protections (lex Quinctia)

Frontinus, De Aquaeductu urbis Romae 129.7–11

Si qui locus circa rivos, specus, fornices, fistulas, tubulos, castella, lacus aquarum publicarum, quae ad urbem Romam ducuntur et ducentur, terminatus est et erit, ne quis in eo loco post hanc legem rogatam quid opponito, molito, obsaepito, figito, statuito, ponito, conlocato, arato, serito, neve in eum quid immittito, praeterquam eorum faciendorum, reponendorum causa, quae hac lege licebit, oportebit. (8) Qui adversus ea quid fecerit, siremps lex, ius causaque omnium rerum omnibusque esto, atque uti esset esseve oporteret, si is adversus hanc legem rivum, specum rupisset forassetve. Quo minus in eo loco pascere, herbam, fenum secare, sentes tollere liceat, eius hac lege nihilum rogatur. (9) Curatores aquarum, qui nunc sunt quique erunt, faciunto ut in eo loco, qui locus circa fontes et fornices et muros et rivos et specus terminatus est, arbores, vites, vepres, sentes, ripae, maceria, salicta, harundineta tollantur, excidantur, effodiantur, excodicentur, uti quod recte factum esse volent; eoque nomine eis pignoris capio, multae dictio coercitioque esto; idque eis sine fraude sua facere liceat, ius potestasque esto. (10) Quo minus vites, arbores, quae villis, aedificiis maceriisve inclusae sunt, maceriae, quas curatores aquarum causa cognita ne demolirentur dominis permiserunt, quibus inscripta insculptaque essent ipsorum qui permisissent curatorum nomina, maneant, hac lege nihilum rogatur. (11) Quo minus ex eis fontibus, rivis, specibus, fornicibus aquam sumere, haurire eis, quibuscumque curatores aquarum permiserunt, permiserint, praeterquam rota calice, machina liceat, dum ne qui puteus neque foramen novum fiat, eius hac lege nihilum rogatur.

Frontinus, On the water-management of the city of Rome 129.7–11

(7) If any area has been or will hereafter be delimited along the channels, tunnels, arches, pipes, tubes, delivery-tanks, or basins of the public waters which are conveyed or will hereafter be conveyed to the city of Rome, then after the passage of this statute no one shall in that area put in the way, construct, enclose, set up, establish, place, locate, plow in or sow anything, nor shall anyone introduce anything into that area, except for making or replacing such things as are permitted or required by this

statute. (8) Whoever shall have done anything contrary thereto, against him in every way the statute, law, and procedure shall apply in every particular as it would or ought to apply if he had broken or pierced the channel or tunnel in contravention of this statute. (9) To the effect that it not be permitted in that area which has been or shall be delimited along the springs and arches and walls and channels and tunnels to graze livestock, to cut hay or grass, to remove brush; or to the effect that in that area those who now are or shall hereafter be water commissioners not arrange that trees, vines, brambles, brush, banks, fences, willow-thickets, and beds of reeds be removed, cut down, dug out, uprooted in such manner as they will think right, nothing of that is proposed by this statute; and on that account they shall have the authority to collect a pledge, to impose a fine, the power of compulsion and administration; and they are to be allowed and have the right and power to do so without personal liability. (10) To the effect that vines and trees (which are enclosed by country residences, buildings or fences) or that fences (which the water commissioners after due examination have exempted their owners from demolishing and upon which have been inscribed or carved the names of those commissioners who gave the permission) not remain, nothing of that is proposed by this statute. (11) To the effect that it not be allowed to whatever persons the water commissioners have permitted or will hereafter have permitted to take or haul up water from such springs, channels, tunnels, or arches, excepting by means of wheel, screw, or machine, provided that there be made neither well-shaft nor any new opening, nothing of that is proposed by this statute.

1. This case presents the rest of the lex Quinctia of 9 BCE (see the preceding case for the first part). What activities does this law prohibit? What exceptions did it make? Compare the lex Quinctia with the senate decree on the clearway (Case 4.22). Which is more restrictive? Which is better law? Why?
2. What problems or situations might have created a need for these new rules on the clearway?
3. What penalty is prescribed for violations of this law? Why are violations of this law compared to damaging the tunnels or conduits of the aqueduct?

4. What procedures does the water commissioner use to enforce the law? What legal protections does he have? Why might he need this legal protection?
5. The last section of the decree confirms existing rights of withdrawal from the aqueduct (note: *haustus* designates not a praedial servitude but a personal right of use because it involved public water). Why is this topic included in a decree on the clearway? What types of technology does the senate decree authorize for exercising these rights? Why does the Senate restrict the use of these technologies?
6. This senate decree appears at the end of Frontinus' treatise, followed only by a brief concluding paragraph in which he expresses what we might call his judicial philosophy:

> I should not deny that those who show no respect for a statute of such excellent justice are worthy of the penalty which is threatened. But those who had been lulled into confidence by administrative neglect over a long period of time deserved to be brought back to their senses with gentleness. (2) Thus with special care I have sought, so far as it lay within my power, to preserve the anonymity of those who had erred. (3) Those who took my admonition seriously and sought the emperor's pardon may look upon me as the means whereby they now enjoy an official grant with imperial favor. (4) Against the others, indeed, I hope that execution of the statute may not be necessary, since in the end it is better to uphold the trust placed in my office even at the risk of provoking indignant reactions. (Front. *Aq.* 130)

   Based on this passage, how assiduously do you think Frontinus enforced these laws when he was water commissioner? If he did not plan to enforce them, what reasons might he have had for quoting them at length? How can we explain Frontinus' approach to law enforcement? Why might he have preferred to use social pressure rather than legal process to protect the aqueducts?
7. A fourth-century constitution instructed the governor's office to see to the removal of trees from the clearway (*CJ* 11.43.1.2 = *CTh* 15.2.1). Why was maintaining the clearway a persistent problem?

Case 4.25. Maintenance at Amiternum

Corpus Inscriptionum Latinarum 12.1853

> Pu]rcatio / [A - - - ad] castellum p(edes) CX; a*f* / [- - - ad castel]lum Ferebra et castellum / [- - - p(edes) - - -] MMCCCXX; ab castello ad co/[- - -]lum ad vinias Anchariorum ped(es)/[- - - a*f* vin]ieis Anchar<ior>um ad castellum qui / [est contra vin]ias Pacianas p(edes) CCCXX; a*f* vinieis / [Pacianeis] ad castellum qui est contra / [villam p(edes)] DCCCCL; a*f* villa Paciana ad castel(lum) / [qui est s]ub segete Paciana p(edes) CCLXXXV; a*f* / [castell]o qui est sub segete ad castel(lum) ad / [compitu]m Traecis p(edes) MCCXC; a[*f*] angulo / [- - -] ad cast(ellum) qui est ad compitum Trae/[cis p(edes) - - - a]b angul(o) Traec(is) ad cast(ellum) qui est sub / [segete] Gavidi p(edes) CCCXLV; ab segete Gavidi ad ca/[stellu]m ped(es) DCCCXXX. S(umma) pe(des) ((octo milia)) DCLXX

Decree on the Amiternum Aqueduct

> Cleaning . . . to the reservoir one hundred ten feet; from . . . to the reservoir Ferebra and the reservoir . . . two thousand three hundred twenty feet; from the reservoir to the hill(?) at the vineyards of the Ancharii . . . feet; from the vineyards of the Ancharii to the reservoir which is across from the vineyards of the Pacii three hundred twenty feet; from the vineyards of the Pacii to the reservoir which is across from the villa, nine hundred fifty feet; from the villa of the Pacii to the reservoir which is below the arable field of the Pacii, two hundred eighty-five feet; from the reservoir which is near the arable field to the reservoir near the crossroads Traecis one thousand two hundred ninety feet; from the corner . . . to the reservoir which at the crossroads Traecis feet . . . ; from the corner Traecis to the reservoir which is near Gavidius' arable field three hundred forty-five feet; from Gavidius' arable field to the reservoir eight hundred thirty feet. Total feet eight thousand six hundred seventy.

1. This inscription preserves a decree about an aqueduct in the territory of the Italian city, Amiternum, and dates to the early first century CE. Its title is only partially preserved, but should probably be restored to read *purcatio* (or *purgatio*), "cleaning." The decree records in Roman

feet the length of the channel between landmarks it traversed, ending with its total distance. How should this information be interpreted? Why was it recorded on the decree? What details support your interpretation?

2. Based on the inscription, what structures were part of the aqueduct (e.g., arcades, reservoirs)? Where were reservoirs located? Draw a picture of the aqueduct's route using information from the inscription.
3. What function or functions could the reservoirs have served? Compare the reservoirs in Rome's water system (Cases 4.12, 4.14).
4. In many irrigation communities, the people who use the water are responsible for maintaining the infrastructure in exchange for their share of the water. That is, they have both rights of management and a right of withdrawal. Is it likely that the aqueduct at Amiternum belonged to such a community? Why or why not?
5. Who paid for repairs of the aqueduct at Amiternum? Although the decree does not answer this question explicitly, what can you infer about the finances? There is no indication in the inscription whether the aqueduct at Amiternum was public or private, although it appears to have run across private land. Typically public roads were maintained and repaired by individuals whose land abutted the roads: is it appropriate to follow the same practice for aqueducts as for roads? Why or why not?

B. Constantinople and Antioch

Case 4.26. Maintenance by Landowners

Codex Justinianus 11.43.1 pr–1 Imp. Constantinus A. ad Maximilianum consularem aquarum (= Codex Theodosianus 15.2.1)

> Possessores, per quorum fines formarum meatus transeunt, ab extraordinariis oneribus volumus esse immunes, ut eorum opera aquarum ductus sordibus oppleti mundentur, nec ad aliud superindictae rei onus isdem possessoribus attinendis, ne circa res alias occupati repurgium formarum facere non occurrant.
>
> 1 . Quod si neglexerint, amissione possessionum multabuntur: nam fiscus eius praedium obtinebit, cuius neglegentia perniciem formae congesserit.

Emperor Constantine Augustus to Maximilianus, Consular Prefect of Waters, 330 CE

> We wish that landowners, through whose fields channels of the aqueducts pass, be free from extraordinary burdens so that the water channels filled with filth can be cleared by their effort. Nor should these landowners be compelled to an added burden of an extra duty, lest they not deal with the cleaning of the aqueduct quickly because they are busy with other duties. (1) But if they neglect it, they will be punished with the loss of their property. For the treasury will take the land of a man who brings harm to the aqueduct by his negligence.

1. In this constitution, the emperor Constantine addresses Maximilianus, the consular official in charge of Rome's aqueducts comparable to the water commissioner in earlier eras. What rules for maintenance does this constitution establish?
2. What mechanisms does Constantine put in place to motivate landowners to clean the aqueduct? Which do you think would work better, the carrot or the stick?
3. The decree from Amiternum in the preceding case sets up a similar system of maintenance for an aqueduct that may have been public or private. Can you identify any differences between the provisions of the decree and this constitution? How does law made by an emperor differ from a civic or community decree? How does the form of the law affect our interpretation of it?
4. Which system would be more effective at keeping the aqueduct clear, the one described by Frontinus or the one adopted in this constitution? Explain.
5. A later constitution required all citizens to contribute to the renovation and construction of aqueducts, with no exemptions for people of high rank (*CJ* 8.11.7 = *CTh* 15.1.23, 384 CE). Why might citizens need this encouragement? Is it likely that the landowners along the aqueduct's route would perform maintenance more reliably than other citizens? Why or why not?
6. In the fifth century CE, the emperors directed city officials in Constantinople to inspect the area around pipes connected to the aqueduct (*CJ* 11.43.6.3, 440? CE). Would inspections improve maintenance? Or did they serve other purposes?

Case 4.27. Reckless Damage

Codex Justinianus 11.43.2 = Codex Theodosianus 15.2.4 Impp. Valentinianus, Theodosius et Arcadius AAA. Pancratio pu.

> Si quis de cetero vetiti furoris audacia florentissimae urbis commoda voluerit mutilare aquam ad suum fundum ex aquaeductu publico derivando, sciat eundem fundum fiscalis tituli proscriptione signatum privatis rebus nostris adgregandum. *CJ* 11.43.2 = *CTh* 15.2.4

Emperors Valentinian, Theodosius, and Arcadius to Pancratius, city prefect, 381 or 382 CE

> If in the future anyone, in the boldness of forbidden madness, wishes to damage the amenities of this most thriving city by diverting water to his own farm from the public aqueduct, he should know that the same farm, identified by written notice of a treasury claim, is to be incorporated into our private property.

1. What kind of damage to the city's aqueduct does this constitution address? Does this constitution address a more specific problem than earlier laws, for example, the lex Quinctia (Case 4.23)? Explain.
2. What penalty do the emperors prescribe for this damage? Other constitutions establish impose a monetary fine (*CTh* 15.2.9) or require the defendant to repair his damage to the aqueduct (*CJ* 11.43.10.1). Which penalty do you think is most fair? most likely to deter illegal diversions? Explain with a hypothetical illustrating the advantages or disadvantages of the different penalties.
3. How do the emperors characterize a person who illegally taps a city aqueduct? Why might the emperors have used such language? What assumptions about imperial power and the rule of law does it reveal?
4. Compare the language of the imperial constitutions with other laws on aqueducts as quoted in Frontinus and as documented in inscriptions. What differences in language and tone do you observe? What problems are repeatedly addressed by the laws? How can you account for both similarities and differences?

Case 4.28. Free Water

Codex Justinianus 11.43.7 Impp. Theodosius et Valentinianus AA. Eutychiano pp

> Ad reparationem aquaeductus huius almae urbis omnia vectigalia, quae colligi possunt ex universis scalis huius inclitae urbis et ex operariis qui Cyzicenii dicuntur, ad refectionem eiusdem aquaeductus procedere: illo videlicet observando, ut nemo eorum qui ius aquae possident quamcumque descriptionem sustineat: nam exsecrabile videtur domos huius almae urbis aquam habere venalem.

Emperors Theodosius and Valentinian to Eutychianus, Praetorian Prefect, between 445 and 447 CE

> For the restoration of the aqueduct, all the revenues of this generous city which can be collected from all the landing docks of this famed city and from the workers who are called Cyziceni, go to the repair of the same aqueduct; but observing this rule, that no one of those who have a water right should pay an assessment of any kind: for it seems abominable that the houses of this generous city have to pay for water.

1. How did the emperors Theodosius and Valentinian finance maintenance of Constantinople's aqueducts?
2. Why was there no fee for water rights, according to the emperors? How else could we explain this imperial policy?
3. Imperial magistrates also contributed to the costs of aqueduct maintenance; for example, consuls were expected to give one hundred of gold for each year they were in office (*CJ* 12.3.3.1 Zeno 451 CE). In contrast, engineers and surveyors who build aqueducts were exempt from taxation (*CTh* 13.4.3). What principles explain the financing of aqueducts at Constantinople?
4. How does the finance model at Constantinople compare with Rome's (see Case 4.6, 4.19, 4.21, 4.26)? Which system would provide a more reliable funding and maintenance, and why?

Case 4.29. Accountability for Repairs

Codex Justinianus 11.43.8 Zeno A. Adamantio pu.

> Hac lege sancimus, ut, si quis amplissimam praefecturam gubernans aurum aquaeductui deputatum ad alterum quodlibet opus non aquaeductibus vel aquae publicae competens extruendum vel curandum putaverit convertendum, de suis facultatibus eandem summam aquaeductus titulo repensare cogatur. (1) Separatus vero arcarius aurum aquaeductus suscipiat gloriosissimorum consulum liberalitate vel ex aliis titulis ad aquas publicas pertinentibus collectum vel postea colligendum.

Emperor Zeno Augustus to Adamantius, City Prefect, between 474 and 479 CE

> By this law we decree that if anyone governing this most magnificent prefecture thinks that gold assigned to the aqueduct should be directed to building or maintaining some other public work and not to the aqueducts or public water, he will be compelled to pay back the same amount from his own resources to the aqueduct account. (1) The treasurer shall receive and keep separate the gold for the aqueduct whether it has been collected or is to be collected later from the generosity of our most illustrious consuls or from other accounts relating to the public waters.

1. How are repairs to Constantinople's aqueducts financed? Which city official is responsible for managing the funds? How has Zeno changed the funding model in Theodosius' and Valentinian's constitution in the previous case?
2. What problems does Zeno attempt to solve with this constitution? Why might the governor divert funds from aqueducts to other public works?
3. How does the emperor attempt to ensure that sufficient funds are available to repair the city's aqueducts? What problems can you anticipate in enforcing this constitution?
4. Compare the right of management for aqueducts in different places and at different times in Rome's history. Who exercises the right? How were these individuals held accountable? Which system do you think

would be most effective at funding and performing maintenance on the aqueducts? Why?

Case 4.30. The Sign of the aquarius

Codex Justinianus 11.43.10.4 Imp. Zeno A. Spontio

> Universos autem aquarios vel aquarum custodes, quos hydrophylacas nominant, qui omnium aquaeductuum huius regiae urbis custodiae deputati sunt, singulis manibus eorum felici nomine nostrae pietatis impresso signari decernimus, ut huiusmodi adnotatione manifesti sint omnibus nec a procuratoribus domorum vel quolibet alio ad usus alios avellantur vel angariarum vel operarum nomine teneantur.

Emperor Zeno to Spontius, between 476 and 491 CE

> We decree that all the water men or guardians of the aqueducts, whom they call hydrophylakes (in Greek), who are charged with the care of all the aqueducts of this royal city, be marked on each of their hands with the blessed name of our reverence, so that by this mark they are clearly known to everyone and not pulled away by the managers of private houses or anyone else to other tasks and not detained for the imperial post or labor.

1. The water men or *aquarii* who managed and repaired the aqueducts were slaves owned by the emperor. What new conditions does this constitution impose on them?
2. While the Romans used branding or tattoos to punish slaves, slave owners also applied these marks to identify slaves as their property. Which purpose seems to best justify this constitution? Why?
3. What rationale does the emperor give for this new procedure? How convincing is the emperor's rationale for branding the water men?
4. Frontinus accuses the water men (*aquarii*) of arranging illegal taps on Rome's aqueducts (*Aq.* 74.2, 109). While there is no evidence for branding the aqueduct crews at Rome, they may also have been branded. Is there anything contradictory about slaves powerful enough to flout the law and yet forced to subject their bodies to branding? How can we explain this paradox?

IV. The Decree on the Venafrum Aqueduct

Case 4.31. Repairs and Special Treatment

Corpus Inscriptionum Latinarum 10.4842.8–20

Venafranorum nomin[e . . . . / Qui riui specus saepta fon[tes . . . .]que aquae [ducend]ae reficiundae / causa supra infraue libram [facti aedi]ficati structi sunt, siue quod / aliut opus eius aquae ducendae ref[ici]undae causa supra infraue libram / factum est, uti quidquid earum r[er]um factum est, ita esse habere itaque / reficere reponere restituere resarcire semel saepius, fistulas canales / tubos ponere, aperturam committere, siue quid aliut eius aquae ducen/dae causa opus [er]it, facere placet dum qui locus ager in fundo, qui / Q(uintus) Sirini (?) L(uci) f(ilius) Ter(etina) [est esseue] dicitur, et in fundo, qui L. Pompei M. f. Ter. Sullae / est esseue dicitur, m[acer]ia saeptus est, per quem locum subue quo loco / specus eius aquae p[erue]nit, ne ea maceria parsue quae eius maceriae / aliter diruatu[r tollat]ur, quam specus reficiundi aut inspiciendi cau/sa : [neue quid ibi pri]uati sit, quominus ea aqua ire fluere duciue poss[it / . . .

Decree on the Venafrum Aqueduct, lines 8–20

In the name of the people of Venafrum . . . . for the sake of repairing whatever canals, conduits, sluices, springs were made or built for conducting water above or below ground or any other work for conducting water above or below ground, it is decreed that any of these things is to be and remain as it has been made and so to rebuild, replace, restore, repair once or more often, to install pipes, channels, culverts and to make an opening in the aqueduct, or if any thing else will be needed for channeling water, provided that whatever place or field enclosed with masonry on the farm, which belongs or is said to belong to Quintus Sirinus, son of Lucius, of the tribe Terentina, and on the estate, which belongs or is said to belong to Lucius Pompeius Sulla son of Marcus of the tribe Terentina, where the water conduit crosses, neither the masonry or any part of it is to be demolished or pulled down, other than to repair or inspect the conduit. Nor shall any private property hinder the water from going, flowing or being conducted . . .

1. The decree on the aqueduct at Venafrum is only partially preserved. The stone is broken and abraded at the top so that only a few words from the first seven lines remain. The readable text begins in line eight, with a section on repairs. What types of repairs and maintenance are included in the right of management at Venafrum? Roman statutes often express the legal rules with several synonyms such as the different terms for repair in this case. Is this just legal formality or do these terms specify different types of necessary maintenance? Can you think of any type of repairs that would not be covered by this decree?
2. What exception does the law authorize for Sirinus and Pompeius? Why might these two landowners have enjoyed special treatment? What problems might result from this exception? What can you infer from this exception about the usual treatment of private property along the route of the aqueduct? See the next case for more protections for landowners.
3. How does the decree explain the purpose of the provisions on repairs? What other policy goals do these provisions advance?

Case 4.32. City, Citizens, and Clearway (Venafrum)

Corpus Inscriptionum Latinarum 10.4842.21–36

Dextra sinistraque circa eum riuom circaque / ea o[pera, quae eius aqu] ae ducendae causa facta sunt, octonos pedes agrum / [u]acuo[m esse placet]; p[e]r quem locum Venafranis eiue, qui Venafranorum / [nomine opus su]m[et], iter facere eius aquae ducendae operumue eius aquae / [ductus faciendor]u[m] reficiendorum quod eius s(ine) d(olo) m(alo) fiat, ius sit liceatque / quaeque ea[rum rer]um cuius faciendae reficiendae causa opus erunt, quo / proxume poterit, aduehere adferre adportare, quaeque inde exempta erunt / quam maxime aequaliter dextra sinistraque p(edes) VIII iacere, dum ob eas res damn[i] / infecti iurato promittatur earumque rerum omnium ita habendarum / colon(is) Ven[afra]nis ius potestatemque esse placet, dum ne ob id opus domi/nus eorum cuius agri lociue, per quem agrum locumue ea aqua ire fluere duciue solet, inuius fiat; neue ob id opus minus ex agro suo in partem agri / quam transire transferre transuertere recte possit; neue cui eorum, per quo/rum agros ea aqua ducitur, eum aquae ductum corrumpere abducere auer/tere facereue, quo minus ea aqua in oppidum Venafranorum recte duci fluere possit, liceat.

Decree on the Venafrum Aqueduct lines 21–36

It is decreed that there shall be eight feet of land clear around the channel and the structures which were built to conduct water. Across this place there is a right and it is permitted for the people of Venafrum and those, who undertake in the name of the people of Venafrum, work that can be done without malice, to make passage for channeling water or repairing the aqueduct's channel or structures, and also to bring in, convey, deliver those things which will be needed for building and repairing these structures by the shortest route possible to the aqueduct, and to leave lying there things which are dumped as evenly as possible within the eight-foot space on the right and the left sides [of the aqueduct], provided that a sworn guarantee against damage is promised for these activities. It is decreed that right and power over all these things belong to the colonists of Venafrum provided that the owner of the land and field across which the water goes, flows, or is conducted, is not unwilling and that he is no less able on account of this work to go, transport, and travel directly from one part of his field across into another, and that no one of those whose fields the aqueduct crosses be permitted to break, violate, divert, or do [anything] to make the water less able to be conducted or flow directly into the town of Venafrum.

1. This case continues the provisions on repairs to the Venafrum aqueduct (Case 4.31). What protections for the aqueduct's infrastructure does the decree establish? Is it the same as the clearway around Rome's aqueducts? What might account for any differences?
2. What legal powers did the town have to perform maintenance? The decree mentions the "the people of Venafrum" (*Venafrani*), but who exactly is meant? Compare the rules for maintenance of other city aqueducts. Which model is the best fit for a small city such as Venafrum?
3. Why might a landowner interfere with the repair of an aqueduct? It is likely that the Venafrum aqueduct delivered water both to the city and to private properties along its route outside the city. How does this

pattern of delivery complicate the enforcement of the provisions on repair?

4. How does the decree protect the rights of individuals whose land abuts the aqueduct? Are these protections adequate? Why or why not? How do these protections compare with the special treatment accorded to Sirinus and Pompeius in the preceding case?
5. A legal guarantee gave the landowner a right to sue for damage caused by the repairs. How adequate was this remedy? What circumstances might make it difficult for a landowner to prove his case?

Case 4.33. Private Delivery at Venafrum

Corpus Inscriptionum Latinarum 10.4842.37–50

Quaeque aqua in oppidum Venafranorum it fluit ducitur, eam aquam / distribuere discribere uendundi causa, aut ei rei uectigal inponere consti|tuere, IIuiro IIuiris praefec(to) praefectis eius coloniae ex maioris partis decuri/onum decreto, quod decretum ita factum erit, cum in decurionibus non minus / quam duae partes decurionum adfuerint, legemque ei dicere ex / decreto decurionum, quod ita ut supra scriptum est decretum erit, ius po/testatem[q]ue esse placet, dum ne ea aqua, quae ita distributa discripta deue qua / ita decretum erit, aliter quam fistulis plumbeis d(um) t(axat) ab riuo p(edes) L ducatur; neue / eae fistulae aut riuos nisi sub terra, quae terra itineris uiae publicae limi/tisue erit, ponantur conlocentur; neue ea aqua per locum priuatum in/uito eo, cuius is locus erit, ducatur. Quamque legem ei aquae tuendae op[e]/ribusue, quae eius aquae ductus ususue causa facta sunt erunt, tuendis/[IIuiri praefect]i [e]x decurion(um) decreto, quod ita ut s(upra) s(criptum) e(st) factum erit, / dixeri[nt]/ [eam . . . . . fir]mam ratamque esse placet.

Decree on the Venafrum Aqueduct, lines 37–43

It is decreed that the duumvir or duumvirs or the prefect or prefects in charge of this colony have the right and power to allot and assign for sale the water that goes, flows, or is conducted into the town of the Venafrani, or to impose or establish a fee, in accordance with a decree so enacted by a majority of the decurions, when no less than two thirds of the assembly are present, as has been written above, provided that the water, allotted and distributed as decreed, shall not be conducted in any other way than by lead pipes within fifty feet of the canal. Nor may these pipes or canals be laid or located anywhere except under ground which belongs to a public road, paths, or boundary lane. Nor should this water be conducted through private property if the owner, whose land it will be, is unwilling. It is decreed that the law which the duumviri and prefects proposed for protecting the water and the structures that have been and will be built to conduct and use the water, be binding and enacted in accordance with the decree of the decurions as written above.

1. Which magistrates have authority over private delivery from Venafrum's aqueduct? What rights and powers does the decree assign to these officials? Or, in other words, which component right or rights do these magistrates exercise?
2. How is private delivery organized at Venafrum? In this case the verb "sell" probably refers to a contract with a fee for use, as it does in Frontinus (Case 4.6). The water contracts at Venafrum may have had a term of five years, like public contracts arranged by the censors in Rome. Alternatively, they could have lasted as long as the same person owned the property (like private delivery from Rome's aqueducts), or they may have been perpetual (like servitudes). How would these different terms affect the costs and benefits for individual and for the city?
3. The Venafrum decree does not limit private grants to *aqua caduca*, as do the laws from Rome and Urso. What are the consequences of this omission? Consider the impact on both private individuals and the public supply.
4. The aqueduct and the water in it were public property of Venafrum, but some of the infrastructure was located outside the aqueduct's clearway, such as the pipes for private delivery: where were they located? A boundary or *limes* marked the division between two parcels when Roman surveyors organized the farms, but it also served as a road or path, something like the gravel roads at one-mile intervals across farmland in some regions of the United States. Given the location of the pipes, what potential problems could arise in exercising the right of management on this infrastructure?

5. How do these provisions add to the protections for private property near the aqueduct? Do you think this protection is sufficient? Why or why not?
6. Compare the system of private delivery at Rome, Constantinople, Urso, and Venafrum: which system do you think is best, and why? Be sure to consider fairness, efficiency, and the policy issues that are articulated for each city.

Case 4.34. Legal Procedure for Claims (Venafrum)

Corpus Inscriptionum Latinarum 10.4842.62–69

> . . .]atio quam colono aut incola[e aut . . .] / da [. . .] i [. . .] is cui ex decreto decurionum, ita ut supra comprensum est, ne/gotium datum erit, agenti, tum, qui inter ciuis et peregrinos ius dicet, iudicium / reciperatorium in singulas res HS X reddere, testibusque dumtaxat X denun|tiand[o q]uaeri placet; dum reciperatorum reiectio inter eum qui aget et / eum quocum agetur ita fi[et ut ex lege, q]uae de iudicis priuatis lata est / licebit oportebit.

Decree on the Venafrum Aqueduct lines 62–69

> . . . as to a colonist or a resident . . . the person to whom the case is assigned in accordance with the decurion's decree, as provided above, when he brings an action, it is decreed that the praetor, who has jurisdiction for cases between citizens and foreigners, grant a recuperatory action for ten thousand sesterces for each individual claim to the person bringing the action, and for questioning of up to ten witnesses by formal summons, provided that the choice of arbiters (i.e. recuperators) between the one who sues and the one who is sued, is made as it is permissible and right according to the law about private suits.

1. This case describes part of the legal procedure for claims about the aqueduct at Venafrum. It is not known whether the decree listed the causes of action or types of disputes, because the stone is broken and part of this section is missing. Who can bring a legal action about the aqueduct? Whose interests does this prosecutor represent?
2. Which magistrate had jurisdiction over these claims? The peregrine praetor was one of Rome's city magistrates who had jurisdiction for

legal matters involving citizens and noncitizens. Legal claims about the Venafrum aqueduct may have been heard in Rome because the aqueduct was an imperial gift. How did the location or venue affect litigants' ability to pursue their claims?

3. What kind of legal action is available for resolving disputes about the Venafrum aqueduct? In a recuperatory a board of *recuperatores* or arbiters served as a jury with three or five members that passed judgment in expedited hearings. What details of the procedure described here would shorten the time to judgment? Why was speed important in resolving disputes about water rights?

Case 4.35 Marking the Venafrum Clearway

Corpus Inscriptionum Latinarum 10.4843

iussu imp(eratoris) Caesaris / Augusti circa eum / rivom qui aquae / ducendae causa / factus est octonos / ped(ibus) ager dextra / sinistraq(ue) vacuus / relictus est

Boundary Stone for the Venafrum Clearway

By the order of the emperor Caesar Augustus, the land eight feet to the right and to the left are to be left vacant around this canal that was made for conducting water.

1. This case presents the text written on a boundary stone from the clearway to the Venafrum aqueduct. Is its description of the clearway consistent with the decree?
2. Why were boundary stones like this erected along the clearway of the Venafrum aqueduct? Would the stone have the same function where the aqueduct ran on arcades as where it ran underground? Boundary stones were also installed along Rome's aqueducts first during the reign of Augustus. They may have been placed about seventy meters apart, although too few have been found in place to be certain of the usual interval.
3. Would boundary stones be effective in deterring damage to the aqueducts or illegal withdrawals, as prohibited in other provisions of the decree? Why or why not?

4. Why does the inscription mention the emperor Augustus? For us, his name shows that he played a role in building the aqueduct, which was one of several public works that he sponsored when he established a colony at Venafrum in the late first century BCE. Why would an emperor sponsor an aqueduct in a small town like Venafrum? How do the politics of building an aqueduct in a small town like Venafrum compare with the situation at Rome or Constantinople?

Bibliography

ABBREVIATIONS

The titles of journals in Classical Studies follow abbreviations in *l'Année Philologique*.

GENERAL WORKS ON ROMAN LAW AND ROMAN WATER LAW

Costa, E. 1919. *Le acque nel diritto romano*. Bologna: Zanichelli.

Diósdi, G. 1970. *Ownership in Ancient and Preclassical Roman Law*. Budapest: Akadémiai Kiadó.

Du Plessis, P. 2015. *Borkowski's Textbook on Roman Law*. 5th ed. Oxford: Oxford University Press.

Fischer, R. 1996. *Umweltschützende Bestimmungen im römischen Recht*. Aachen: Shaker Verlag.

Franciosi, G. 1997. "Regime delle acque e paesaggio in età repubblicana." In *Uomo, acqua e paesaggio: Atti dell'incontro di studio sul tema irreggimentazione delle acque e trasformazione del paesaggio antico*, edited by A. Coen and S. Quilici Gigli, 11–19. Rome: "L'Erma" di Bretschneider.

Geißler, K. 1998. *Die öffenliche Wasserversorgung im römischen Recht*. Berlin: Duncker & Humblot.

Gerez Kraemer, G. M. 2008. *El derecho des aguas en Roma*. Madrid: Dykinson.

Glick, T. 1970. *Irrigation and Society in Medieval Valencia*. Cambridge, MA: Harvard University Press.

Hausmanninger, H., and R. Gamauf. 2012. *A Casebook on Roman Property Law*. Translated by G. S. Sheets. Oxford: Oxford University Press.

Honoré, A. M. 1961. "Ownership." In *Oxford Essays in Jurisprudence*, edited by A. G. Guest. Oxford: Oxford University Press.

Jakab, E. 2015. "Property Rights in Ancient Rome." In *Ownership and Exploitation of Land and Natural Resources in the Roman World*, edited by P. Erdkamp, K. Verboven, and A. Zuiderhoek, 107–31. Oxford: Oxford University Press.

Longo, G. 1966. "Sull'uso delle acque pubbliche in diritto Romano." In *Ricerche romanistiche*, 149–77. Milan: A. Giuffrè. Originally published in *Studia in memoria di Umberto Ratti*, edited by E. Albertario, 51–96. Milan: A. Giuffrè, 1934.

Lucarelli, A. 2012. "La nature juridique de l'eau entre bien public et bien commun." In *L'environnement, notre patrimoine commun, et son État gardien*, edited by P. Halley and J. Sotousek, 143–55. Cowansville: Éditions Yvon Blais.

Masi Doria, C. 2003. "Modificazione e estinzione di rapporti giuridici reali per causa delle acque: Un esempio della relazione tra nature e ius; Diritto romano e codificazioni." In *Modelli teorici e metodologici nella storia del diritto privato*, AAVV, 277–304. Naples: Jovene.

Santucci, G., A. Simonati, and F. Cortese, eds. 2011. *L'acqua e il diritto*. Trento: Litotipografia Alcione.

Watson, A. 1968. *The Law of Property in the Later Roman Republic*. Oxford: Clarendon Press.

EDITIONS AND COMMENTARIES OF ROMAN SOURCES

Amanuensis. Copyright 2015. http://www.riedlberger.de/08amanuensis.html

Beltrán Lloris, F. 2006. "An Irrigation Decree from Roman Spain: The Lex Rivi Hiberiensis." *JRS* 96:147–97. First published in *l'Année Epigraphique* (*AE*) 1993 1043.

Birks, P., A. Rodger, and J. S. Richardson. 1984. "Further Aspects of the Tabula Contrebiensis." *JRS* 74:45–73.

Crawford, M. H. 1996. "Lex Colonia Genetivae Iuliae." In *Roman Statutes*, edited by M. H. Crawford, 1:393–454. London: Institute of Classical Studies.

Crawford, M. H. 1996. *Roman Statutes*. 2 vols. London: Institute of Classical Studies.

Crook, J. A. 1996. "Leges de aquis." In *Roman Statutes*, edited by M. H. Crawford, 2:729–30. London: Institute of Classical Studies.

Crook, J. A. 1996. "Lex Sulpicia." In *Roman Statutes*, edited by M. H. Crawford, 2.727–28. London: Institute of Classical Studies.

Evans, H. B. 1994. *Water Distribution in Ancient Rome: The Evidence of Frontinus*. Ann Arbor: University of Michigan Press.

Frier, B. W., ed. 2016. *The Codex of Justinian: A New Annotated Translation*. Cambridge: Cambridge University Press.

Maganzani, L. 2012. "Cd. Aqua Vegetiana." In *Revisione ed integrazione dei Fontes Iuris Romani Anteiustiniani (FIRA), studi preparatori*. 1, *Leges*, edited by G. Purpura, 159–64. Turin: G. Giappichelli Editore.

Maganzani, L. 2012. "Edictum Augusti de aquaeductu Venafrano." In *Revisione ed integrazione dei Fontes Iuris Romani Anteiustiniani (FIRA), studi preparatori*. 1, *Leges*, edited by G. Purpura, 125–34. Turin: G. Giappichelli Editore.

Maganzani, L. 2102. "Lex rivi Hiberiensis." In *Revisione ed integrazione dei Fontes Iuris Romani Anteiustiniani (FIRA), studi preparatori.* 1, *Leges,* edited by G. Purpura, 171–86. Turin: G. Giappichelli Editore.

Maganzani, L. 2012. "Senatusconsulta de aquis e lex Quinctia de aquaeductibus." In *Revisione ed integrazione dei Fontes Iuris Romani Anteiustiniani (FIRA), studi preparatori.* 1, *Leges,* edited by G. Purpura, 135–52. Turin: G. Giappichelli Editore.

Maganzani, L. 2012. "Tabula aquaria di Amiternum." In *Revisione ed integrazione dei Fontes Iuris Romani Anteiustiniani (FIRA), studi preparatori.* 1, *Leges,* edited by G. Purpura, 121–24. Turin: G. Giappichelli Editore.

Maganzani, L. 2012. "Tabula di Lamasba." In *Revisione ed integrazione dei Fontes Iuris Romani Anteiustiniani (FIRA), studi preparatori.* 1, *Leges,* edited by G. Purpura, 195–213. Turin: G. Giappichelli Editore.

Purpura, G., ed. 2012. *Revisione ed integrazione dei Fontes Iuris Romani Anteiustiniani (FIRA), studi preparatori.* 2 vols. Turin: G. Giappichelli Editore.

Rechtshistorie: A Gateway to Legal History. https://www.rechtshistorie.nl/en/roman-law

Richardson, J. S. 1983. "The *Tabula Contrebiensis*: Roman Law in Spain in the Early First Century B.C.: I." *JRS* 73:33–41.

Rodgers, R. H., ed. 2004. *Frontinus: De Aquaeductu Urbis Romae.* Cambridge: Cambridge University Press.

Rodgers, R. H. 2003. Translation of Frontinus, On the Water-Management of the City of Rome. http://www.uvm.edu/~rrodgers/Frontinus.html

Roman Law Resources. http://iuscivile.com/

Shaw, B. D. 1982. "Lamasba: An Ancient Irrigation Community." *Ant. Afr.* 18:61–103.

The Roman Law Library. https://droitromain.univ-grenoble-alpes.fr/

Ware, E. F. 1985. *Roman Water Law.* Reprint, Littleton, CO: Fred B. Rothman. First published, 1905.

Watson, A., trans. 2009. *The Digest of Justinian.* 4 vols. Rev. ed. Philadelphia: University of Pennsylvania Press.

THE ACTIO AQUAE PLUVIAE ARCENDAE

Agnati, U. 2000. *Le Dodici Tavole: il versetto VII, 8 e l' "actio aquae pluviae arcendae."* Cagliari: Ed. AV.

Bretone, M. 2007. "Labeone e l'ordine della natura." In *Testi e problemi del giusnaturalismo romano,* edited by D. Mantovani and A. Sciavone, 249–69. Pavia: IUSS Press.

Burckhard, H. 1881. *L'Actio aquae pluviae arcendae.* Erlangen: Palm & Enke.

Donadio, N. 2014. "'Locus inferior naturaliter superiori seruit': di un'antica *regula iuris* in tema di scolo dell'acqua piovana tra fondi attigui." *RIDA* 3e sér., 61:149–93.

Gerkens, J.-F. 1995. "Exégèse de Paul. D. 39,3 (*de aqua et aquae pluviae arcendae*), 2,6." *RHD* 63:11–26.

Kacprzak, A. 2007. "L'actio aquae pluviae arcendae ed il concetto labeoniano di natura." In *Testi e problemi del giusnaturalismo romano*, edited by D. Mantovani and A. Sciavone, 271–98. Pavia: IUSS Press.

Rodger, A. 1972. *Owners and Neighbors in Roman Law*. Oxford: Clarendon Press.

Sargenti, M. 1940. *L'actio aquae pluviae arcendae: Contributo alla dottrina della responsabilita per danno nel diritto romano*. Milan: A. Giuffrè.

Sitzia, F. 2016. "D. 39. 3. 24 e « opus agri colendi causa factum." *SDHI* 82: 99–115.

Sitzia, F. 1999. Aqua pluvia *e* natura agri: *Dalle XII tavole al pensiero di Labeone*. Cagliari: Edizioni A.V.

Sitzia, F.1977. *Ricerche in tema di "actio aquae pluviae arcendae": Dalle XII tavole all'epoca classica*. Milan: A. Giuffrè.

SERVITUDES

Bannon, C. J. 2016. "Ancient Roman Water Rights and Commons Theory." In *Politics of Fresh Water: Access, Conflict and Identity*, edited by C. M. Ashcraft and T. Mayer, 14–27. New York: Routledge.

Bannon, C. J. 2009. *Gardens and Neighbors: Private Water Rights in Roman Italy*. Ann Arbor: University of Michigan Press.

Basile, R. 2012. *'Usus servitutis' e tutela interdittale*. Milan: CEDAM.

Bonneau, D. 1984–1985. "Les servitudes de l'eau dans la documentation papyrologique." In *Sodalitas: Scritti in onore di Antonio Guarino*, edited by V. Giuffrè, 5:2273–85. Naples: Jovene.

Capogrossi Colognesi, L. 1999. *Proprietà e diritti reali: Usi e tutela della proprietà fondiaria nel diritto romano*. Rome: Il Cigno Galileo Galilei.

Capogrossi Colognesi, L. 1966. *Ricerche sulla struttura delle servitù d'acqua in diritto romano*. Milan: A. Giuffrè.

Grosso, G. 1969. *Le servitù prediali nel diritto romano*. Turin: G. Giappichelli Editore.

Grosso, G. 1932. "Sulla servitù di *aquae haustus*." *BIDR* 40:401–36.

Martin. S. D. 1986. "The Case of the Collapsing Watercourse: Builders' Responsibility for Damage in Classical Roman Law." *Law and History Review* 4:423–38.

Masuelli, S. 2009. *La refectio nelle servitù prediali*. Naples: Jovene.

Möller, C. 2010. *Die Servituten: Entwicklungsgeschichte, Funktion und Struktur der grundstückvermittelten Privatrechtsverhältnisse im römischen Recht*. Göttingen: Wallstein.

Rainer, J. M. 2013. "Die Überwindung des Ersitzungsverbotes von Dienstbarkeiten der lex Scribonia durch Ulpian." In *Liber amicorum: Christoph Krampe zum 70. Geburtstag*, edited by M. Armgardt, F. Klinck, and I. Reichard, 279–88. Berlin: Dunker & Humblot.

Rodger, A. 1989. "The Position of Aquae Ductus in the Praetor's Edict." In *New Perspectives in the Roman Law of Property*, edited by P. Birks, 177–84. Oxford: Clarendon.

Solazzi, S. 1949. *La tutela e il possesso delle servitù prediali.* Naples: Jovene.

Solazzi, S. 1948. *Specie ed estinzione delle servitù prediali.* Naples: Jovene.

INTERDICTS: RIVERS AND SEAS

Albanese, B. 1991. "L'edictum vetus su qui flumina retanda publice redempta habent." *Annali de Seminario Giuridico della Università di Palermo* 41:17–29.

Albertario, E. 1930. "Le derivazioni d'acqua dai fiumi pubblici in diritto romano." *BIDR* 38:197–214.

Alburquerque, J. M. 2002. *La protección o defensa el uso colectivo de las cosas de dominio público: Especial referencia a los interdictos de publicis locis (loca, itinere, viae, flumina, ripae).* Madrid: Dykinson.

Anagnostou-Canas, B. 1994. "Les différends concernant l'eau dans l'Égypte romaine." In *Les problèmes institutionnels de l'eau en Égypte ancienne et dans l'Antiquité méditerranéenne*, edited by B. Menu, 15–28. Cairo: Institut français d'archéologie orientale.

Bannon, C. 2017. "Rivers, Rights, 'Romanization.'" In *Ancient Law, Ancient Society*, edited by D. P. Kehoe and T. A. J. McGinn, 66–83. Ann Arbor: University of Michigan Press.

Bonneau, D. 1994. "Usage et usages de l'eau dans l'Égypte ptolémaïque et romaine." In *Les problèmes institutionnels de l'eau en Égypte ancienne et dans l'Antiquité méditerranéenne*, edited by B. Menu, 47–71. Cairo: Institut français d'archéologie orientale.

Bonneau, D. 1982. "Le souverain d'Égypte, judge de l'usage de l'eau." In *L'Homme et l'eau en Méditerranée et au Proche Orient. 2, Aménagements hydraulics, état et législation*, edited by F. Metral and J. Metral, 69–80. Lyon: GIS, Maison de l'Orient, Presses Universitaires de Lyon.

Bonneau, D. 1971. *Le fisc et le Nil: Incidences des irrégularités de la crue du Nil sur la fiscalité foncière dans l'Égypte grecque et romaine.* Paris: Editions Cujas.

Brugi, B. 1930. "Fiumi compresi nei lotti dei coloni romani." In *Studi in onore di Pietro Bonfante nel XL anno d'insegnamento*, 361–66. Milan: Fratelli Treves Editore.

Campbell, B. 2012. *Rivers and the Power of Ancient Rome.* Chapel Hill: University of North Carolina Press.

Capogrossi Colognesi, L. 2014. "La lex rivi Hiberiensis e gli schemi delle servitù d'acqua in diritto romano." In *Lex Rivi Hiberiensis: Diritto e tecnica in una comunità di irrigazione della Spagna romana*, edited by L. Maganzani and C. Buzzacchi, 75–91. Naples: Jovene.

De Marco, N. 2004. *I* loci publici *dal I al III secolo: Le identificazioni dottrinali, il ruolo dell'usus, gli strumenti di tutela.* Naples: Satura.

Di Lella, L. 2004. "La tutela interdittale dei luoghi pubblici." In *Espaces intégrés et ressources naturelles dans l'Empire romain*, edited by M. Clavel-Lévèque and E. Hermon, 193–96. Besançon: Presses Universitaires de Franche-Comté.

Di Porto, A. 2013. Res in usu publico *e "beni comuni": Il nodo della tutela*. Turin: G. Giappichelli Editore.

Di Porto, A. 1988. "La tutela della salubritas fra editto e giurisprudenza: Il ruolo di Labeone." *BIDR* 30:459–570.

Dursi, D. 2017. *Res communes omnium. Dalle necessità economiche alla disciplina guiridica*. Naples: Jovene.

Fiorentini, M. 2010a. "L'acqua da bene economico a 'res communis ominum' a bene colletivo." *Analisi Giuridica dell'Economia* 1:39–78.

Fiorentini, M. 2010b. "*Fructus* e *delectatio* nel uso del mare e nell'occupazione delle coste nell'età imperiale romana." In Riparia *dans l'Empire romain pour la définition du concept*, edited by E. Hermon, 263–82. Oxford: J. and E. Hedges.

Fiorentini, M. 2003. *Fiumi e mari nell'esperienza giuridica romana*. Milan: A. Giuffrè.

Frier, B. W. 2019. "The Roman Origins of the Public Trust Doctrine." *JRA* 32:641–47.

Grosso, G. 1931. "Appunti sulle derivazioni dai fiumi pubblici nel diritto romano (Aproposito di uno studio di Emilio Albertario)." *Atti Reale accademia delle scienze di Torino: Classi de scienze morali, storiche e filologiche* 66:369–91.

Kehoe, D. P. 2008. "Economics and the Law of Water Rights in the Roman Empire." In *Vers une gestion intégrée de l'eau dans l'Empire romain: Actes du colloque international Université Laval, octobre 2006*, edited by E. Hermon, 243–51. Rome: "L'Erma" di Bretschneider.

Maddalena, P. 1970. *Gli incrementi fluvial nella visione giurisprudenziale classica*. Naples: Jovene.

Maganzani, L. 2012. "Le comunità di irrigazione nel mondo romano: Appunti sulla documentazione epigrafica, giuridica, letteraria." In *Revisione ed integrazione dei Fontes Iuris Romani Anteiustiniani (FIRA), studi preparatori*. 1, *Leges*, edited by G. Purpura, 103–19. Turin: G. Giappichelli Editore.

Marzano, A. 2017. *Harvesting the Sea: The Exploitation of Marine Resources in the Roman Mediterranean*. Oxford: Oxford University Press.

Masi Doria, C. 2014. "Litus maris: definition et controverses." In Riparia, *un patrimoine culturel: La gestion intégrée des bords de l'eau*, edited by E. Hermon and A. Watelet, 233–42. Oxford: Archaeopress.

Meuret, C. 1996. "Le règlement de Lamasba: des tables de conversion appliquées à l'irrigation." *Antiquités africaines* 32: 87–112.

Mommsen, T. 1881. "Inscrift aus Caiatia." *Hermes* 16:495–98.

Nörr, D. 2008. "Prozessuales (und mehr) in der *lex rivi Hiberiensis*." *ZRG* 125:108–88.

Orestano, R. 1935. "Concessione personale e concessione realie dello ius aquae ducendae ex castello (contributo all'esegesi dell fr. 1.38–44 D. 43.20 di Ulpiano)." *BIDR* 43:297–313.

Pavese, M. P. 2004. *Fundus cum vadis et alluvionibus: Gli incrementi fluviali fra documenti della prassi e riflessione giurisprudenziale romana.* Rome: "L'Erma" di Bretschneider.

Rodger, A. 1987. "The Rise and Fall of Roman Lakes." *RHD* 55:19–29.

Santini, P. 2012. "*. . . si piscari prohibeatur, utile interdictum competere. . .* : Alle radici di un equivoco in tema di tutela interdittale delle acque." In *Per una comune cultura dell'acqua dal Mediterraneo all'America del Nord,* edited by F. Nasti and F. Reduzzi, 60–70. Cassino: Università degli studi di Cassino e del Lazio Meridionale.

Schiavon, A. 2011. "Aqua e diritto romano: 'invenzione' di un modello?" In *L'acqua e diritto,* edited by G. Santucci, A. Simonati, and F. Cortese, 117–81. Trento: Litotipografia Alcione-Lavis.

Solazzi, S. 1941. "*Usus proprius.*" *SDHI* 7:373–420.

Stagl, J. F. 2017. "Die Funktionen der *utilitas publica.*" *ZRG* 134 (1): 514–24.

Tomás, G. 2001. "Limitations à la propriété riveraine et libre navigation fluviale." *RIDA* 48:361–72.

Uribe, P., A. Magallón, and J. Fanlo. 2012. "New Evidence on Roman Water Supply in the Ebro Valley: The Roman Dam of Muel (Zaragoza, Spain)." In *The Archaeology of Water Supply,* edited by M. Żuchowska, 75–83. British Archaeological Reports: International Series 2414. Oxford: Archaeopress.

Vigano, R. 1969. "Sull'edictum de fluminibus retandis." *Labeo* 15:168–77.

Zoz, M. G. 2007. "Idee vecchie e nuove in tema di acque pubbliche interne." In *Fides humanitas ius: Studi in onore di L. Labruna,* 9:6079–6113. Naples: Editoriale Scientifia.

AQUEDUCTS

Aicher, P. 1995. *Guide to the Aqueducts of Ancient Rome.* Wauconda, IL: Bolchazy-Carducci.

Ashby, T. 1935. *The Aqueducts of Ancient Rome.* Oxford: Clarendon.

Atlas Project of Roman Aqueducts. https://www.romaq.org/

Bedello Tata, M., É. Bukowiecki, M. A. Ricciardi, L. Lombardi, A. Carbonara, M.-C. Vittori, P. Vori et al. 2006. "Le acque e gli acquedotti nel territorio Ostiense e Portuense: Ritrovamenti e ricerche recenti." *MEFRA* 118 (2): 463–526.

Bedon, R. 1997. *Les aqueducs de la Gaule romaine et des régions voisines.* Limoges: Presses Universitaires de Limoges.

Biavaschi, P. 2014. "Dalla scrittura su tabulae alla scrittura sulla pelle: Il valore del documento scritto nelle costituzioni del titolo De Aquaeductus del Codice Teodosiano." In *Ravenna Capitale,* 95–118. Santarcangelo di Romagna: Maggioli Editore.

Bruun, C. 2015. "Water Use and Productivity in Roman Agriculture." In *Ownership and Exploitation of Land and Natural Resources in the Roman World*, edited by P. Erdkamp, K. Verboven, and A. Zuiderhoek, 132–49. Oxford: Oxford University Press.

Bruun, C. 2012. "Roman Emperors and Legislation on Public Water Use in the Roman Empire: Clarifications and Problems." *Water History* 4:11–33.

Bruun, C. 2007. "Why Did Frontinus Write *de aquaeductu*?" *JRA* 20 (2): 460–66.

Bruun, C. 2004. "The Impossibility of Reaching an Exact Value for the Roman *quinaria* Measure." In Frontinus, *De aquaeductu urbis Romae*. Edited by R. H. Rodgers, 342–46 Cambridge: Cambridge University Press.

Bruun, C. 1991. *The Water Supply of Ancient Rome: A Study of Roman Imperial Administration*. Helsinki: Societas Scientiarum Fennica.

Buonocore, M. 1994. "Fra topografia ed epigrafia: L'acquedotto di *Amiternum* (L'Aquila)." *JAT* 4:185–94.

Burnand, Y. 1983. "La documentation épigraphique sur les aqueducs de la Gaule et de la Germanie romaines." In *Journées d'études sur les aqueducs Romains, Lyon (26–28 mai 1977)*, edited by J.-P. Boucher, 51–73. Paris: Les Belles Lettres.

Cantarelli, L. 1901. "La serie dei curatores aquarum." *BCAR* 29:180–214.

Coste J., and P. Schutzmann-Bolzon. 1970. "Roma (Agro romano): Il cippo arcaico della tenuta Sbardella." *NSA*, ser. 8, 24:364–71.

Crook, J. A. 1986. "*Lex 'rivalicia'* (*FIRA* 1 no. 5)." *Athenaeum* 74 (n.s. 64): 45–53.

Crow, J., J. Bardill, and R. Bayliss. 2008. *The Water Supply of Byzantine Constantinople*. London: Society for the Promotion of Roman Studies.

De Kleijn, G. 2001. *The Water Supply of Ancient Rome: City Area, Water, and Population*. Amsterdam: Gieben.

Del Chicca, F., ed. 2004. *Frontino. "De aquae ductu urbis Romae."* Rome: Herder.

de Robertis, F. M. 1938. "Costituzione 'ex castello' e costituzione 'aliunde' nella 'servitus aquae ducendae' (a proposito del fr. 9 Dig. 8, 3, Paulus, libro 1. Sententiarum)." *Annali della Facoltà di Giurisprudenza, Università degli studi, Bari* 1:61–98.

Hainzmann, M. 1975. *Untersuchungen zur Geschichte und Verwaltung der Stadtrömischen Wasserleitungen*. Vienna: Verband der wissenschaftlichen Gesellschaften Österreichs.

Hinker, H. 1992. "Grundzüge des öffentlichen römischen Wasserrechts." In *Vestigia iuris romani: Festschrift für Gunter Wesener zum 60. Geburtstag am 3. Juni 1992*, edited by G. Klingenberg, H. Stiegler, and J. M. Rainer, 177–86. Graz: Leykam.

Hodge, A. T. 2013. "Aqueducts and Water Supply." In *A Companion to the Archaeology of the Roman Republic*, edited by J. DeRose Evans, 285–95. Chichester: Wiley-Blackwell.

Hodge, A. T. 1991. *Roman Aqueducts and Water Supply*. London: Duckworth.

Kahane, H. R. 1940. "Italo-byzantinische Etymologien: *scala*." *Byzantinisch-neugriechische Jahrbücher* 16:33–58.

König, A. 2007. "Knowledge and Power in Frontinus' *On aqueducts*." In *Ordering Knowledge in the Roman Empire*, edited by J. König and T. Whitmarsh, 177–205. Cambridge: Cambridge University Press.

Lanciani, R. 1975. *Le acque e gli acquedotti di Roma antica*. Roma: Edizioni Quasar. Reprint of "Topografia di Roma antica: I commentarii di Frontino intorno le acque e gli acquedotti; Silloge epigrafica aquaria." *Memorie della Romana Accademia dei Lincei*, ser. 3, 4:215–616.

Maganzani, L. 2004. "L'approvvigionamento idrico degli edifici urbani nei testi della giurisprudenza classica: Contributi giuridici alle ricerche sugli acquedotti di Roma antica." In *Acque per l'utilitas, per la salubritas, per l'amoenitas*, edited by M. A. Gallina, 185–220. Milan: Edizioni ET.

Mateo, A. 1996. "Sobre la supuesta lex Sulpicia rivalicia." *RIDA* 62:287–308.

Mommsen, T. 1850. "Römische Urkunden." *ZRG* 15 (3): 287–371 = *Gesammelte Schriften* 3:75–124. *Gesammelte Schriften*. 8 vols. Berlin: Weidmann, 1907.

Pagano, M. 1996. "Note su alcuni acquedotti romani in Campania." In *Cura aquarum in Campania*, edited by N. De Haan and G. C. M. Jansen, 101–8. Leiden: Stichting Babesch.

Palma, A. 1987. "Derivazioni di acqua 'ex castello.'" *Index* 20:439–57.

Peachin, M. P. 2004. *Frontinus and the* curae *of the* curator aquarum. Stuttgart: Franz Steiner Verlag.

Reduzzi Merola, F. 2007. "*Mutilare commoda urbis* e derivazioni abusive d'acqua." In *Scritti in onore di G. Nicosia*, 485–94. Milan: A. Giuffrè.

Roman Aqueducts. http://www.romanaqueducts.info/

Tarpin, M. 2002. Vici *et* pagi *dans l'occident romain*. Rome: École française de Rome.

Taylor, R. A. 1997. "Torrent or Trickle? The Aqua Alsietina, the Naumachia Augusti, and the Transtiberim." *AJA* 101:465–92.

Vallocchia, F. 2012. *Studi sugli acquedotti pubblici romani*. 1, *La struttura giuridica*. Naples: Jovene.

Waters of the City of Rome. Last modified 27 September 2017. http://www3.iath.virginia.edu/waters/

GENERAL WORKS ON WATER AND THE ENVIRONMENT IN THE ROMAN WORLD

Arenillas, M., and J. C. Castillo. 2003. "Dams from the Roman Era in Spain: Analysis of Design Forms." In *Proceedings of the First International Congress on Construction History*. Madrid: Instituto Juan de Herrera.

Argoud, G., L. Marankou, V. Panagiotopoulos, and C. Villain-Gandossi, eds. 1992. *L'eau et les hommes en Méditerranée et en mer Noire dans l'Antiquité*. Athens: Centre National de Recherches Sociales and Centre de Recherches Néo-Helléniques.

Beltrán Lloris, F. 2014a. "Irrigation Infrastructures in the Roman West: Typology,

Financing, Management." In *Infrastruktur und Herrschaftsorganisation im Imperium romanum*, edited by A. Kolb, 121–36. Berlin: De Gruyter.

Beltrán Lloris, F. 2014b. "I pagi e l'organizzazione dell'irrigazione in Caesar Augusta." In *Lex Rivi Hiberiensis: Diritto e tecnica in una comunità di irrigazione della Spagna romana*, edited by L. Maganzani and C. Buzzacchi, 55–73. Naples: Jovene.

Bergamini, M., ed. 1991. *Gli Etruschi maestri di idraulica*. Perugia: Electa, Editori Umbri.

Bianco, A. D. 2007. Aqua ducta, aqua distributa: *La gestione delle risorse idriche in età romana*. Turin: Silvio Zamorani.

Biundo, R. 2008. "*Aqua publica:* propriété et gestion de l'eau dans l'économie des cités de l'Empire." In *Le quotidien municipal dans l'Occident romain*, edited by C. Berrendonner, M. Cébeillac-Gervasoni, and L. Lamoine, 365–77. Clermont-Ferrand: Presses Universitaires Blaise Pascal.

Biundo, R. 2007. "Gestion intégrée de l'eau dans l'histoire environnementale: savoirs traditionnels et pratiques modernes." *Index* 35:415–23.

Biundo, R. 2006. "La gestion publique de l'eau: finances municipales et centre du pouvoir à l'époque impériale." In *Vers une gestion intégrée de l'eau dans l'Empire romain*, edited by E. Hermon, 163–74. Rome: "L'Erma" di Bretschneider.

Bonneau, D. 1964. *La crue du ile: divinité egyptienne*. Paris: Librairie C. Klincksieck.

Bruun, C. 2013. "Water Supply, Drainage, and Water Mills." In *The Cambridge Companion to Ancient Rome*, edited by P. Erdkamp, 297–313. Cambridge: Cambridge University Press.

Bruun, C. 2006. "Inscriptions on Lead Pipes." In *The Horace's Villa Project 1997–2003*, edited by B. Frischer and J. Crawford, 295–301. Oxford: Archaeopress.

Butzer, K. W., J. F. Mateu, E. K. Butzer, and P. Kraus. 1985. "Irrigation Agrosystems in Eastern Spain: Roman or Islamic Origins?" *Annals of the Association of American Geographers* 4:479–509.

Cangelosi, E. 2014. Publica *e* communis: *Acqua, mondo romano e beni comuni*. Rome: Aracne editrice.

Clavel-Lévèque, M., and E. Hermon, eds. 2004. *Espaces intégrés et ressources naturelles dans l'Empire romain*. Besançon: Presses Universitaires de Franche-Comté.

Coen, A., and S. Quilici Gigli, eds. 1997. *Uomo, acqua e paesaggio*. Rome: "L'Erma" di Bretschneider.

De Haan, N., and G. C. M. Jansen, eds. 1996. *Cura Aquarum in Campania*. Leiden: Stichting Babesch.

De Ruggiero, E. 1895. "Aqua-aquaeductus." In *Dizionario epigrafico di antichità romane*. 1:537–88. Rome: Istituto Italiano per la Storia Antica.

Di Porto, A. 2014. *Salubritas e forme di tutela in età romana*. Turin: G. Giappichelli Editore.

Eck, W. 2008. *Roms Wassermanagement im Osten: Staatliche Steuerung des öffentlichen Lebens in den römischen Provinzen.* Kassel: Kassel University Press.

Eck, W. 1995. *Die Verwaltung des römischen Reiches in der hohen Kaiserzeit.* Basel: Reinhardt.

Eck, W. 1987. "Die Wasserversorgung im römischen Reich: Sozio-politische Bedingungen, Recht und Administration." In *Geschichte der Wasserversorgung.* Vol. 2, *Die Wasserversorgung antiker Städte,* edited by G. Garbrecht, 49–100. Mainz am Rhein: Von Zabern.

Ellis, S. 1996. "Pooling Resources: The Use of Water for Social Control in the Roman Empire." *Theoretical Roman Archaeology Conference* 6:144–50.

Erdkamp, P., K. Verboven, and A. Zuiderhoek, eds. 2015. *Ownership and Exploitation of Land and Natural Resources in the Roman World.* Oxford: Oxford University Press.

Evans, H. B. 2002. *Aqueduct Hunting in the Seventeenth Century: Raffaello Fabretti's "De aquis et aquaeductibus veteris Romae."* Ann Arbor: University of Michigan Press.

Fagan, G. 1999. *Bathing in Public in the Roman World.* Ann Arbor: University of Michigan Press.

Franciosi, G. 1997. "Regime delle acque e paesaggio in età repubblicana." In *Uomo, acqua e paesaggio,* edited by A. Coen and S. Quilici Gigli, 11–19. Rome: "L'Erma" di Bretschneider.

Franconi, T. 2017. *Fluvial Landscapes in the Roman World.* Portsmouth, RI: Journal of Roman Archaeology.

Garbrecht, G., ed. 1995. *Meisterwerke antiker Hydrotechnik.* Wiesbaden: Teubner.

Garbrecht, G., ed. 1987. *Geschichte der Wasserversorgung.* Vol. 2, *Die Wasserversorgung antiker Städte.* Mainz am Rhein: Von Zabern.

Garbrecht, G. 1983. "Ancient Water Works: Lessons from History." *Impact of Science on Society* 1:5–16.

Halley, P., and J. Sotousek, eds. 2012. *L'environnement, notre patrimoine commun, et son État gardien.* Cowansville: Éditions Yvon Blais.

Harris, W. V. 2013. *The Ancient Mediterranean Environment between Science and History.* Leiden: Brill.

Hermon, E., ed. 2010. Riparia *dans l'empire Romain: pour la définition du concept.* Oxford: J. and E. Hedges.

Hermon, E. 2009. "La gestion intégrée des ressources naturelles: Pour une conscience environnementale des jurists et arpenteurs romains." In *Société et climats dans l'empire romain,* edited by E. Hermon and L. Labruna, 113–28. Naples: Editoriale scientifica.

Hermon, E., ed. 2008. *Vers une gestion intégrée de l'eau dans l'Empire romain.* Rome: "L'Erma" di Bretschneider.

Hermon, E., and L. Labruna, eds. 2009. *Société et climats dans l'Empire romain.* Naples: Editoriale scientifica.

Hermon, E., and A. Watelet, eds. 2014. Riparia, *un patrimoine culturel: la gestion intégrée des bords de l'eau.* Oxford: Archaeopress.

Higginbotham, J. 1997. Piscinae: *Artificial Fishponds in Roman Italy.* Chapel Hill: University of North Carolina Press.

Horden, P., and N. Purcell. 2000. *The Corrupting Sea: A Study of Mediterranean History.* Oxford: Blackwell.

Hughes, J. D. 2014. *Environmental Problems of the Greeks and Romans.* 2nd ed. Baltimore: Johns Hopkins University Press.

Jaillette, P., and F. Reduzzi Merola. 2008. "L'eau à usage agricole dans la législation romaine de l'époque tardive." In *Vers une gestion intégrée de l'eau dans l'empire romain,* edited by E. Hermon, 229–41. Rome: "L'Erma" di Bretschneider.

Jansen, G. C. M., ed. 2000. *Cura Aquarum in Sicilia.* Leiden: Stichtung Babesch.

Jashemski, W. F., K. L. Gleason, K. J. Hartswick, and A.-A. Malek. 2017. *Gardens of the Roman Empire.* Cambridge: Cambridge University Press.

Kamash, Z. 2013. *Archaeologies of Water in the Roman Near East 63 BC–AD 636.* Piscataway, NJ: Gorgias Press.

Keenan-Jones, D. 2015. "Somma-Vesuvian Ground Movements and the Water Supply of Pompeii and the Bay of Naples." *AJA* 119 (2): 191–215.

Keenan-Jones, D. 2013. "Large-Scale Water Management Projects in Roman Central-Southern Italy." In *The Ancient Mediterranean Environment between Science and History,* edited by W. V. Harris, 233–56. Leiden: Brill.

Knapp, C. 1919. "Irrigation among the Greeks and Romans." *The Classical Weekly* 12, no. 10: 73–74, and 12, no. 11: 81–82.

Koloski-Ostrow, A. O., ed. 2001. *Water Use and Hydraulics in the Roman City.* Dubuque, IA: Kendall/Hunt.

Kosso, C., and A. Scott. 2009. *The Nature and Function of Water, Baths, Bathing, and Hygiene from Antiquity through the Renaissance.* Leiden: Brill.

Lagóstena Barrios, L. G., J. L. Cañizar Palacios, and L. Pons Pujol, eds. 2010. *Aquam perducendam curavit: Captación, uso y administración del agua en las ciudades de la Bética y el occidente romano.* Cádiz: Universidad de Cádiz.

Le Gall, J. 1953. *Le Tibre: fleuve de Rome dans l'Antiquité.* Paris: Presses Universitaires de France.

Leveau, P. 1994. "Dal paesaggio naturale al paesaggio coltivato: Dati archeologici relativi ai grandi lavori agricoli in età romana; Il drenaggio delle paludi nella Bassa Provenza." In *Landuse in the Roman Empire,* edited by J. Carlsen, P. Ørsted, and J. E. Skydsgaard, 73–78. Roma: "L'Erma" di Bretschneider.

Leveau, P., and J.-L.Paillet. 1976. *L'alimentation en eau de Caesarea de Mauretanie et l'aqueduc de Cherchell.* Paris: Éditions L'Harmattan.

Malissard, A. 1994. *Les romains et l'eau: Fontaines, salles de bains, thermes, égouts, aqueducs.* Paris: Les Belles Lettres.

Maganzani, L. 2014. "Le règlement des *riparia* dans les communautés d'irrigation dans le monde romain." In Riparia, *un patrimoine culturel: la gestion intégrée des bords de l'eau,* edited by E. Hermon and A. Watelet, 225–31. Oxford: Archaeopress.

Maganzani, L., and C. Buzzacchi, eds. 2014. *Lex rivi Hiberiensis: Diritto e tecnica in una comunità di irrigazione della Spagna romana*. Naples: Jovene.

Malouta, M., and A. Wilson. 2013. "Mechanical Irrigation: Water-Lifting Devices in the Archaeological Evidence and in the Egyptian Papyri." In *The Roman Agricultural Economy,* edited by A. Bowman and A. Wilson, 273–305. Oxford: Oxford University Press.

Manning, J. G. 2018. *The Open Sea: The Economic Life of the Ancient Mediterranean World from the Iron Age to the Rise of Rome.* Princeton: Princeton University Press.

Marano, Y. A. 2015. "'Watered . . . with the Life-Giving Wave': Aqueducts and Water Management in Ostrogothic Italy." In *Ownership and Exploitation of Land and Natural Resources in the Roman World,* edited by P. Erdkamp, K. Verboven, and A. Zuiderhoek, 150–69. Oxford: Oxford University Press.

Maruotti, L. S. 2009. *La tutela dell'ambiente nella sua evoluzione storica: L'esperienza del mondo antico*. Turin: G. Giappichelli Editore.

McCormick, M., U. Büntgen, M. A. Cane, E. R. Cook, K. Harper, P. Huybers, T. Litt et al. 2012. "Climate Change during and after the Roman Empire: Reconstructing the Past from Scientific and Historical Evidence." *Journal of Interdisciplinary History* 43 (2): 169–220.

Menu, B., ed. 1994. *Les problèmes institutionnels de l'eau en l'Égypte ancienne et dans l'Antiquité méditerranéenne*. Cairo: Institut français d'archéologie orientale.

Metral, F., and J. Metral, eds. 1982. *L'Homme et l'eau en Méditerranée et au Proche Orient.* 2, *Aménagements hydraulics, état et législation*. Lyon: GIS, Maison de l'Orient, Presses Universitaires de Lyon.

Ohlig, C., Y. Peleg, and T. Tsuk, eds. 2002. *Cura Aquarum in Israel*. Siegburg: DWhG.

Oleson, J. P. 2012. *The Oxford Handbook on Engineering and Technology in the Classical World*. Oxford: Oxford Universitiy Press.

Oleson, J. P. 1984. *Greek and Roman Mechanical Water-Lifting Devices: The History of Technology.* Toronto: University of Toronto Press.

Purcell, N. 1996. "Rome and the Management of Water: Environment, Culture and Power." In *Human Landscapes in Classical Antiquity: Environment and Culture,* edited by G. Shipley and J. Salmon, 180–212. London: Routledge.

Quilici Gigli, S. 1983. "Sistemi di cunicoli nel territorio tra Velletri e Cisterna." In *Archeologia laziale.* Vol. 5, edited by S. Quilici Gigli, 112–23. Rome: Consiglio nazionale delle ricerche.

Rainer, J. M. 1987. *Bau- und nachbarrechtliche Bestimmungen im klassischen römischen Recht.* Graz: Leykam Verlag.

Rey-Coquais, J. P. 1992. "L'eau dans la Syrie antique: inventaire epigraphique." In *L'eau et les hommes en Méditerranée et en mer Noire dans l'Antiquité*, edited by G. Argoud, L. Marankou, V. Panagiotopoulos, and C. Villain-Gandossi, 383–95. Athens: Centre National de Recherches Sociales and Centre de Recherches Néo-Helléniques.

Rodrígez Neila, J. F. 1988. "Aqua publica y politica munipical romana." *Gerión* 6: 223–52.

Saliou, C. 1994. *Les lois des bâtiments: Voisinage et habitat urbain dans l'Empire romain; Recherches sur les rapports entre le droit et la construction privée du siècle d'Auguste au siècle de Justinien*. Beirut: Institute français d'archéologie du Proche-Orient.

Sánchez, E. 2015. "*Erogationes extra urbem* in Iberian Aqueducts: Additional Evidence for Irrigation in Roman Hispania." *Water History* 7:289.

Šašel, J. 1973. "Trajan's Canal at the Iron Gate." *JRS* 63:80–85.

Segarra Lagunes, M. M. 2005. *Il Tevere e Roma: Storia di una simbiosi*. Rome: Gangemi Editore.

Shaw, B. D. 1984. "Water and Society in the Ancient Maghrib: Technology, Property and Development." *AntAfr* 20:121–73.

Shilling, B., and P. Stephenson, eds. 2016. *Fountains and Water Culture in Byzantium*. Cambridge: Cambridge University Press.

Squatriti, P. 2002. *Water and Society in Early Medieval Italy, AD 400–1000*. Ann Arbor: University of Michigan Press.

Taylor, R. 2000. *Public Needs and Private Pleasures: Water Distribution, the Tiber River, and the Urban Development of Ancient Rome*. Rome: "L'Erma" di Bretschneider.

Thomas, R., and A. Wilson. 2001. "Water Supply for Roman Farms in Latium and South Etruria." *PBSR* 62:139–96.

Thommen, L. 2012. *The Environmental History of Ancient Greece and Rome*. Translated by P. Hill. Cambridge: Cambridge University Press. Originally published as *Umweltgeschichte der Antike*. Munich: Beck, 2009.

Thonemann, P. 2011. *The Maeander Valley: A Historical Geography from Antiquity to Byzantium*. Cambridge: Cambridge University Press.

Traina, G. 1988. *Paludi e bonifiche del mondo antico: Saggio di archeologia geografica*. Rome: "L'Erma" di Bretschneider.

Wacke, A. 2002. "Protection of the Environment in Roman Law?" *Roman Legal Tradition* 1:1–24.

Wescoat, J. L. 2000/2001. "The Landscape of Roman Water Law." *Environmental Design: Journal of the Islamic Environmental Design Research Centre* 18 (1/2): 88–99.

Wikander, Ö., ed. 2000. *Handbook of Ancient Water Technology*. Leiden: Brill.

Wilson, A. I. 2012. "Hydraulic Engineering and Water Supply." In *The Oxford Hand-*

book on Engineering and Technology in the Classical World, edited by J. P. Oleson, 285–318. Oxford: Oxford University Press.

Wilson, A. I. 2011. "Urban Water Storage, Distribution, and Usage in Roman North Africa." In *Water Use and Hydraulics in the Roman City*, edited by A. O. Koloski-Ostrow, 983–96. Dubuque, IA: Kendall/Hunt.

Wilson, A. I. 2008. "Villas, Horticulture and Irrigation Infrastructure in the Tiber Valley." In Mercator Placidissimus: *The Tiber Valley in Antiquity*, edited by F. Coarelli and H. Patterson, 731–68. Rome: Quasar.

Wilson, A. I. 2000. "Industrial Uses of Water in the Ancient World." In *Ancient Water Technology*, edited by Ö. Wikander, 127–49. Leiden: Brill.

Wilson, A. I. 1999. "Deliveries *extra urbem*: Aqueducts and the Countryside." *JRA* 12:314–31.

Wilson, A. I. 1998. "Water Supply in Ancient Carthage." In *Carthage Papers*, edited by J. T. Peña, 65–102. Portsmouth, RI: Journal of Roman Archaeology.

SELECTED STUDIES OF WATER AND ENVIRONMENTAL LAW IN CONTEMPORARY SOCIETIES

Baden, J. A. 1998. "A New Primer for the Management of Common-Pool Resources and Public Goods." In *Managing the Commons*, edited by J. A. Baden and D. S. Noonan, 51–62. 2nd ed. Bloomington: Indiana University Press.

Baden, J. A., and D. S. Noonan, eds. 1998. *Managing the Commons*. 2nd ed. Bloomington: Indiana University Press.

Burden, P. D. 2015. *Earth Jurisprudence: Private Property and the Environment*. London: Routledge.

Coates, P. 1988. *Nature: Western Attitudes since Ancient Times*. Berkeley: University of California Press.

Cole, D. H. 2000. "New Forms of Private Property: Property Rights in Environmental Goods." In *Encyclopedia of Law and Economics*, edited by B. Bouckaert and G. De Geest, 274–314. Cheltenham: Edward Elgar.

Cole, D. H., and E. Ostrom. 2012a. *Property in Land and Other Resources*. Cambridge: Lincoln Institute of Land Policy.

Cole, D. H., and E. Ostrom. 2012b. "The Variety of Property Systems and Rights in Natural Resources." In *Property in Land and Other Resources*, edited by D. H. Cole and E. Ostrom, 37–64. Cambridge: Lincoln Institute of Land Policy.

Dietz, T., N. Dolšak, E. Ostrom, and P. C. Stern. 2002. "The Drama of the Commons." In *The Drama of the Commons*, edited by E. Ostrom, E. U. Weber, S. Stonich, P. C. Stern, N. Dolšak, and T. Dietz, 3–35. Washington, DC: National Academy Press.

Fagan, B. 2011. *Elixir: A History of Water and Humankind*. New York: Bloomsbury.

Fernea, R. A. 1963. "Conflict in Irrigation." *Comparative Studies in Society and History* 6 (1): 76–83.

Fischer, D. 2009. *The Law and Governance of Water Resources*. Cheltenham: Edward Elgar.

Freyfogle, E. T. 1996. "Water Rights and the Common Wealth." *Environmental Law* 26 (1): 27–51.

Getzler, J. 2004. *A History of Water Rights at Common Law*. Oxford: Oxford University Press.

Hunt, R. C., and E. Hunt. 1976. "Canal Irrigation and Local Social Organization." *Current Anthropology* 17:389–411.

Johnston, C. N., W. F. Funk, and V. B. Flatt. 2010. *Legal Protection of the Environment*. 3rd ed. St. Paul, MN: Thomson/West.

Juuti, P. S., T. S. Katko, and H. S. Vuorinen, eds. 2008. *Environmental History of Water*. London: IWA Publishing.

Ostrom, E. 1991. *Governing the Commons*. Cambridge: Cambridge University Press.

Ostrom, E., E. U. Weber, S. Stonich, P. C. Stern, N. Dolšak, and T. Dietz, eds. 2002. *The Drama of the Commons*. Washington, DC: National Academy Press.

Pearce, F. 2006. *When the Rivers Run Dry: Water—the Defining Crisis of the Twenty-First Century*. Boston: Beacon Press.

Perry, C. J., M. Rock, and D. Seckler. 2002. *Water as an Economic Good: A Solution, or a Problem?* Colombo, Sri Lanka: International Irrigation Management Institute.

Reich, P. 2013. "The Historical, Comparative, and Convergence Trifecta in International Water Law: A Mexico-U.S. Example." *Environmental Law Reporter* 43 (6): 10509–13. Revised and reprinted as "The All-American Canal and the Civil-Common Law Divide." *Western Legal History* 27 (2014): 185–98.

Solomon, S. 2010. *The Epic Struggle for Wealth, Power, and Civilization*. New York: Harper/Perennial.

Index